SIMON CADELL

SIMON CADELL

THE AUTHORISED BIOGRAPHY

BRIAN SLADE

FONTHILL

Fonthill Media Language Policy

Fonthill Media publishes in the international English language market. One language edition is published worldwide. As there are minor differences in spelling and presentation, especially with regard to American English and British English, a policy is necessary to define which form of English to use. The Fonthill Policy is to use the form of English native to the author. Brian Slade was born and educated in the United Kingdom; therefore, British English has been adopted in this publication.

Fonthill Media Limited
Fonthill Media LLC
www.fonthillmedia.com
office@fonthillmedia.com

First published in the United Kingdom and the United States of America 2018

British Library Cataloguing in Publication Data:
A catalogue record for this book is available from the British Library

Copyright © Brian Slade 2018

ISBN 978-1-78155-679-5

Typeset in 10pt on 13pt Sabon
Printed and bound in England

CONTENTS

Acknowledgements

When I first stayed with Beckie Croft's family, I became more aware of the responsibility that comes with trying to document somebody's life, particularly a character so widely adored as Simon Cadell. As I shared a beer with Simon's youngest son, Alec, that responsibility became more acute as I realised that I was documenting the life of a father that he had only known for the first six years of his life. I hope that I have at the very least reminded both he and older brother Patrick of the fondness with which their father is remembered to this day.

The family dynasty stretches back more than 130 years now and is still going strong in the acting profession. It is therefore with the utmost respect and humility that I acknowledge the family's incredible support, cooperation, and warmth throughout the research for this book. Beckie Croft's support has been incredible, allowing me to approach any subject and borrow any materials in order to produce this biography. Simon's two sons, Alec and Patrick, have a charm and amiability about them that has surely been passed through from their father and I thank them for allowing me to document his career.

Simon's twin siblings, Selina and Patrick, found time in their hectic lives to support and encourage me and it has been a pleasure and privilege to explore their family heritage. Simon's mother, Gillian, remains a lady of great spirit. To share a glass of wine with her and discover that I was now her favourite person called Brian was a genuine honour. Penny Croft and Peter Farago, and indeed the wider Croft family, were very tolerant of my intrusion into their lives at a time when they were still dealing with the family estate at Honington Hall. I am grateful for their time and their stories, and I promise not to call Peter 'sir' again.

Simon had a host of wonderful friends who were falling over themselves to give their time. Special thanks go to Gyles Brandreth. While I know he and Simon had a friendship where their affection for one another was an unspoken bond, it was, I am sure, difficult to recall his best friend without a tinge of regret, so I am grateful for the enthusiasm and friendliness afforded to me and for putting me in touch with the family at the very start of the project.

To Stephanie Turner, a huge debt of gratitude. Interviewing the most significant lady prior to Beckie was always of concern, especially knowing what a significant part of Simon's life she was. Her kindness and co-operation were gratefully received and the suggestion that Simon 'is in good hands' was extremely reassuring.

To Joanna Lumley, my thanks for trying so hard to make time in your schedule when up to your eyes in interviews around the release of *Absolutely Fabulous* at the cinema. Making me feel like I was doing Joanna a favour by talking to her was indicative of the charm of her personality and I am thankful for the shot in the arm our interview gave me.

To Nick Renton and Patricia Lord, who allowed me to share a morning croissant and a trip down memory lane at Patricia's home on the morning after the great Academy Awards mix-up of 2016, where one of her former clients had collected an Oscar for *Moonlight*. It was one of the highlights of my research and the warmth and hospitality shown were matched only by their obvious love of Simon.

There are a host of other friends and colleagues of Simon's who gave up their time to answer emails, discuss things on the telephone, or meet for a chat over a cup of tea. Not everything discussed made it into this book, and plans simply did not gel with some people that were unable to help, but I am nonetheless appreciative of the time spent discussing Simon with me. As much as I would love to acknowledge them all with individual comments, space dictates that I issue a group thank you, and so my sincere gratitude to Polly Adams, James Arthur, Sir Alan Ayckbourn, Sarah Berger, Andrew Benson, Gillian Bevan, Simon Butteriss, John Caird, Esta Charkham, Ray Cooney OBE, Rob Cope, Carol Drinkwater, Rob Eaton, Chris Ellis, Clive Emsley, Christopher Gee, Briony Glassco, Constantine Gregory, Kim Grant, Evgeny Gridnoff, Michael Hadley, Carol Hayman, Giles Havergal, Richard Heffer, Janet Henfrey, Jeffrey Holland, Jane How, Trevor Hughes, Tim Luscombe, David McKail, Anthony May, Kevin Moore, Jane Morgan, Kenn Oldfield, John Oxley, the late Tim Pigott-Smith OBE, David Schofield, Dr Martin Scurr, Michael Simkins, Neil Stacy, Tony Staveacre, Nick Turnbull, Philippa Vaizey, Rudolf van den Berg, Charlie Waite, and David Webb.

In addition to my thanks for the above content contributions, I also appreciate the help given with regards to the provision of images. Most have come from Simon's own personal collection opened so kindly by Beckie Croft. My thanks however also go to Mohamad Ansar, Derek Balmer, Gyles Brandreth, Patrick Cadell, Rob Cope, Penny Croft, Peter Farago, Richard Heffer, Joanna Lumley, Ruth Madoc and Tristram Kenton.

My additional thanks to Alan Sutton, Jamie Hardwick, and the staff at Fonthill Media, along with the many agents who facilitated my contact with their clients.

On a personal note, I would like to thank my own family and friends for putting up with a large amount of aftermath stories of 'I spoke to xyz today.' Their support and belief in my ability to deliver this project kept me going and this book wouldn't have made it without them. Specifically, I would like to thank Doreen Squire, Darren Slade, Raymond Slade, Adam Slade, Nathan Slade, Sarah Slade, David Squire, Clifford Price, Colin and Poppy Mckee, Marty Mckee, Andy Preston and the whole bridge crowd, and my number one fan, Talulah Mckee.

Last, but certainly not least, to Simon Cadell. The most common description of Simon was that he was such a charming man. When I asked Nick Renton what aspect he recalled most of Simon, he opted for naughtiness. It is quite clear that while Simon oozed charm, there was always a glint of cheekiness in his eyes. As much as I am clearly the poorer for never having met the man himself, having gotten to know his extended family and friends I built enough of a picture of him to be crestfallen when writing the final chapter of his story. I hope to have done him some level of justice within these pages and upon its release I will be sure to raise a glass in your direction sir ... the right vintage of course!

Foreword

Simon Cadell was an interesting human being. Even if you did not know, like, and love him over more than thirty years, as I did, I think you will find this book intriguing because Simon was rather a fascinating character. He was essentially an actor. He had other interests of course—literature, life's pleasures, wine, cigars, art, history, and politics—but first and foremost, first and last, he was an actor. That was what made him tick.

I met him first in 1964, at school, when he was thirteen and I was fifteen. I had written a stage adaptation of an Arthur Conan Doyle short story and for my school production, on the recommendation of our drama teacher, cast Simon in lead role. On 7 March 1964, I recorded in my diary: 'I am very excited with my Sherlock Holmes. He is key to the whole thing, of course, and I feel that I have found a star in the making. He is 13 and quite small, but he can do it.' He certainly could. Jeremy Brett in his prime was quite wonderful as Holmes, but, believe me, Simon, at thirteen, was even better.

Looking at my diary, I am amused to note that on the same day—7 March 1964—I travelled from school to London to the Prince Charles Theatre off Leicester Square to see an evening of music hall, in which the top of the bill was Sir Donald Wolfit performing 'The Death of Bill Sikes'. These were the so-called 'Swinging Sixties', but Simon and I were in another world, happily regaling one another with stories about (and impressions of) a raft of great actors all born more than half a century earlier—Donald Wolfit, Ralph Richardson, Laurence Olivier, Michael Redgrave, and the rest. While our contemporaries were discovering the Beatles and the Rolling Stones, we were busy impersonating Noël Coward, Jack Buchanan, and Flanagan and Allen.

As you will discover in the pages that follow, Simon came from a theatrical family and his own family heritage, as well as the heritage of the theatre and the details of his craft, were endlessly fascinating to him. From the time we met at school until his untimely death, I suppose I saw everything he did, from *Hamlet* to *Hi-de-Hi!*, from *Zigger Zagger* to *Travels with My Aunt*. Knowing Simon and his family—his remarkable parents, his delightful uncle, his gifted siblings, his beautiful wife and sons (to whom my wife and I are proud godparents)—has been one of the principal joys of my life and I rather assumed I knew the whole story. But thanks to Brian Slade, I have discovered lots I did not know. This is a wonderful celebration of a very special talent and of an actor who, unusually, is remembered with huge affection twenty years after his passing.

What do I remember best of Simon? In a phrase, the pleasure of his company—his wicked wit, his zest for life, his generosity. Chekhov said, 'When an actor has money he doesn't send letters, he sends telegrams.' That was Simon. He lived life to the full and when death came his way, he took it on board with extraordinary grace and humour. When he was in hospital, dying, I remember the nurse pulling back the bedclothes to give him an injection and saying, 'It's just a little prick,' only to have Simon grin his lopsided grin at her and reply, 'There's no need to be insulting.'

While, other than in photos and reviews, there is no record of many of his most memorable performances (his Mercutio, his Oswald in *Ghosts*, and his beyond-belief-brilliant comic turn in *Tons of Money* at the National Theatre), happily much of his best work, from *Blott on the Landscape* to *Hi-de-Hi!*, is preserved on film. Somewhere on the internet, you will be able to find Simon and Patricia Hodge doing a routine from *Noël and Gertie*. Find it if you can: it is immaculate. Few could put over a certain type of song better than Simon. I chose his version of 'I've Grown Accustomed to Her Face' from *My Fair Lady* as my favourite 'Desert Island Disc'. And no one could read a book better for the radio than he did. He was one of the great voice-over artistes. There are still a couple of London underground stations where you can hear him calling out, 'Mind the gap'. They may be only three short words, but, oh boy, does he make the most of them!

I am so glad Brian Slade has produced this account of Simon's life. He has done it with respect, affection, authority, and the cooperation of Simon's family and friends. He has been conscientious in badgering us for information. While I was trying to unearth a particular photograph he wanted—of Simon and his mother chatting with Sir John Gielgud on the stage of the Oxford Playhouse at a gala I produced there in 1973—I recalled Gielgud's list of the qualities that define a 'star' performer: 'Energy, an athletic voice, a well-graced manner, certainty of execution, some unusually fascinating originality of temperament. Vitality, certainly, and an ability to convey an impression of beauty or ugliness as the part demands, as well as authority and a sense of style.' That describes what Simon Cadell brought to his craft precisely. He was such a fine actor and such a lovely man. I hope you enjoy his story.

Gyles Brandreth
2018

Prologue

During the early stages of research for the book you are about to read, I went out for a catch-up over a glass of wine with a friend who regularly worked shifts of differing hours. While bemoaning how many television quiz shows he had become addicted to on days of early finishes, he highlighted a positive. 'I do get to see some reruns of some of the great comedy shows from when I was growing up,' he said. 'You forget how good they really were. This week I've been watching *Yes, Minister* and *Hi-de-Hi!*'.

It is of no great surprise that my friend should reflect on the quality of the shows; while appealing to vastly different ends of the comedy spectrum, each was in its own right a classic of its time. Yet what was so interesting, however, was his summation of the appeal of them. He continued, 'the writing on *Yes, Minister* was so good, so clever. When watching it now, with European sentiment as it currently is the show still carries a lot of relevance. *Hi-de-Hi!* was still laugh-out-loud funny—it was Simon Cadell, so good at being deadpan. It was hysterical really. And I believe he died quite young.'

Yes, Minister had been a massive worldwide success, but the assessment that the writing of that show was what appealed to him the most (without disrespecting the masterful performances of the leading trio of quality comic actors) was most interesting when contrasting it with the appeal of *Hi-de-Hi!*—the performance of the leading man. Simon Cadell somehow projected himself into the memory for his performance above those of the great Paul Eddington, a good friend of Simon's, and Nigel Hawthorne; this was no mean feat given the critical acclaim that adorned *Yes, Minister* and its equally successful follow-up, *Yes, Prime Minister*.

The comments also projected the sadness that accompanied the topic of discussion. In one short conversation, my friend had brought together the all too common perception of Simon—that the pinnacle of his work was Jeffrey Fairbrother, the fish-out-of-water entertainments manager of Maplins

Holiday Camp, and that his tragically early passing at the age of just forty-five somehow defined his legacy in tandem with the bawdy sitcom for which his name had become synonymous.

At the time of the above conversation, I had not shared the information that I was in the process of writing a biography of Simon. So many things can go wrong during a book project that I felt it necessary to withhold that information from all but my closest friends until further down the line towards publication. It was, however, extremely comforting that more than twenty years after Simon's untimely passing, he remains an actor worthy of discussion among friends and I felt reassured me that this was a project that needed to bear fruit.

The public perception of Simon Cadell is very much of a man in the Jeffrey Fairbrother mold. He resisted appearing on chat shows and found live television made him unbearably nervous, so beyond his stage and screen persona, there was little evidence to persuade Joe Public that he was something other than a fourth-generation privileged product of a publicly educated theatrical dynasty.

I hope that the information in these pages shines fresh and previously unseen light on a much-loved and sadly missed talent. During the interviews and correspondence exchanges, the most common way to refer to Simon seemed to be with the prefix of 'dear', so much so that I began to wonder if he had actually been christened 'Dear Simon John Cadell.' There are many who believe that he was one of the best actors of his generation and his best years were still ahead of him.

I would like to think that the chapters in this book will enlighten those who remember only the hapless Jeffrey Fairbrother, the reprehensible Nazi Hauptmann Reinicke, or the gently bemused Larry Wade.

Those who knew his work in greater depth will, I hope, reacquaint themselves with this hugely-talented, kind, conflicted, devilishly playful but deeply honourable and charming man who made a generation laugh and cry.

Blood Will Out

'I'm sorry mother but I've made up my mind and nothing you can do can make me change it.'[1]

Simon Cadell uttered these words ten years after leaving the renowned Bristol Old Vic Theatre School. However, he was not arguing with his mother, Gillian, spirited head of drama at the Guildhall. He was actually in character, standing up to sitcom writer Jimmy Perry, bizarrely playing his mother in an audition for Perry and his writing partner David Croft's new comedy show pilot, *Hi-de-Hi!*. Perry, as a disapproving matriarchal figure, was unimpressed with her son's sudden choice to change career from Cambridge professor to holiday camp entertainments manager.

As with the role he was hoping to land, it was a pivotal moment in the young Cadell's life as he attempted to convince the BBC's creative comedy geniuses that he would be the perfect actor for the role of the bemused professor Jeffrey Fairbrother, set to break with family expectations and defect to a holiday camp that provided holidays for 'working class people.'[2]

'Blood will out,' said Perry as the appalled mother, reminding her son of his breeding.[3] It was a somewhat prophetic line. While Simon would never need to convince his parents of the nature of the theatrical blood coursing through his veins, it was nonetheless symbolic of a battle from three generations previous that had set the Cadell acting dynasty in motion.

The first man in Simon's family tree to decide that he wanted to tread the boards was Perceval Clark, Simon's great-grandfather on his father's side. Perceval's father was a fruit broker and a member of The Salters' Company. As was common in those days, expectation was that Perceval would follow in his father's footsteps to some degree. To hear the words 'I want to go into the theatre' was a shock, and the statement from the offspring was dismissed out of hand. Perceval was unwavering in his desire to break away from his father's preferred career choice, but without his family's support, he chose instead to join the military.

Although conferred with a Bachelor of Arts from Worcester College, Oxford in 1860, by 1861, Perceval Clark was serving in the British Army. Having initially been assigned to the 16th Light Dragoons, he became cornet in the 9th Light Dragoons in February 1861. By July 1863, he had worked his way up to lieutenant in the 9th Lancers, a cavalry regiment.

The 9th Lancers had been deployed to India. Order had been restored after the rebellion battles of 1857–8, and it was in this company that Perceval would apply himself after the death of his father.

On his visits home, he struck up a romance with Alice Margaret Richards, a West Country lady, and the pair would marry near Clifton, Somerset in December 1864. Perceval would return intermittently from his military obligations and the couple would have a flurry of children throughout the early years of their marriage, with five daughters arriving on the scene through to 1871. Perceval was clearly determined that his name should live on and took the somewhat bizarre step of including his name as a middle name for each of the girls.

By the time their youngest daughter, Louise, was born, Perceval had moved to the 84th Foot Regiment, and had seen further service in Jamaica prior to his retirement from active service. His desire to appear in the performing arts, however, was still not pursued for some time.

Simon would later recall the details of his great-grandfather's path into the theatre; aside from some of the precise details, he was correct in his storytelling. Just a few months after the birth of Perceval and Alice's only son in 1881 (their sixth child, somewhat inevitably named Perceval), Perceval was forty-four years old; just a few months later, and with his father no longer present to frown upon his career choice, he was free to answer what he felt was his calling. So it was then that Perceval Clark took his first steps into acting.

The first recorded appearance of Perceval Clark, and the starting point of what would become a thriving acting dynasty, was in February 1882 playing with the Irving Amateur Dramatic Club in *The Critic*, a satirical piece by the Irish playwright Richard Sheridan. Perceval played the part of Sir Fretful and his early reviews were positive.

This early foray led to more significant roles as the late arrival to acting began to gain sustained positive feedback in amateur circles. He joined Mr and Mrs F. H. Macklin's Comedy Company, touring in a production of W. S. Gilbert's *The Engaged* and by the end of the year, he had accumulated a significant body of work and garnered enough positive reviews to suggest that making acting his profession rather than an amateur pastime would be a justifiable decision.

Perceval's role of Sir Anthony, Old Dornton in *The Road to Ruin* saw the first signs of artistic traits that would be passed through the generations. Of his performance, the *Western Evening News* remarked: 'Mr Perceval Clark as Sir Anthony had his first chance here of showing his best powers as a comedian, and turned it to excellent account.'[4]

By now, Perceval's family were settled in a home at Bedford Park in Chiswick, and in 1885, Perceval's theatrical career took its most positive turn when he joined the company of Squire Bancroft at The Haymarket. The timing was acute, as Perceval lined up in *Masks and Faces*, with Mrs Bancroft appearing in her final role as Peg Woffington and Mr Bancroft as Triplet.

Perceval appeared as Colley Cibber before changing role to James Burdock during the run, the latter proving to be the character he would portray at the farewell performance in front of the Prince and Princess of Wales as on 20 July 1885, Mr and Mrs Bancroft bade adieu from theatrical management.

At a subsequent farewell dinner, Perceval was presented with a silver snuff box engraved on behalf of the Squire Bancroft Company and this is still in the possession of the Cadell family today.

A few months after the *Masks and Faces* run was completed, Perceval Clark took a rather unusual step in his career. At the age of forty-seven, having spent three years touring in comedy plays and carving a positive, albeit delayed reputation, he chose to alter his name. On 13 June 1885, he announced that he had changed his surname by deed poll from Clark to Perceval-Clark. Already having a son named Perceval, the change to Perceval Perceval-Clark is certainly a curious one, perhaps intended to ease the confusion for the five daughters.

The reason for this alteration is lost to history and even the generations since are unaware of why he made the change, but subsequent notices and reviews for the remaining days of his brief acting career show an inconsistent adoption by the presses of his new legal persona.

Throughout the remainder of his acting career, Perceval Perceval-Clark was rarely without work. Reviews of his performances, mostly comedic roles, were almost entirely healthy. He was also admired for his character accents and imitations, skills that would prove a significant part of Simon's arsenal several generations on.

Despite his keenness to act, in 1890, the performances stopped. Perceval's final notice was for an appearance as Shallow in *The Merry Wives of Windsor*, back with the Haymarket Company. There is again no known reason for this abrupt end, nor is anything recorded as to what immediate career path Perceval Perceval-Clark opted to follow in the aftermath. However, he did become master at The Salters' Company in 1899, curiously following in the footsteps of his father, and was regularly seen giving after dinner speeches around the turn of the century.

While Perceval's much-delayed foray into the arts may have been relatively short-lived, seemingly lasting only ten years, it had set in motion a career path for descendants that is still going strong to this day. The next person to step out onto the stage would be his only son—a new Perceval Perceval-Clark would soon tread the boards.

Perceval Perceval-Clark the younger was much like his father. His desire was to be in the theatre, but he was aware of what he felt were his military obligations. By 1901, he was a second lieutenant in the 2nd Hertfordshire Volunteer Battalion, part of the Bedfordshire Regiment. He served time in South Africa during the Second Boer War and by the time he resigned his commission in 1903, he had become second lieutenant in the 4th East Surrey Regiment.

Upon his release from duty, Perceval set about emulating his father in the arts. His first known toe in the water came on a sunny day in June 1906 at a fete to benefit the Radcliffe Infirmary and Oxford County Hospital. While the principal feature of the fundraising event was standard stalls selling craftwork and produce, the out-patients' hall hosted a number of amateur entertainments, the cast of which included one Perceval Perceval-Clark.

Whatever those 'dramatic entertainments' as they were known entailed, they were clearly enough to encourage young Perceval, and in September that same year, he had an uncredited walk-on role believed to be his genuine stage debut, at the Court Theatre in Bernard Shaw's *John Bull's Other Island*.[5]

He followed this with his first known official stage credit, appearing in Pinero's *The Times* at Terry's Theatre, for which he received positive reviews, the *London Evening Standard* describing Perceval's performance as 'admirable'.[6]

The Cadells (in its original form, Cadell is pronounced as one would pronounce saddle. Simon won a battle with his sister many years later over pronunciation) were a deeply artistic family based in Edinburgh. Simon's great-grandfather, Francis Cadell, painted in his spare time when not a practising doctor, and he married Mary Hamilton Boileau, a distinguished lady of French descent. Their artistic talents were thriving in genes that would flourish in their offspring.

Born in 1884, Jean Dunlop Cadell was probably the best known of the Cadell dynasty prior to Simon and his siblings—certainly theatrically at any rate—but she was by no means alone in achieving success in her chosen field. Her older brother was the famous Scottish colourist Francis Campbell Boileau Cadell (FCBC for short, or Bunty to those closer to him). They also had a younger sibling, Arthur, the only one of the trio not to pursue a career in the arts.

There are interesting parallels in the descriptions of Bunty's character when compared to Simon Cadell. At a memorial exhibition in June 1942, five years after FCBC's death, Stanley Cursiter in his introduction described Bunty's wit as 'constant and brilliant—caustic, sardonic, Rabelasian, or lightly bantering.'[7]

In Tom Hewlett's biography of FCBC, *Cadell,* the author refers to a previous work, Guy Peploe's *Critical Memoir*, in which Bunty was further described as a man whose worked showed 'an intense love of life, a sensuous enjoyment of good living'—certainly plenty of Simon traits there.[8]

Schooling for the Cadell children began at the Edinburgh Academy. In further parallels with Simon, who would find school a chore that simply delayed progression to his chosen career, Bunty was distracted in his education. It failed to serve any purpose, simply because his heart was not in it. An often-reported story came from Bunty's spell at the Royal Scottish Academy Life School. Admonished by the school's president for painting left handed, he was warned that this would prevent him from any success since no previous artists had attained artistic merit with such an apparent affliction. Bunty allegedly took great delight in responding, 'Sir, did not Michaelangelo paint with his left hand?' The rebuttal prompted a hasty exit from the president. When quizzed by a fellow student as to how he knew of this fact, Bunty is said to have replied, 'I didn't know, but nor did the President.'[9]

It became clear that Bunty needed something more stimulating than turn-of-the-century Edinburgh if his talents were to flourish. In support of their son's intention to paint for a living, his parents took him to France in 1899. There, he hoped to study with the great Impressionists and flourish among the artistic scene in turn of the century Paris. As a sixteen-year-old, he was enrolled into Académie Julian. As the family planned an extended stay to support Bunty's artistic education, Jean, Francis's younger sibling by a year, went with them, learning French and attending finishing school in the capital.

The angst of Perceval Perceval-Clark Senior's decision to pursue a career that was against his family's wishes were mirrored by Jean Cadell. Times were very different for women who chose to have a prominent career of any kind, let alone one in the arts. While Bunty's talents were encouraged, much like the challenges faced by her future husband's family, Jean's parents, Francis and Mary, did not approve of her desire to appear in the theatre.

Surrounded by all the creativity one could imagine, it was perhaps inevitable that a more standard domestic career for Jean was not something she could contemplate. Her announcement that she wished to pursue acting was turned down flat. The family's history was in medicine, law, and publishing. There was no room for such frivolity, especially for a young woman.

As the family returned to Scotland in the first few years of the twentieth century, Bunty's artistic pursuits continued to be encouraged, and rightly so. He began to exhibit his work locally in Edinburgh and as his talents flourished in reputation and expertise, he ran annual exhibitions for like-minded artists from around Scotland in the years prior to the First World War.

While her free-spirited brother gathered influence from trips to Venice and Munich, and expanded his talents after falling for the charms of the Isle of

Iona, Jean was forced to tread a different path. She was only able to give limited vent to her dramatic leanings by joining a small group of young girls who would tour local houses in *tableau vivant*.

Roughly translated as 'living pictures', *tableau vivant* was very much a real-life variation on a particular scene. Often involving complete stillness, the contributors would depict a particular moment or emotion much in the ways a painter would bring such life to a canvas.

Jean and thirteen compatriots would take up their still positions to background music. One would announce the scene, depicting pity, love, or some such emotional state, and after a short time holding the poses, the music would be changed and the group moved on to another emotive positioning.

At the completion of the various scenes, a Shakespearean sonnet would be read by one of the members; this was very much Jean Cadell's forte. This would be her moment to shine and whenever a sonnet was read, she would carry the task with gusto.

It was after one of these *tableau vivant* performances that a card was thrust into Jean's hand by a stranger. The man was George Alexander, manager of the Theatre Royal at Drury Lane. A successful actor in his own right, he is now best remembered as having bought the rights to two of Oscar Wilde's most famous works, *The Importance of Being Earnest* and *Lady Windermere's Fan*, when Wilde was desperately short of money. Alexander would go on to be knighted for his services to theatre.

The theatre manager was impressed by what he had seen, telling twenty-one-year-old Jean that he felt that she was very talented and that she should come to London to pursue an acting career. Sadly for Jean, she knew all too well that her parents were still against her dramatic desires and such a move was impossible. *Tableau vivant* was a safe way for her to let her artistic talents out without turning her back on the life of domesticity at home in Edinburgh that her parents wished her to follow. Alexander bid the young lady farewell but suggested that should her family circumstances change, she should get in touch.

Jean remained in Scotland, continuing to perform in amateur dramatics in order to try and satisfy her theatrical leanings while still conforming to her parents' wishes.

Mirroring the first documented appearance of the second-generation Perceval Perceval-Clark, Jean Cadell is first noted appearing at the Queen Street Hall in Edinburgh in a benefit performance for the Royal Infirmary. The piece was a farce entitled *Niobe, All Smiles*, and Jean was noted for giving a 'lively rendering of the role of Hattie, the emancipated modern schoolgirl.'[10] Given the restrictions placed upon her, perhaps a little personal yearning was placed into her portrayal.

Jean would continue to perform in an amateur capacity, including one historical performance in February 1904, again a benefit at the Queen's

Hall in Edinburgh. In aid of the artist M. Pierre Langdale, she lined up in performances of *Sunset* and *The Bogus Bandit* alongside both of her brothers. Arthur, Bunty, and Jean would all earn praise from the local press in what would surely have been a one-off moment of history within the Cadell family.

When Jean's father became ill, unable to live to the same standards that the family were used, he was forced to close his medical practice and take the drastic step of moving to Munich. It was a brief and somewhat doomed move. Jean's mother Mary died unexpectedly and only months later, her father Francis also passed away after fighting his illness for several years.

Now twenty-five years of age, Jean had been respectful to her parents' desires and had followed them on their various travels. Yet with Bunty's artistic talents in full flow, she was now free to choose her own path. Since their parents' death and Arthur's departure to serve with the military in India, Jean and Bunty had developed a close bond. She went to her elder brother with a request. With George Alexander's card still in hand, she asked to borrow money for a train fare to the English capital. 'I'm going to London to find this man,' she announced. Ever the supportive sibling, Bunty agreed to Jean's request. Leaving Bunty in Edinburgh to continue with his painting exhibitions, Jean arrived in London in 1906. It would be a while before she would cross paths with George Alexander.

Just days after Perceval Perceval-Clark made his first tentative steps into acting as an amateur, Jean Cadell was set for her stage debut in the West End. With a minor role in *The Inspector-General*, simply credited as The Sergeant's Wife, it would be a momentous step for the young Scotswoman, but one not to appease the critics.

The play was originally a Russian piece and was the second of two productions at the Scala Theatre produced by The Incorporated Stage Society, the other being *The Invention of Dr. Metzler*. It was rounded upon unanimously by the press, the *London Evening Standard* suggesting that the company had, 'added two tiresome and commonplace pieces to its repertory.'[11] The *London News* was equally scathing, suggesting that the programme to accompany the performance was in fact far more entertaining than the production itself.[12]

Thankfully for Jean, the extent of her own role meant that the only mention she attained was a collective comment that the minor roles taken by her and a significant number of other actors had been played 'ably.'[13] Hardly startling praise, but some consolation in the light of the production's own general reception.

For Jean's career to take off, she needed to be brave and she needed something far more substantial than *The Inspector-General* to support her burgeoning talent. While she had been dodging the criticism fired at her first professional play, over at the St James's Theatre, George Alexander had been producing Pinero's *His House in Order* to much acclaim prior to a transfer to the Theatre Royal.

Jean decided that the support of this man was what her career needed and so in 1907 she arrived at the stage door of the Theatre Royal. With little more than the money from her brother and a crumpled business card to her name, she faced a man who opened the stage door and who questioned the young lady as to who she was and what she wanted.

'I've got this card,' she announced to the stranger, and with that her future in the theatre was set to follow a smoother course. True to his word, Alexander found her a role and Jean joined the cast in the character of the French governess, Mademoiselle Thome. Although a comparatively minor character, Jean was able to claim a regular income as the play enjoyed a substantial run.

Simon Cadell's sister, Selina, pondered the spirit of her grandmother, such a young girl with no particular experience to speak of, hundreds of miles from home and with no parents to call upon should her move have proved fruitless. 'That was brave,' Selina justifiably believes. 'She stayed with George Alexander and his family for two years. She lived with their family and she became part of the company. He started her career.'

When the company moved onto its next production, *The Thief*, Jean remained with it to take the part of Isabel Layton. She followed this with a role in *On the Other Foot*, a one-act comedy preceding *The Reformer* at the Gaeity Theatre. This was most notable for the name of one of her two co-stars, one Owen Nares. Nares belonged to the Howell family tree, from which Gillian Howell, Simon's mother, would emerge.

In 1909, the paths of the two fledgling careers of Jean Cadell and Perceval Perceval-Clark would finally cross. In April of that year, The Scottish Players Company leased the Royalty Theatre in Glasgow for the summer season and proposed to introduce the Glasgow Repertory Theatre, a proposition deemed ambitious by the press of the time.

The *Scotsman* announced that the intention of the company was threefold: 'To represent such plays as touring companies rarely, if ever, play; to stimulate popular interest in the more important towns in dramatic art; and to place Scotland, if possible, in the plane of being able to boast a real drama of her own.'[14]

The season was not without its challenges. It was reported that George Bernard Shaw, on hearing of plans for the entire season to be made up of his plays, wrote to the manager of the company saying, 'I won't let you have a blessed one of them except "*You Never Can Tell*." Anybody can start a Shaw Theatre, which is what the Court virtually was.'[15] He was referencing the significant spell of Shaw plays produced at the New Court Theatre in Sloane Square.

The opening play was indeed Shaw's comedy *You Never Can Tell*. Notices were generally positive, both for the play and the intentions of the company. Perceval took the part of Phillip Clandon and received praise for a performance of 'infinite spirit,' although in reviews of this opening piece there is no mention of Jean.[16]

With no option of a subsequent Shaw play, the second piece for the company was Ibsen's *An Enemy of the People*, where Perceval appeared as Billing. This was swiftly followed by *Admiral Guinea* and *The White Dove*.

Jean and Perceval finally took credited roles together on stage in Arnold Bennett's *Cupid and Common Sense*, where they aptly played husband and wife, Willie and Edna Beach. The production was a romantic comedy, but it was received with comparatively small audiences and disappointing reviews. The *Scotsman* was considerably more critical of the play than its cast, suggesting that the story, set in a Staffordshire district was 'not a strong dramatic work.'[17] It was, however, kinder on the young novices within the cast:

> Willie Beach, a lad who is tempted to forgery to save his father from ruin, but who retrieves his character abroad, and returns home with a wealthy wife, had a satisfactory exponent in Mr Perceval Clark ... Miss Jean Cadell acted brightly as the young American wife of Mr Beach.[18]

At this point in their careers, it was clear that Perceval's roles were far more central to the plays they were involved in than Jean's. Of course, strong female leads were significantly fewer in number at the time, but while Perceval's reviews were consistently positive, it was rare that anything suggested a future of significant progression in the industry. For *Cupid and Common Sense*, however, *The Era* did see something in Jean, noting, 'Miss Cadell had only a small part to play, but she showed an ease, a vigour, and humour in her acting which promise well for her future career.'[19] As the repertory season blossomed, so did the relationship between Perceval and Jean, and in early summer of 1910 the pair were married.

The intention of what turned out to be several years residency for the Scottish Players at the Royalty Theatre had been to impress upon the paying public of Glasgow that this was their theatre. The ever-changing parade of plays covered a vast array of writing talent, old and new, and for the next year the reception was positive for almost everything that was presented before the people and press of the Scottish city—even if audiences were not always plentiful in numbers.

In the summer of 1911, Jean returned to London in a play that would have fitted neatly into the aims of the rep circuit that she had left behind in Glasgow. Graham Moffat's three-act comedy *Bunty Pulls the Strings* opened on 5 July at the Playhouse to rave reviews. Set in the 1850s, it was a play about the small village life of a Scottish elder with more than an inkling of childishness in the way he treated his now grown-up children.

The play received plaudits both from the critics and the notoriously difficult to please Glaswegian contingent of the audiences, to whom the play represented, 'more like a transcript from life than a drama.'[20] The *London Daily News* went so far as to suggest that, 'All London would want to see it if all London only knew how good it is.'[21] It would not be long before all London found out.

After a week at the Playhouse, *Bunty Pulls the Strings* moved over to the Haymarket for an extended spell. The audiences flocked in and even as the original cast, including Jean, moved on, the production at the Haymarket was forced into additional matinee performances to accommodate demand.

While Jean was experiencing her biggest success yet, Perceval was across town in *Sally Bishop*, a dramatisation at the Prince of Wales of a Temple Thurston novel. Although a Perceval-Clark, Jean continued to be known as Cadell professionally after her marriage. Life was good for the Perceval-Clarks.

More success was to follow as New York's theatre-goers eagerly awaited the arrival of *Bunty Pulls the Strings*. While a new cast continued to draw the crowds at the Haymarket, the original cast opened in Manhattan on 9 October 1911 at the Comedy Theatre. Jean was welcomed with open arms by the American theatre-going public.

Following on from her first venture into Broadway theatre, Jean returned to stage acting with her husband, reprising their roles from *Cupid and Common Sense* before the pair performed in a variety of moderately successful productions for the Stage Society and the Play Actors Association.

With the outbreak of war, Jean's brothers and husband all volunteered their services, with somewhat mixed fortunes. While Bunty was busy being promoted to lieutenant with the 9th Royal Scots regiment, Jean's husband Perceval was having a rather less successful time returning to duty with the 8th Battalion of the East Surrey Regiment.

Upon declaration of war in August 1914, Perceval completed the necessary documents to re-enlist for the infantry of his old regiment. His return to service lasted barely six months. In September 1914, he had been given the temporary rank of captain, but by March the following year, Perceval had been admitted to the Military Hospital of Purfleet. Described then as 'poorly nourished and of nervous temperament,' he was complaining of sciatic pain and was nursing calf and knee injuries.[22] Each of these conditions were said to have come from getting wet at Purfleet Camp.

After ten days at Colchester Hospital, Perceval began undergoing treatment at the Officer's Convalescent Home in Bath, and while signed off from active duty the wheels were put in motion for him to submit his resignation.

Although praised for his desire to assist his country in its hour of need, medical and officer reports were quite convinced that Perceval Perceval-

Clark's talents lay elsewhere. His commanding officer, Major Searle, described him as being, 'very slow and apathetic having never shown himself as fit for his present rank.'[23]

The comments were not intended to be in any way dismissive of Perceval's good intentions to do his duty, but such was the urgency to have an active military man in his role, the necessary protocols had to be invoked. The suggestions of an apathy towards the enforced military surroundings he found himself in were a bizarre precursor to some of the comments directed at Simon Cadell by teachers during his education.

In concluding that Perceval had no future as a Captain in the military, the 18th Headquarters documentation confirmed that, 'Capt. Perceval-Clark belongs to the dramatic profession and volunteered his services for patriotic motives but I do not consider he is fit to command a company in his field.'[24] Simon would find that his schoolmasters were of a similar belief in terms of his drifting to more dramatic and less physical pursuits.

Having initially been returned home for convalescence, Perceval Perceval-Clark did indeed relinquish his commission from the 8th Battalion on 23 April 1915. Perceval was able to spend time with Jean, and the couple would welcome their first and only child in the winter of 1915, John Cadell Perceval-Clark.

2

A Talent to Amuse

John Cadell Perceval-Clark was welcomed into the world on 13 December 1915. Jean Cadell's career was temporarily placed on hold, being seen for the final time prior to John's arrival at a garden party in aid of a theatrical orphanage on 20 July, appearing in a little-known play, *She Loves Me, She Loves Me Not*.

For Perceval, now fully recovered from his brief military exploits and the ailments he collected alongside them, came a role in the tail end of a run of *The Man Who Stayed at Home*. Telling the story of a British spy who is disparaged for seemingly not enlisting, the play had an extended run from its initial appearance at the Royalty in 1914. Jean herself had appeared in the first round of casting while Perceval was re-enlisting. Such was the play's success that a film was made, with Jean reprising her role of Miss Myrtle. When the play was recast for a transfer to the Apollo, Perceval joined as Perceval Pennicuik while Jean grappled with her only experience of parenthood.

So strong were Jean's theatrical instincts, however, that she would not be away from the stage for long. On 27 March 1916, with John barely three months old, she was back in front of a theatre audience, appearing in *Kitty Mackay*, another Scottish three-act comedy proving very popular with its audiences and providing a reunion of sorts with some of Jean's pals from the cast of *Bunty Pulls the Strings*.

Jean and Perceval were rarely off stage over the next seven years, sometimes together, sometimes not. Notable success continued to prove more difficult for Perceval than for Jean, who in 1923 reprised a role from two years previous in a revival of *At Mrs Beam's* at the Everyman. Her interpretation of Mrs Shoe, a gossiping inmate of a boarding house, won much acclaim and within a few years, she was heading back across the Atlantic ahead of another Broadway success, reprising the role at New York's Guild Theatre.

Reviews for the transfer to Broadway were positive and the presence of Jean in the cast, an almost entirely isolated British voice among a plethora of

Americans, meant that they took to her interpretation of Mrs Shoe with ease. The *Sporting Times* quoted an unnamed New York critic and gender aside, were one to attribute the quote to Simon Cadell, one would barely have reason to believe that it was not written about him: 'Her technique is something to be envied and her diction is perfect. Of particular interest is her perfect timing of every method of expression.'[1]

Somewhat inevitably for the only child of a pair of West End theatrical performers, one of whom was sharing her time between London and New York, John Perceval-Clark's childhood was one of nannies and eventually, boarding school. For his younger years, Fettes in Edinburgh was John's base, before seeing out the remainder of his education at Loretto, Scotland's oldest boarding school, prior to heading off to Oxford. He loathed both his boarding schools.

While his parents continued their work, John grudgingly excelled in Scotland. When not in education he would spend time with Jean's brother, Bunty, and one famous painting shows sixteen-year-old John sat on a deserted beach looking wistfully out to sea.

It would be wrong to suggest in any way that Perceval Perceval-Clark's career floundered during this time—far from it. He was rarely out of work throughout the 1920s and into the 1930s, although his last role of significance came in 1932, when he appeared at the Apollo as Mr Purefoy in Austen Allen's comedy *Pleasure Cruise* alongside Jean and the play's leading man, Owen Nares.

Jean's career, however, was in overdrive. In addition to her continued stage success, the 1930s saw her film career take off on both sides of the Atlantic, perhaps most notably for her appearance as Mrs Pearce in the 1938 production of *Pygmalion*, starring Leslie Howard and Wendy Hiller.

While his parents were thriving on stage, John was soldiering through his schooldays. Although an intelligent and quiet young man, the key to his survival through boarding school days was his sporting ability—cricket, hockey, and even boxing would take up his free time. Yet none of these pursuits was as successful as rugby.

John was a tall boy and his rugby talents were seized upon on his arrival at Loretto in 1929. He would lead the forward line to much acclaim for various school fifteens through to the end of his time at the school in 1935, even representing Scotland against England at Twickenham in the annual public schoolboys' match. Indeed, he would continue to represent the school as part of the Old Lorettonians and then further his oval ball talents after taking up further education at Oxford.

Despite this sporting prowess, John's future lay elsewhere. Although boarding miles away from the theatrical life that his parents were living, he still took his first sampling of theatrical involvement at Loretto. On 30 March

1933, John made his stage debut at the age of seventeen in *The Taming of the Shrew* as the shrew.

Appearing as the female lead was not something that John was pleased about. Selina Cadell recalls: 'He did act at school and played Kate in *The Taming of the Shrew* which always made him cross because he had to play a woman's part.'[2] This was of course a Shakespearean production, not a pantomime that called for hearty laughs from a pantomime dame. It was a performance at least given praise by the unnamed reviewer within the school's *Lorettonian* publication, who informed that: 'Perceval-Clarke [*sic.*] made a vicious Shrew.'[3]

Performing as Kate may not have sat well with John, but he nonetheless reappeared in further stage productions, tackling Shakespeare a year later in a more conventional manner as Prospero in *The Tempest*. Once again, praise was forthcoming. The anonymous reviewer was gushing as he recalled that John 'was Prospero as Shakespeare drew him; powerful and tenacious of purpose, yet tolerant, and above all, human.'[4]

Despite his dislike of his boarding school education, John remained committed to doing his duty as a member of the school, even becoming head boy and taking a brief spell as editor of the *Lorettonian*. He concluded his time at the school with a brief appearance as the young man in the Gertrude Jennings one-act farce, *The Bathroom Door*, perhaps a sign of the comedic talents that would be passed on to his son.

John moved from Loretto to Oxford, where he continued to excel. Although his rugby skills were put to good use, he also became a rowing blue. He never participated in the annual boat race with Cambridge, but it remained an important part of his calendar.

For the Perceval-Clarks, the close of the decade was a sad one. Jean's brother Bunty passed away in December 1937. He had been ill for some time and works were not selling well. Jean would forward funds to help the situation and visit as often as she could, but after an operation for a cancerous growth in his head, Bunty would spend much of his final year confined to a nursing home before succumbing to his fate at the age of just fifty-four. Just a few months later, Jean's husband Perceval also passed away, bringing to an end the various combinations of Perceval Clarks and Perceval Perceval-Clarks in the theatrical world.

In early 1939, John Cadell Perceval-Clark decided to drop the Perceval-Clark from his name. Whether it was a career move to either mirror his mother's name or merely to simplify it from the more cumbersome double-barrelled surname is known only to history. Simon's brother Patrick believes it is most likely that at this stage in his father's life, he was aware that a career in the acting profession would be better suited to the surname of Cadell. However, Patrick also recalls being told by his mother that, 'if he didn't take his mother's name, and with Bunty having had no children, there would be no more Cadells for that branch of the family.'[5]

After graduation from Oxford, John initially did follow his parents into the theatre. He debuted in March 1940 at the Mercury Theatre, Notting Hill Gate in T. S. Eliot's *Murder in the Cathedral*, playing one of the four knights quizzing Thomas Becket. A few months later, he appeared in Noël Coward's *I'll Leave It to You*, but the onset of war would soon reach the young Cadell. By March 1941, John was on probation with the RAF as an acting pilot officer.

John's eyesight was not of the required standard to be a flying member of the air force, but still determined to do his duty, his skills were applied elsewhere as he progressed to flight officer. Selina recalls: 'He was in charge of troops that were carried from Halifax, Nova Scotia back to Southampton—Canadian troops. He was on these huge ships that took six weeks to cross the Atlantic.'[6]

With John away in the military, her husband and brother departed, Jean Cadell meanwhile continued with what she did best—immersing herself in the theatre. In 1943, she committed to joining a tour with the Stanford Holme Company, offering productions with support from the Council for the Encouragement of Music and the Arts.

The CEMA, renamed the Arts Council after the war, was government funded with the intention of bringing the arts to wartime workers across the country. In July 1943, Jean joined the company as they began a brief pre-London tour of the north with the Chines play, *Lady Precious Stream*, written in the 1930s by a previously unknown student, S. I. Hsiung.

Jean was one of the headline performers alongside Stanford Holme himself, his wife Thea Holme, O. B. Clarence, and Phyllis Joyce. After a few weeks of touring, the company would arrive to perform at Regents Park Outdoor Theatre to much critical acclaim.

The production consisted of a substantial cast, twenty-two in all, and among the supporting players as one of the maids was a young talent by the name of Gillian Howell. Born in 1922, Gillian did not hail from a theatrical background. However, with Owen Nares already an established force in the West End, with whom Jean Cadell had already starred several times, it was not a profession viewed with the same misapprehension as the previous generations of Cadells and Perceval-Clarks.

Gillian's grandfather was Bulmer Howell who had been a civil law student at Corpus Christi College, Oxford. After graduating from Corpus Christi, he had co-founded the legal firm of Neish, Howell & Haldane in 1875. Bulmer's wife, Amy Nares, was a daughter of the famous naval officer Sir George Strong Nares, who commanded the Challenger expedition and British arctic expedition in the 1870s. Owen Nares was a grandson of Sir George's brother, also named Owen. When Bulmer retired from the legal business in 1928, his son Owen Bulmer Howell assumed his place on the London Board of the Scottish Union and National Insurance Company.

Gillian had not been born into theatre, but her desire to appear on stage was developed at an early age, something shared with her only sibling, older brother Peter Howell. Peter himself would go on to have a long and distinguished career on stage as well as being seen frequently on television and film.

With a talent for performing beyond simply acting, Gillian's first stage appearance came in 1932 as part of The Poster Ballet, a troop of young dancers performing in support of a special fundraising event at Drury Lane for the Royal General Theatrical Fund. This was swiftly followed by a well-received performance of *The Water Babies* by the same group, with Gillian starring as Tom, the central character of a young chimney sweep who transforms into a water baby after falling into a river.

By 1942, Owen Nares had taken his distant relative under his wing and Gillian received her greatest acting opportunity to date, appearing with Owen in *Rebecca*. Nares had already starred as Max de Winter to some acclaim in 1940, so the reprise was a welcome boost for Gillian.

When Gillian joined the cast of *Lady Precious Stream*, she tweaked Jean Cadell's interest. Both strong-willed ladies with a twinkle in their eye and a determination to succeed, Jean recognised a potential matchmaking opportunity between the young theatrical performer alongside her and her son. 'Come and have tea on Sunday and meet my son,' insisted Jean when John was on leave from his RAF role.

Jean's efforts were a success as Gillian and John, affectionately known as Gruff, struck up a happy relationship. As John reached flight lieutenant towards the latter stages of the war, the romance blossomed. In February 1945, their engagement was announced and on 10 April 1945, the pair were married at the King's Chapel of the Savoy, London. The couple remained married until John's passing in 1989.

After the conclusion of the war, John returned to the theatre, a world he already knew well via his mother and now further populated by the colleagues of his new bride. Yet for John, the acting bug had not bitten quite as much as it had his parents. In the short-term, regular acting jobs presented themselves and much like his father before him, John found a steady flow of work, starting with appearing alongside Gillian in *The Thracian Horses*. This production was also covered by the BBC in the summer of 1946.

There followed a role among a lengthy cast at The Piccadilly, with Edith Evans and Godfrey Tearle headlining in *Anthony and Cleopatra*. Performances in *Mid Channel*, *Little Holiday*, *Uprooted*, and *Easy Money* followed, all with pleasing enough reviews, but it was becoming clear to the gentle, somewhat reserved John that acting was not for him.

The fine diction of both the Cadells and the Perceval-Clarks lent themselves well to audio work, and so John found himself leaning towards further pieces for the BBC via the Home Service. He began to step away from acting roles as Selina recalls: 'He worked for the BBC as an announcer in the days when an announcer did a lot more than they do now. He also did a lot of outside broadcasts. I think he did some very early commentary from OB.'[7]

John also took his vocal talents to an early panel show, *Answer Next Week*, which promised, 'a problem programme including posers on chess, crime, law and bridge.'[8] The show rather sank, despite the talents of host Norman Hackforth, famous for being accompanist to Noël Coward, and Ian Messiter, then a junior producer at the BBC but who would most famously bring *Just A Minute* to the airwaves. The duo had considerably more success with *Twenty Questions*.

In 1949, Gillian fell pregnant. She had been appearing in *The Heiress* at The Haymarket. Friendships had been formed with the leading players in what was a veritable cornucopia of acting talent. When the production arrived from Broadway, the principal roles were played by Ralph Richardson and Peggy Ashcroft, a pairing that Simon himself would have his big West End breakthrough alongside years later. Producing was John Gielgud, and when the cast changed over during its hugely successful run, Wendy Hiller and Godfrey Tearle took over the roles of Catherine Sloper and her father, Austin. Another family friend was among the lower order in the cast, one Donald Sinden to whom Simon would credit much of his comedic development.

For most first-time parents, the term 'mother and baby doing well' would be the most important five words they could utter after the birth of their first child. For John and Gillian Cadell, this would be said with immense relief more than anything, and the ability to say them was not something that was necessarily a foregone conclusion.

Gillian went into labour on 19 July 1950. The birth of her son was far from straight-forward, in an age where difficult childbirths could often be disastrous. Simon's head was badly positioned and after several failed delivery attempts both mother and baby were in danger. John and Gillian were warned—something had to give as there was a distinct possibility that mother or son, or possibly both, could be lost. The delivery staff did not think both could be saved.

Doctors turned to the forceps to try and complete the birth, a far more common practice at the time of Simon's arrival. With one desperate final attempt, the baby was grabbed around the head with the forceps and pulled into the world. Simon John Cadell was born somewhat battered and bruised and against the odds, he and Gillian survived the traumatic arrival. Gillian suffered badly and was unable to even see her first-born child for the first four days of his life, after which Simon was reunited with his mother in a rather bruised state.

There would be a long term physical impact to Simon from the process. The endearing lop-sided look that would make him so recognisable, but cause him so much internal anguish, was in part a reaction to the birth, his jaw growing in an awkwardly disjointed line.

Gillian returned to the stage once fully recovered, appearing in well received performances of *Pygmalion*, *Trelawny Of The 'Wells'*, and *The White Carnation*. However, when her pregnancy in 1953 yielded twins, she decided to call time on her stage career. Juggling the West End with an infant child was challenging enough; to do so with a toddler and twin babies was one step too far, especially if her career dictated a return to repertory theatre. The new Cadell arrivals had appeared in far less traumatic circumstances, with the world welcoming Selina Jane and Patrick Mally Francis on 12 August 1953. Perhaps inevitably, both would achieve considerable success within the arts.

When John stepped away from the BBC, he joined the Christopher Mann agency as a junior agent. He did not give up performing entirely, still presenting some early children's television shows in 1952 and subsequently writing and narrating his own children's stories, *The Cow that Blew her Horn* and *The Cow Goes for a Sail*. He even became a semi-regular guest on *Woman's Hour*.

The remainder of John's career would be as a theatrical agent within his own firm after moving away from the Christopher Mann Agency to create John Cadell Ltd, which he ran from Berkley Square and later, the Cadell's Highgate home. He was highly respected, even if his gentlemanly nature and quiet demeanour did not necessarily seem to be the qualities needed in the cutthroat world of artist representation. Agent Patricia MacNaughton, now Patricia Lord, who worked with John in his early agency years at the Christopher Mann Agency, remembers: 'He appeared to be very modest, self-deprecating and absolutely good at the job. He eventually felt that he didn't want to be imprisoned in this rather grand agency and he went off to start out on his own. Everything I can say about John is good, he was a really good man.'[9]

Gillian gave up acting but turned her attention to teaching drama. She became head of the respected Guildhall and garnered a fine reputation for nurturing young talent and launching their careers. Sarah Berger, who appeared with Simon in the 1984 production of *Raffles*, remembers Gillian fondly: 'Gill was lovely. She was very kind to me and in fact was instrumental in me getting my career break as Abigail [Williams, in *The Crucible*] when I was still at drama school—it was her that put me forward for it.'[10]

Patricia Lord joined her friend at Guildhall several times for work. She remembers the talents that made Gillian's time there such a success:

She was always very interested in what you were doing, and very shrewd. She had a kind of falcon's eye and she'd look at you in a very, very pleasant way, but it was like a very hard mirror—but embracing as well, never cynical. I thought they couldn't have had a better head of acting. Intellectually, really on it, but completely embracing all the problems of young actors, of which she had a lot of experience.[11]

As an older brother, Simon was already a performer as a child, as his younger sister Selina remembers:

He was bossy as a child. He had this certainty, being very reassuring if you wanted reassurance. But when he was little, that could be quite alarming. I remember once when I was quite little I said something about God—'God knows,' or something like that. Simon said, 'Selina, who gave you permission to use that word? You're not allowed to use that word.' I said, 'Why not?' and he replied, 'Because I invented that word and if you need to use it you have to ask me first.' He got me into so much trouble of course because if I then heard other people say it I used to tell them, 'My brother Simon invented it.' So he was naughty, quite naughty.[12]

Selina also recalled his talent for voices and entertainment:

He was always amusing, acting, putting on funny voices—almost driving us slightly bonkers, me and my twin brother. He would get bored in a waiting room and get up and do a silly walk. And he'd know, he'd know his audience were amused by it. From a very young age, he was entertaining.[13]

Something that was always noted of Simon, even when at school, was his apparent age beyond his years. When writing his book, *The Right Vintage: A Wine Lover's Companion*, he noted that, 'I've always looked older than I am, a characteristic which is useful and fun in extreme youth, less alluring in middle age.'[14]

When talking about Simon's talent to amuse, Selina noted that, 'He was always very good with adults. He had a lot of friends that were older than us. He was a very unusual person I suppose.'[15]

Although education for all three Cadell children would be taken at boarding schools, there was still enough time in their childhood to become as engrossed in the acting profession as the generations before them had been. 'We were brought up watching films,' remembers Selina. 'We went to the Everyman every week as children. We thought films were iconic ... we saw everything that came out. Simon's physical comedy was connected to Peter Sellers, Jacques Tati ... Peter Sellers was a huge influence on Simon.'[16]

Simon also developed his dreams of stardom from the more serious offerings of the time, having a particular fondness for *Casablanca*, as well as any offering from Fred Astaire. Selina continues, 'He absolutely loved Fred Astaire. He knew the words to all the songs. Not completely unlike him to look at, the same kind of palette. He loved Bogart too.'[17]

In Simon's introduction to *Right Vintage*, he recalled fondly his visits to the Everyman with Uncle Peter:

> My uncle used to take me to see Marx Brothers movies. The cinema screen had no curtain. Instead the screen itself was lit in a distinctive shade of green. There we sat in green dimness waiting for the film to start and my uncle would start to laugh in anticipation of what we were about to see ... quite often I and the rest of the small audience would be chortling away as the film began. It was at this cinema that I saw many classic films for the first time, including a late-night showing of *Casablanca*. A packed audience of aficionados greeted the entrance of major characters with a short but intensive round of applause and at the end there was a thunderous ovation lasting several minutes as though the audience were trying to reach through the screen and beyond the intervening years to thank those responsible for their enjoyment.[18]

As much as Simon enjoyed these cinema trips, theatre was what really grabbed him and he was treated to a host of performances that developed both his skills and his desire to tread the boards, like his father before him, remembering:

> My father was taken to shows from a very early age by his mum. He saw a matinee of Ellen Terry, the last charity matinee she ever did. He saw Grock the Clown on stage—he saw all these people, so I was taken to a wide variety of things. I saw the last Crazy Gang show, but I also saw Gielgud's Prospero, transferred from Stratford Memorial Theatre to Drury Lane in Peter Brook's production of *The Tempest*, and these were when I was four, five, or six. I can still remember them, I can still see and hear Gielgud giving one of the last great speeches of Prospero.[19]

Childhood at this stage was a contented one for Simon and his siblings. Jean Cadell would take her trio of grandchildren for tea at the top floor of Derry & Toms department store in Kensington. By now, Jean was in her late seventies, and Patrick Cadell recalls his grandmother with affection as, 'a very sweet woman, with hearing aids—a stubborn but sweet elderly Scotswoman.'[20]

Christmas for the family was also a period of great enjoyment for the children. John and Gillian had become the best of friends with Donald and Diana Sinden. Donald was a client of John's at the agency and Diana and Gillian had formed a strong friendship when the pair had been acting in the 1940s, and it was a bond that would remain strong until Diana's death in 2004.

Christmas Eve would see a visit to the Sindens' home, followed by a party on Christmas Day itself, and it was courtesy of this familial bond that Simon became friends with the Sindens' oldest son Jeremy. Unsurprisingly, Jeremy would also go on to find fame as an actor, with parts in popular successes such as *Brideshead Revisited* and with a recurring role as Anthony Mortimer in soap opera *Crossroads*.

On the rare occasion that Simon would clash with his parents, he would seek solace with another pair of family friends, Jean and Jack Flower. Jean had been an actress herself and Jack was an antiques dealer. It was under their guidance that Simon learned much of his fondness for the finer things in life. Patrick Cadell recalls of the influential pair:

> Jean was Simon's godmother and Jack was an extraordinarily gregarious character. He was an antiques dealer in Buckinghamshire and he was extremely kind and colourful. They adored Simon and Simon adored them. Jack was a bon viveur and I think they did influence Simon's love of fine wines and good food because that was something very much of them. Jack was quite a character—old school and rather dashing, rather grand, and a charming, charming man.[21]

All was well for young Simon at this point, but education was about to throw him completely off course.

The Hall School in Hampstead was where Simon would head for his education. He was not keen on school and the idea of boarding school in particular did not impress him one bit. He went to school because he had to, not because he wanted to. Perhaps there is nothing unusual in that, but it was a theme that drove Simon to distraction throughout his entire education.

By 1958, Simon's class reports were developing a certain pattern, and reflecting a distinct lack of progress in many areas. His writing was described as microscopic and his spelling dismissed as very weak, and as a boy he was deemed to be self-conscious and easily distractible. Further to his apparent lack of English skills, there were long periods of absence. Illness was a common cause for his absence, but not the sole one.

Patricia Lord was regularly called upon to deal with an escape attempt from the school, normally achieved via a window in the toilets. Patricia went on to be Simon's agent and one of the first people to whom Simon would look for reassurance on the quality of his acting performances:

> He kept on running away. I'd recently acquired a Mini-Minor. The headmaster would ring John and he in turn would say, 'Patricia, you

wouldn't kindly go down to Victoria and pick him up would you?' so I
would pick up this rather scared looking little boy and bring him back to the
office, where John would have to hang around a bit until lunchtime when his
mother came to get him.[22]

In class, Simon was regularly scoring lowest in tests. Self-consciousness was
a regular criticism along with his lack of written skills. By the end of 1960,
the early years at Hall had not lifted Simon to any great heights. His teachers
seemed forlorn in their hopes for him, recognising that perhaps there were
other things on Simon's mind.

The most positive comments within his reports were that Simon was
'kindly and well-behaved', but the conclusion was that, 'It does not look
like an academic future for him and we must not swamp his real virtues in
striving for it.'[23]

The Cadell parents were perplexed as to what to do next. They bore no
grudge with the school, but in a letter to The Hall School in September 1960,
they conceded that, 'we have come to the conclusion that another term at The
Hall cannot benefit Simon and the sooner he makes the change the better. We
shall therefore not send him back this term.'[24]

They were so comfortable that the issues were not with the school that they
went out of their way to tell the headmaster that Patrick was to stay where he
was, a vote of confidence for the exasperated teaching staff.

The family letter continued, 'It is agreed on both sides that some alternative
to Hall is required for Simon and it is very unlikely that he will make progress
where he is in his present state of mind. It is simply a case of incompatibility.'[25]
In fact, the Cadells had already discussed with the school the potential for
removing Simon from their classes in January that same year, but had decided
against that option in the hope that he would settle.

The Hall School hierarchy made a number of suggestions as to where
Simon might go for the next stage in his education, but none of them was
taken. Instead, as the inability to fathom why his education was proving such
a problem continued, Simon was requested to sit something known as the
Stanford-Binet Intelligence Scales.

Dyslexia was of course not really diagnosed nor understood in the early
1960s. Even though the term was first used in the nineteenth century, at the
time of Simon's education, people with the condition were normally dismissed
as simply having limited intellectual capacity or no inclination to learn.
Dyslexia Action indeed today note that school reports often used to warn
parents not to expect much from their child.[26]

Perhaps for this reason, Simon was sent to be assessed. The Stanford-Binet
tests were primarily used to look for some level of deficiencies in a child's
intellectual or behavioural capabilities. They focused on cognitive reasoning—

verbal, visual, and quantitative—and short-term memory. The theory was that the results would then give a child's estimated mental age along with an IQ score.

The results for Simon proved everything the Cadells might have expected. There was nothing even remotely wrong with Simon's intelligence—in fact, exactly the opposite. Aside from being noted as having been less observant than he could have been during a practical planning exercise, the two-hour test gave him very encouraging results. Given that at the time of the tests he was only ten years and two months old, his mental age of fourteen garnered from the results was an undoubted relief for his parents.

What was especially noteworthy among the comments were those around his English skills. Simon had been heavily criticised throughout his education thus far for his writing abilities. However, his test results showed, 'He has a particularly large vocabulary for his age and was successful with other tests which have an English basis well in advance of his years. His immediate verbal memory was very good indeed and showed advanced powers of association.'[27]

The conclusion to his report, which gave him an IQ of 138, representing a 'superior mental ability of a considerably advanced and most satisfactory level,' was to give a major insight into the reasons for Simon's apparent lack of success throughout his entire academic years. [28]

> It looks as if Simon needs to be led to prove his ability to himself. He certainly should be able to make really good scholastic progress, so it is most important to stimulate his effort and help him develop good habits of work, so that he can go steadily and happily.[29]

The key to this conclusion was the 'stimulate his effort' section, but the cold reality was that scholastic progress would not be made. His dyslexia would at times cause him issues, but his greatest foe was simply a lack of stimulus. He did not want to be there. Studying was not what he wanted to be doing. He was in a rush to his destiny of performing, and very little in an educational establishment was going to satisfy that desire.

The Doyen of Bedales Drama

By the time Simon Cadell had left The Hall School in Hampstead, he had already had enough of education establishments. It was a distraction. Nothing seemed to be of relevance to his future career, and those areas where he genuinely needed assistance were going largely unaided.

The next step from The Hall School was Dunhurst, a prep school for ages up to thirteen and from where, if accepted, the pupils would move on into Bedales senior school. Set amid the beauty of the South Downs in Hampshire, it was here that the Cadells hoped Simon would find a better level of success and perhaps more importantly, contentment. It was an optimistic hope based perhaps more on desire than on faith in the establishment, as Simon's problems persisted.

Dunhurst, like its parent school, had an approach to education that was rather more freeing than the traditional methods. Here, creativity was something to be embraced and given wings to fly. That was certainly something that would have appealed to Simon and his parents. Seeing education as an obstacle to his theatrical desires, any establishment that would nurture his dramatic leanings would certainly have increased the chances of Simon at least staying in school.

'Hand, head and heart' was the principal philosophy adopted by John Haden Badley when he founded Bedales in 1893, believing that these were the three core elements of an education.[1] Badley wrote in 1923 that the focus of the school was to be upon, 'the development of creative intelligence, and with the intellectual and emotional tendencies, the formation of interests, purposes and ideals.'[2] Theatre director John Caird, who would come into Simon's life at drama school, recalls Bedales as being, 'a brilliant place for just letting children be themselves and letting them find their own scholastic level.'[3]

Badley also harboured a belief of the basic needs of life being not dissimilar to those Simon would strive for during his entire life—'something to work at, someone to work with and sometime to live for.'[4] In a press interview many years later, when asked what made him jolly, Simon replied, 'Good work, travel, nice parties, good argument and having one's friends around one.'[5] This was certainly not too far from Badley's philosophy, albeit Simon's was perhaps a tad more indulgent.

In principal then, the approach of the school and the goals that it purported to strive towards sounded like they should have provided Simon with greater creative freedom and a less formalised education against which to rebel. Dunhurst and Bedales were, however, still boarding schools. Time away from his family was still something that did not appeal to Simon, regardless of how things progressed on a scholastic level. A regular boarder could expect to see his parents perhaps at half-term, but otherwise he would have no face-to-face contact with them for several months—not something that Simon found very palatable.

In 1961, Simon arrived at Dunhurst, still repelled by the routine of education, unhappy to be there and as a result, somewhat distanced from his new classmates. It was an uninspiring start, with the same criticisms emanating from staff at Dunhurst to those levelled at him at The Hall School—poor mathematics, trouble forming written words and a general malaise with regard to having to be involved with the school at all. Amid it all, Simon spent considerable time off sick, a trend that continued to follow him throughout his education.

By the end of autumn term, however, Simon had begun to come to terms with his fate. He was more reconciled with the staff, who all felt that with more effort on Simon's part, he would be able to carve out a respectable, if unspectacular, result from his education. Of particular note during this time was the recognition of some of his dramatic skills. Said to work with imagination during eurythmic lessons and developing an understanding of singing, there were areas where he clearly could relate his dreams of theatrical stardom to the freedom of the classes on offer.

While class performance improved, it did nothing to settle Simon's restlessness, however. Lacking concentration, he was said to be accepting of a lower standard than he was capable of reaching simply because he was disinclined to commit to the things that did not interest him. By 1962, his headmaster noted that despite Simon's classwork improving in many areas he spent, 'far too much of each day hoping for an excuse to go to bed.'[6] Simon was bored and he missed his family.

With Simon's continued irritation with boarding school life, and with Selina and Patrick arriving to further their own education as well, John and Gillian considered a move away from the city in order to allow the children to become day pupils. Their work being so focused on London, such a move was going to involve considerable commuting and so when offers on potential houses fell through, John admitted a certain relief, knowing that the poor commuting routes would have made life somewhat difficult.

In an effort to find a happy compromise that still helped ease the pains of separation from the children's kith and kin, the Cadells spent £1,500 on a cottage in nearby Froxfield, a 4-mile journey from Bedales School grounds, and here the pair would regularly appear at weekends to try to appease their homesick children and give Simon reason to resist the ongoing urge to escape from school. Of their localised retreat, Selina remembers:

> We were having nervous breakdowns from being sent to boarding school. I was absolutely miserable aged eight at boarding school, so they very sweetly, thinking it would help, bought this little cottage called Wyke Green Cottage. It was a tiny two up, two down, and it was absolutely sweet so we became weekly borders.[7]

Patrick had settled well to Bedales life, embracing and enjoying his time there from day one, but Selina mirrored Simon's unhappiness. The approach of buying the cottage seemed to be one that did start to ease Simon's concerns. Becoming more a part of the school community and noted for being less tense, only his continuing English language skills were being consistently highlighted as concerns.

The move also coincided with his first acting role. Now more at home in his peer group, albeit reluctantly so, Simon took on the lead role in a production of *Ivan the Fool* at the New Hall in Dunhurst. The show went down well with pupils and staff, with headmaster Paul Townsend recognising that it was appreciated by everyone.[8] The school did note, however, that Simon was very dependent on those weekend escapes to Froxfield.

In April 1963, John Cadell received confirmation that Simon would indeed be accepted into the main school at Bedales. Nothing changed in terms of Froxfield. After consultation with the school, it was felt that the success of the experiment during his time at Dunhurst should not be risked by making Simon board on campus at weekends. The pattern would continue therefore of Bedales dorms midweek and Froxfield at weekends, at least for the foreseeable future.

From an educational perspective, life continued much as before at Bedales—a mixed bag of results depending largely on Simon's interest in the subject at hand. Sports carried no interest for him, with the exception of swimming and cricket. When a sports master encouraged him to drop on the ball during a rugby lesson, Simon promptly performed a kind of dying swan collapse, which resulted in his departure to the headmaster's office—a far cry from his father's prowess with the oval ball.

'Get up Cadell,' shouted the frustrated games master. According to Simon when recounting the exchange many years later, the teacher promptly kicked him in the shin. Simon rose from his swan's deathbed and kicked the master back, turning to storm to the headmaster's office. Here he announced that he would not take any further part and so he was given the new responsibility of mowing the grass. Unsurprisingly, his sports master chastised him in his end of year report, suggesting that, 'If Simon were to forget his aspirations for acting and concentrate on the activity being done, there would be a great improvement.'[9] Of course, he would not and so there was not any change.

The escape attempts did not fully cease, but the headmaster had a somewhat more pragmatic approach to them according to Selina: 'He said, "Well you can run away all you like, but you'll have to come back." I think that kind of took the sting out if it a bit. I think Simon was a bit disappointed.'[10]

One runaway attempt eventually put a stop to the escapes. After having enough of dealing with them, the headmaster promptly called the authorities. Instead of being met by Patricia when he stepped off the train, Simon was met by the transport police. There was of course nothing to charge him with, so he was promptly returned to Bedales on the next train and that was the end of his attempts for freedom.

In his first autumn term, the colourful head of drama at Bedales, Rachel Carey Field, approached another pupil at the school, Gyles Brandreth, about a future dramatic production. Brandreth was two years older than Simon, but with an equal obsession with all things theatrical and he was looking around for some acting talent. He was about to stage a production, with junior pupils, of *A Study in Sherlock*, described as, 'a forgotten fragment from the memoirs of John H. Watson, M.D.'[11]

Rachel Carey Field was quite the character, as Simon's younger brother Patrick remembered:

> She was an extraordinary woman—passionate and rather scary, and Victorian in some ways. She absolutely adored Simon because he was her star pupil. She ran drama and the wardrobe department, and the Bedales wardrobe department became extraordinary because people would contribute from all over the place. Even the Petersfield Players would come and borrow costumes for their amateur productions.[12]

Field came to Brandreth and informed him that, 'we've got an interesting young man that could be in your play that's just come up from Dunhurst—this twelve-year-old boy called Simon Cadell.'[13] Brandreth's one-act play was missing its most vital component, a believable Sherlock Holmes. So on Field's recommendation, he met with this recommended discovery.

'I was looking for my Sherlock Holmes and I met this twelve-year old boy. He looked like my idea of Sherlock Holmes,' recalls Brandreth. 'Strong nose, strong face, blonde hair slicked back. He had a sort of elegant maturity about him as a twelve-year-old which was extraordinary.'[14]

Brandreth instantly cast Simon in the lead role and his faith, and that of Rachel Carey Field, was rewarded with a standout performance, incredibly convincing for one so young. Gyles went as far as to remark of Simon in his diaries that, 'My Holmes is quite excellent, and will one day be the doyen of Bedales Drama.'[15]

'He was outstanding from the get go—he *was* Sherlock Holmes,' Brandreth recalls. 'We had a very serviceable boy playing Watson and a very good young lady playing Mrs Hudson, but Simon stood out from the crowd. He handled the pipe as though he had been born smoking a pipe.'[16]

Simon and Gyles got on famously and became instant pals, remaining best friends until Simon's death more than thirty years later. Brandreth was in love with the theatre. He aspired to achieve something in that field, although his talents did not restrict him to one specialised aspect. He just knew that he had to be involved in the theatrical world in some capacity.

Brandreth became aware of Simon's acting heritage, and the knowledge that Simon and his agent-father and actress-mother knew all the theatrical royalty of the day intrigued him. This mutual love of the theatre would not necessarily have been enough to sustain a solid friendship, but as the duo got to know each other it became clear that there was a deeper friendship to be had that would keep them bosom pals for life.

'We got on famously right from that start,' remembers Gyles of the early days of their friendship. 'I was in love with the theatre and I liked the idea of Simon's heritage. But we were also on the same wavelength.'[17]

This was the early 1960s. The free spirit of the decade was appearing with rock 'n' roll bands gaining an edgy and more rebellious tone. Every new chart-topper seemed to be rebelling against the shackles of society and continuing the breakaway spirit of the 1950s music scene.

The new friends were listening to their own vinyl, a live album that made number fourteen on the Billboard chart in America in 1955. Yet it was not rock 'n' roll. It was Noël Coward. This was a recording of Coward's Desert Inn show in Las Vegas.

Gyles and Simon both had a copy, and as they listened to one another's record collection, it became clear that not only did they yearn for a career in the theatre, but they had a mutual admiration for the glamour of the old-time music hall elegance of the likes of Coward, Jack Buchanan, and Flanagan and Allen.

Patricia Lord, so often the recovery service for the would-be escape artist, believed that this was when Simon became more accepting of Bedales, even if he was not particularly contented:

> He wanted to be at home—he loved his comforts and he wanted to get out to the interesting life of London. He had such extremely interesting parents and

I think he just wanted to be grown up. But then it got better when he found
Gyles. The moment he and Gyles got together I think they were planning
and plotting their adult careers, doing plays ... but he now had a mate and
he settled down.[18]

Of the escape attempts, Gyles is reflective of Simon's reasons:

I was essentially a conventional person. It would never have occurred to me
to run away, I didn't have that independent spirit, whereas Simon was his
own master. He wanted to do what he wanted to do. I never felt that he was
particularly unhappy, he just didn't think school was necessary—he felt he
should be doing other things. He knew he was going to be an actor and this
all seemed to be totally superfluous.[19]

As the boys became friends, Gyles would accompany Simon at times for the
weekend visits to Froxfield. Here he would bask in the remarkable world that
his new friend came from and could see first-hand why his young pal might
yearn to escape. Simon was already a part of the grown-up world.

'At the age of fourteen, he could already smoke a Gitanes and blow a
perfectly formed blue smoke ring,' remembers Brandreth of his unusually
learned younger friend. 'He could tell the difference between a Chablis and
a Sauternes at a hundred paces, whereas I could barely tell the difference
between red and white! He was a very sophisticated animal.'[20]

Talk was almost always about the theatre, which was music to Gyles's
ears, and there was a remarkably adult feel to the time spent at the cottage.
Brandreth remembers:

Simon's parents would try and come down most weekends, so I would go with
Simon to their cottage where it was a wonderful life. Wine was drunk—not
by me, I was fairly innocent. It seemed almost bohemian—well, not bohemian
but a theatrical atmosphere. Because the parents were both theatrical people
all the talk was of the theatre, so that suited me wonderfully well.[21]

Yet at the end of these weekends, they would return to Bedales. While Gyles
was a major reason for Simon staying the course, it was not enough to
encourage him to greater academic achievements.

Simon continued at the school, but he was not 'of the school' as his best
friend was. Gyles threw himself into the community of Bedales, creating
productions, befriending the aged school founder, J. H. Badley, engaging in
regular games of Scrabble with him at his cottage. Yet Simon remained more
of an outsider, and so as his studies failed to yield anything concrete, the
friendship was pivotal to him.

Within the dormitories, Bedales insisted that there be a variety of age groups. Simon and Gyles requested that they be placed in the same dormitory as one another and their requests were adhered to. The pair became what Gyles believes was seen as, 'a rather quaint and odd little couple.'[22] They spent much of their time together, choosing to lose themselves in the bygone world of Coward, Cole Porter, and Flanagan and Allen and recounting stories of the theatrical heavyweights of Richardson, Gielgud, and Olivier.

Within the confines of their dorm, when they were not pining for times past in the theatre, Simon and Gyles were concocting many plans for the remainder of their education. One such enterprise was for a revue of sorts in which the children of the school performed sketches and songs under the title of *A Merry Evening*. The pair decided to perform as a double act.

In what seems a remarkably poignant piece to have come from such a young pair, Simon played a debonair, sophisticated, and highly successful actor. Set at a hotel in the South of France, overlooking the Mediterranean, he was found sipping his champagne cocktail and enjoying a little caviar. It was the good life for this version of Simon.

The bringer of such luxuries was a waiter of a similar age whose life has clearly not been such a success. The more affluent of the pair does not recognise that the waiter was at school with him. The duo launched into a routine that owed something to 'I Remember It Well', from the Lerner and Loewe musical *Gigi*, in which Honore and Mamita exchange distinctly differing reminiscences of their youth.

Following on from the success of *A Study in Sherlock*, Brandreth's next production was *Thirty Minutes in a Street*. This larger scale production was another success; Simon was once again the standout performer among a cast of forty. The principal theory of the performance was that it would dip briefly into the lives of the unnamed people in an unnamed street. Simon was assigned the role, predictably, of an actor, although he was required to wear a monkey suit for his performance.

By now, it was becoming clear that Simon's destiny was the stage. Gyles was not the only person utilising his friend's talents. Drama teacher Rachel Carey Field was staging a production of *A Passage to India* (the hugely successful film adaptation in 1984 would involve Simon's brother, Patrick, as assistant director) and *Measure for Measure*, in which Simon starred as Pompey (after whom the Cadells named their dog). Simon's advanced talents were described as being, 'as good as two packets of glucose to a harassed producer.'[23]

What Field was now seeing was that Simon did not need to be the top of the billing. His talents were far and away the best at the school's disposal, and so she felt it was kinder to some of those who needed more of a helping hand to give them some of the more senior parts. It was a testament to both Simon's character and confidence that this did not worry him. He was happy to be in the plays, but he knew that there were greater rewards further down the line than school children adulation.

Of his performance as Major Callendar in *A Passage to India*, Field recollected in Simon's report card that he had dropped a line in one performance and needed a prompt during another: 'He was furious, but of course he didn't show his annoyance until afterwards. He's got this marvellous conviction and authority already, but so far he seems completely unspoilt by his talents.'[24]

The only apparent potential blockage in Simon's progress on the stage was his dyslexia. Sight-reading remained an issue, something he fought hard to overcome. During one reading for an exam, he pulled off a 'superb' reading of a passage meant for somebody two grades higher than him, and Rachel Carey Field also pondered as to whether his reading issues were subsiding.

Simon's speech report, however, did note a particular defence mechanism that he used to mask his reading fears. He had a tendency to hold on to consonants for too long in an attempt to try and anticipate the words ahead. 'It will work with some authors, but not with all!' was the remark on the report card.[25]

One battle that continued through Bedales was Simon's propensity to be unwell. He missed entire terms through illness. Gyles Brandreth recalled that this was the reason that their next production together never materialised. That third play was due to be one called *Harlequinade*, by Terence Rattigan, and Simon was again going to play the lead. They had rehearsed in the previous term, but only a few weeks into the new one, Simon returned home. There he stayed while Gyles, after briefly considering stepping into the role himself, replaced him with Mervyn Riches, a student teacher who Gyles felt was the only person capable of taking on the tricky role that he had earmarked for his friend.

Simon's schooldays were often broken up by significant spells out through illness. One such occasion was after a bought of appendicitis, Simon undergoing an appendectomy. There was considerable disagreement between the Cadells and the school as to whether the appropriate action had been taken with the right level of urgency, and in the end the parties agreed to disagree.

What it did mean was that Simon once again missed an entire term and was playing catch-up with his studies. In a somewhat despairing letter to the Cadells, the school admitted to discussing the lack of prospects of Simon achieving anything worthwhile on the academic front. These days, issues with dyslexia would be dealt with more sympathetically, but in 1965, it was decided by the staff that there was little to be done apart from keeping alive to the problem. They acknowledged that there was a marked difference between Simon's written and oral work, but interpreted that as simply a suggestion that his apparent maturity when talking to his teachers was suggestive of him being more capable than he actually was.

The friendship between Simon and Gyles continued to flourish. In addition to their theatrical pleasures, another bond they shared was their dislike of sporting pursuits. Simon was already keen to avoid any further involvement after his earlier run-in during rugby. Gyles came up with a novel solution, remembering:

> I decided to form what we called the Weeds XI. I rather cleverly got the headmaster, Tim Slack, to be in charge of it because I thought that being the headmaster he'd always be called away for important meetings—and so it proved. We were the weakest, we just wanted to get out of our shorts and into the warm as quickly as possible.[26]

During the holidays, Simon and Gyles continued with their unconventional childhood. When able to get out and about, not for them the ordinary pursuits of pre-pubescent teenagers. They wanted to absorb theatrical performances that they could discuss and mimic.

One such occasion saw Simon manage to secure tickets to a performance by Marlene Dietrich. They took their places up in the gods of the stalls at the Golders Green Hippodrome. They gobbled up the manufactured theatrics on offer and adored the evening, but the pair were not satisfied with simply enjoying the performance.

Simon wanted some extra story to mark the occasion and had therefore decided that they needed to see Dietrich as she left the theatre. Whether he had worked it out for himself, or whether it was a secret tactic that his father had let him in on, he believed that there would be a decoy car awaiting the departure of the Hollywood legend. Those forming queues around the stage door and the awaiting car would surely be disappointed.

At the front of the theatre, Simon and Gyles's patience and ingenuity would be rewarded. The swamped car at the side of the theatre was indeed a decoy, and the one next to which the two excitable teens stood would soon play host to the Hollywood goddess. Brandreth remembers the story with relish:

> Marlene climbed up on the top of this car, wearing a miniskirt with a slit up the side, throwing out to the adoring fans, including Simon and me, signed photographs. When she had to get off the car Simon and I had positioned ourselves so that we were the recipients of Marlene Dietrich's legs. So she sat herself down on the roof of her car, wiggled her way towards the edge, and we assisted. Simon took one leg, I took the other, and there we were holding the thighs of Marlene Dietrich as she slipped off the roof of her limousine.[27]

As it became clear that academia was not to be Simon's forte, he made another attempt to expedite his acting career. It was decided that he should apply to join the National Youth Theatre. The company had been set up in 1956 with the intention of nurturing and championing young talent in preparation for a career in the dramatic arts. At the Duchy Hall, pupils from Alleyn's School in Dulwich had been invited to perform Michael Croft's production of *Henry IV Part II*, and it is reported that at the after party the suggestion was made that an organisation be formed for young people to stage plays during the school holidays.

That Simon got in was no great surprise and perhaps evidence of how the plays at Bedales were fun to him, and necessary to maintain his interest in remaining there, but he was already looking to a wider stage. Success at the NYT would be, as it is for pupils today, a significant entry on a fledgling CV.

Undoubtedly, the principle success of Simon's time with the company was *Zigger Zagger*, a Peter Terson play directed again by Michael Croft. If ever something would become an indication of Simon's talents, this was it. *Zigger Zagger* told the story of Harry Philton, a young football hooligan about to leave school at the age of fifteen. While football was the wrapper for the story, the fundamental theme was the apparent futility in the life of this boy, set free into a world where his lack of opportunities and qualifications seemed set to doom him to a life of emptiness.

The action of the play, saving on stage design, was all set within a stadium. The backdrop therefore was the large company of actors. They would appear from the stands for any more specific role they had in the play and then retreat back to their seats when complete.

Simon was not to play the part of Harry, nor of Zigger Zagger himself. These roles had long been assigned to Nigel Humphries and Anthony May. Simon was to play the football club chairman, who tires of carrying the responsibilities of the misbehaving hooligan element plaguing his club.

Simon's character was not actually written into the play until a week before the opening night. He owed his appearance to crowd trouble at the beginning of the new football season. Peter Terson had tired of the responses of the powers at the leading football clubs. Michael Croft recalled that: 'One of these was so fatuous that we could not resist using it, and so the chairman was born.'[28]

Esta Charkham played the mother of Harry. She recalls the unconventional approach to the development of the show: 'We were getting new scenes every day. It was written on the back of envelopes because that's how Peter Terson wrote.'[29]

Bob Eaton, who played the role of the star striker in the play, Vincent, recalls the same aspect to Simon's portrayal that would become thematic for much of his career—his remarkable ability, seemingly a natural one, to appear older than he was.

'His portrayal of a middle-aged, sleazy, football club chairman was extraordinary for someone of his age,' Eaton remembers. 'He just seemed to know what was going on, sophisticated beyond his years. And he was very likeable, so this sophistication didn't get up anybody's nose.'[30]

Anthony May likened Simon's performance to those to be found within Ealing comedies, remarkable for one so young: 'He was a little out of the times ... a cross between Ian Carmichael and Terry-Thomas.'[31]

Terson arrived for that final week's rehearsal and was so impressed with Simon's abilities that he hastily added additional involvement for the role to capitalise on his talents. 'For any of us that particularly had instinctive comedy bones, they would go away and the next day you'd come back and there would be more,' recalls Esta Charkham of the development of the play.[32]

The production was very well received, collecting a variety of awards despite being an amateur play. For pretty much the entirety of his career, production programmes would note *Zigger Zagger* as the play that first announced Simon's arrival in the theatre.

While Esta Charkham recalled the success of the show and the impact it had on its participants and its audiences, she also recounted early signs of the devilish side of Simon's humour:

> There was a song in the show that the youth leader, an actor called Gareth Thomas, sang which was, 'I've Seen Better Days,' in a very rich Welsh voice and he used to sing it on stage by himself. Simon, waiting to come on in braces and a suit, would stand in the wings and do a strip to it. Of course, the entire crowd on the rostrum would just shake with laughter and we got into terrible, terrible trouble. He twiddled his braces and he was just one of the funniest men in the world ... the wickedest, naughtiest, rudest, smuttiest sense of humour. Because we were all kids, it made us laugh even more because it was so naughty.[33]

Simon's path in his chosen profession was becoming clearer. Alongside his acceptance into the NYT was his application to join the Bristol Old Vic Theatre School.

Back at Bedales, Simon recounted the tales of his success to his best friend. Gyles knew that despite his young pal's attempts to persuade him to go to drama school, his destiny lay down a different path, with Oxford University beckoning as it had with his father.

The friendship between Gyles and Simon would never break and never really alter. Conversation was almost always about what plays they had seen, what plays they were working on, or what plays they had finished working on.

As it turned out, one of the first jobs for Gyles' future wife, Michèle, when she left university was at a museum in Bristol, so the pattern of enjoying the good life was barely interrupted by the geographical distance, with Simon going straight to the Bristol Old Vic.

As for Bedales, Simon's final report card in the summer of 1967 presented a far more contented finish. Education had perplexed and frustrated him throughout, seeing it as an annoyance that interrupted him on his chosen path. In that final term, while more absences meant that he missed some of his exams, his teachers were entirely supportive of him as he went out into the world.

'Simon is leaving Bedales a boy of great charm, but one of character and integrity too,' wrote one teacher, while another wrote of his 'delicious comedy timing' and Rachel Carey Field remarked that he had, 'made Bedales so pleasant, simply by being around.'[34]

Attending all classes willingly and getting fully involved in them as well, Simon seemed to have broken free of the shackles of education now that places with the Bristol Old Vic Theatre School and the National Youth Theatre were secured.

His speech tutor perhaps summed things up best. While acknowledging that Simon still had issues with sight-reading that he found exhausting, his teacher recognised:

> He has a real gift for making people laugh at and with him. I'm sure the Bristol and Youth Theatre successes have finally given him that much-needed confidence, even about sight-reading. He has come to realise that he can cope with a part at sight and give a performance because of his instinct for the rhythm and feel of a part. I am especially glad about the NYT because competition is stiff and he can always feel, with absolute, 'Alone, I did it!'[35]

4

Play It Straight

By the summer of 1967, Simon Cadell was free from conventional education. Bedales had provided him with some acting experience as well as a lifelong best friend in Gyles Brandreth, but these few attractions were not substantial enough compensations to entertain even the remotest thoughts of proceeding into any form of further education.

With some experience in the National Youth Theatre under his belt, Simon arrived at the Bristol Old Vic Theatre School, an institution revered the world over. Actor Paul Darrow, whose tutelage began in the 1970s, commented that, 'Every actor or actress takes great pride in being able to say, "Oh yes, I was with the Bristol Old Vic." It is the first "credit" we list in the programme of accomplishments.'[1]

Former principal Chris Denys described having the Bristol Old Vic Theatre School on your professional CV as the acting equivalent of having been to Oxford or Cambridge, making it very likely that you will be seen for any role that one is applying.[2]

To gain his entry, having not been seen in productions by the staff, Simon had to go through the ritual of a weekend audition. His NYT colleague and future roommate, Michael Hadley, remembers this qualifying process well:

> There was an audition weekend that we had. There was a little group of you where you did some very specific exercises which I found very strange—I think Simon did as well. Simon had his tights, I had rugby shorts and a rugby shirt so Simon looked hysterical in his tights. I think he settled into the intake's funny boy straight away.[3]

Through a host of vocal and physical exercises along with scenes from plays and improvisation work, Simon was convincing enough to earn himself a place in the group that would arrive at the school in the late summer of 1967.

To Simon then, this was something of a Holy Grail, and a destiny somewhat fulfilled. No more running away for home, this was where he was meant to be.

The Bristol Old Vic Theatre School started life in 1946. Four months after the end of the Second World War, the London Old Vic Company signalled its intention to start a resident theatre company in Bristol. The company opened in February 1946 with a production of *The Beaux' Stratagem*, a George Farquhar comedy; Simon himself would appear in a version of this during his own time with the company.

After battling some initially unconvinced authorities, the Bristol Old Vic Company announced its plans to establish a theatre school that would not only provide training for its pupils, but also a route into the profession for those deemed worthy of such a reward. It achieved its aims and garnered a reputation for the high quality of its graduates that continues to this day.

Having left school at the first conceivable opportunity, Simon was the baby of the intake for that summer. His peers were largely made up of those who had either already served some level of apprenticeship in local theatre groups, or had decided to continue their education at university level, either to dig deeper into acting theory or to gain some qualifications to fall back on should the profession be unkind to them once their years at Bristol were over.

Simon had a few advantages when the time came to join his new colleagues. His father's experience as a theatrical agent meant that he had already been exposed to the great and the good of the profession that Simon's new friends aspired to join. Furthermore, Simon's experience with the National Youth Theatre meant that he went to Bristol with a friend in tow; this was very important for a teenager whose abilities at finding his place among his peers had been questioned so often by former teachers.

Gillian Cadell, forever a driving force in Simon's career, took her son off to see Esta Charkham's father, a tailor on Saville Row, to deck him out in his first suit. She then packaged him and his NYT colleague Michael Hadley into her car and headed off for the West Country.

After scouring the city for something affordable but of an acceptable standard, Gillian found the pair a bed and breakfast that would give the boys half-board accommodation, sharing a room, at a reasonable rate. Hadley recalls:

We were together at 59 Waverley Road with a Mr and Mrs Hobbs and their two boys. It was an extraordinary family. Mr Hobbs was very secretive in lots of ways. He had a huge electric model railway set up in the attic and he never let his wife go up there, he always padlocked the door. On one occasion he caught us on the landing and said, 'Would you like to come and see my hobby?' There was this huge electric train set. We were only allowed to see it, not operate it. It was still the holy of holies. Simon had hysterics about it whenever it was mentioned.[4]

It was a window to a rather different world to the one in which Simon and his friend had been brought up, Hadley remembering that, 'There were occasions where we'd come back at half past twelve, one o'clock in the morning and the television would literally be smoking from having been on all day from the moment they got up. They'd both be snoring, asleep in their chairs … it was a bit of an eye-opener for us.'[5]

The intake for the school was small in number in comparison to most, as few as twenty students in a year. With so few new faces it is staggering to look back at the collective talent that comprised Simon's first year. Among the future stars who shared his time there were Jeremy Irons, Tim Piggott-Smith, Christopher Biggins, and John Caird.

With such a close group, there were none of the threats of peer groups that could normally befall a student new to his surroundings. As such, Simon's nervous devices and tender years (he and Biggins were the youngest members) were never really an issue.

In his own autobiography, Biggins commented that there were no problems with social alienation in the group: 'Being different was fine—in fact, it was something to be applauded if not actually encouraged.'[6]

John Caird concurs that the atmosphere was one of mutual cooperation, where differentiating traits were almost the norm. 'I guess we were all quite happy with each other's idiosyncrasies,' he reflects. 'We were very interestingly chosen by the principal, Nat Brenner. He loved interesting characters … I think his sense was that theatre needed characters. Just skill or good looks wasn't something that interested him as much as larger than life characters.'[7]

When recalling his first impressions of Simon in their very first week at school, Caird unsurprisingly remembers how Simon's actual age seemed to be masked by a more aged look and theatrical certainty:

My first impression was that he was a strange mixture of extraordinary confidence and almost childishness. He was the most sophisticated of us in the sense that he knew more about professional theatre than anybody else because of his upbringing, but he was emotionally very immature. He'd rubbed shoulders with actors and theatre people all his life. So he had a sort of glamour about him in the sense that his anecdotes were about people that we aspired to be. It became something of an in-joke that Simon knew everybody, no matter how famous they were, even though he was just a boy.[8]

With digs and a first-year companion sorted, the business of learning his craft from the equally colourful characters would shape Simon's first few years as an actor.

The aforementioned Nat Brenner had taken over as principal at the school in 1963. Sometimes, when describing somebody as an all-rounder, it can imply that they never found a level of expertise. That was not the case for Brenner. He had tried his hand at every aspect of the theatre on both sides of the curtain, and excelled at it all.

Brenner was a hard taskmaster, but the students were everything to him and therefore helping them to maximise their talents was a driving force in his approach to life at the school. 'He loved the students, but he was also quite cynical and hard-bitten,' remembers Caird. 'He was never over-impressed by any student, but he was fond of everybody and very good at casting the plays.'[9]

Among Brenner's particular favourite works were those of the Russian playwrights. Being of Ukrainian descent, things like Chekhov and working-class Russian plays were frequent choices. Yet he was equally at home with farces. Brian Rix farces were in full swing at the time, with *Uproar in the House*, starring Nicholas Parsons and *Carry On* favourite Peter Butterworth, set to open at the Whitehall.

'Nat would talk about the Eldridge farceurs,' remembered Tim Pigott-Smith. 'Simon and I loved replicating bits of business Nat had told us that these guys had done.'[10] These were skills that would stand Simon in good stead as he regularly returned to farces during his theatrical career.

Brenner was clearly a massive influence on Simon. Indeed, when researching the principal, many descriptions of his character could be mistaken as a direct description of Simon's own personality. Among the traits attributed to Brenner are being a fan of well-spoken English, a socialist leaning in his political views, traditionalist in his theatrical opinions, with an acerbic wit and a wonderful way with a one-liner, and of course, he was a consistent chain smoker, a habit Simon was already proficient in.

Of course, the school was not all about Brenner. He was surrounded by a talented staff who had specific areas of expertise to impart on the group. Perhaps the chief influence among the other teachers was Douglas Dempster. He was tasked with some direction duties along with the rather unusual combination of improvisation and fencing classes. Dempster was an experienced farceur himself and he could see the comic potential in Simon's skills at this stage. The technical knowledge of the profession that Simon became so well-known for was nurtured and encouraged. John Caird recalled of Dempster:

> He made us laugh a lot. That goes a long way in drama school. If your teacher is demonstrating the work to you in a way that makes you laugh then you know how it's done. Directors should try not to demonstrate, whereas in drama schools there is always an apprenticeship element. Teachers, if they got exasperated, could say 'oh, like this' and you'd practice until you could do it like them. Dougie was like that.[11]

Improvisation skills learnt from Dempster were another talent that helped Simon years later, particularly when he became recognised as the much-despised Reinicke in *Enemy at the Door*. With the Nazi officer as his only established on-screen persona at the end of the 1970s, Simon agreed to appear in a short-lived television improvisation show for Granada entitled *Take the Stage*.

The theory behind *Take the Stage* was that a local theatre group would compete against established actors in a series of improvisation games. After a debut run-through with Michael Horden as chairman, Trevor Peacock took over the moderator role when the series was commissioned.

The format was that each show would contain a number of stars from a pool of talent representing Granada that included Rula Lenska, Michael Elphick, Victor Spinetti, Victoria Wood, and Diane Keen among others. Nick Turnbull, deviser and producer of the show, recalls Simon's talents well:

> The perceived public imagination of Simon had been fostered by this rather po-faced German character [Reinicke]. So it was a delight for everybody to find out that he was nothing like that at all.
>
> He was a great improviser and a great supporter of the show. He had a genuine skill at humour—it was that understated, slightly wry, slightly mischievous but brilliant humour. You could put him in the middle of the stage, get him to say nothing and he'd still be captivating. He could hold an audience without even thinking about it.
>
> The show was always recorded in the evening and so actors would turn up at odd hours during the day but generally you'd have a few pretty boring hours in the green room where everybody said hello to everybody else and then a kind of moribund silence settled on people. It's at that point that you recognised true spirit and the real troopers. If ever I suggested to forget about the coffees and just have some fun, he was always the first one to get up and say, 'Right, what are we going to do? I'm going to be a captain of a boat.' And off we'd go. He was incredibly supportive.[12]

It was a sadly short-lived project. During a strike that saw *Emmerdale Farm* taken off air, *Take the Stage* was inexplicably offered up for the vacant early evening slot, one that it was not designed for. Critics did not take to it and ITV audiences just did not like it not being *Emmerdale Farm*, so it disappeared all too quickly. The format did get very successfully reinvented more for television appeal when *Whose Line Is It Anyway?* appeared a few years later.

Simon's other teachers of note included vocalist John Oxley, movement and dance teacher Lynn Britt, movement teacher Rudy Shelley, and vocal and speech coach Katy Stafford.

Simon was not somebody who really needed a speech coach. His diction was of such quality that there was little that he could be taught in this area. For

Stafford's classes, Simon had little need and so his old school habits returned, albeit in slightly less disruptive ways as he mercilessly mimicked his tutor.

Austrian-born Rudi Shelley's movement classes were somewhat more of an unusual experience. Shelley had arrived in the very first year of the school opening. His classes were more about the craft and techniques as opposed to the acting itself. His role was to teach the appropriate posture and movement for a performer, including in his class lessons on how to walk around a room with a lemon clenched between the buttocks. Carol Hayman, who would cross paths with Simon years later in a Saturday Night Thriller *Where Is Betty Buchus?*, remembers from her own time at the Old Vic Theatre School that should her posture fall, she would hear the mixed accent call of, 'Carolynne, you are not squeezing your lemons!'[13]

Lynn Britt would add the dance teaching to the curriculum, and one can only imagine what Simon made of the two hours of classical ballet lessons. Completing the line-up was John Oxley, who carried the responsibility of teaching the pupils to sing, or at least enhance their existing vocal skills. He recalls Simon's vocal talents being, 'particularly well-suited to Noël Coward, being so typically English.'[14]

When reflecting on the changing times since theatre school, Tim Pigott-Smith believed that the need for singing skills has changed somewhat since the group's time at the school, commenting that:

> I think quite a lot of us wouldn't have got into drama school now. One of the ways you can work in the theatre now is through musicals in the West End. The balance of straight plays to musicals is completely reversed. Our training was fairly rigorously classical. We did a musical, a lovely version of *The Duenna* and Simon was very funny in that. We talked a lot about that when rehearsing because I was uncomfortable in my part in it. It's just a different requirement, but Simon moved effortlessly from one to the other.[15]

In those early days, it quickly became obvious to all around him, both pupils and staff, that Simon possessed what it would take to propel him to stardom, and his talents were not restricted to one specific genre. In particular, his comic skills were getting honed, even though throughout his career, he rebelled against being classed as a comic actor. He told David Shadbolt in 1990 that, 'I am not a comedy actor, I am an actor. If you can play comedy, you can play anything. I hate the idea of a division between comedy and everything else, it's wrong, there is humour in even the darkest plays.'[16]

Despite possessing the necessary comedic skills, Simon was keen to amuse while he learnt and the more outrageous overplaying side of his personality would sometimes need to be kept in check. In school, his teachers were keen that he not overplay his comic talents. Although they recognised that comedy would be a successful avenue for him, he was often admonished by them for overplaying for a laugh. John Caird recalls:

> Quite often he would be pulled up by his teachers—Nat or Dougie—Shelley was very hard on him for getting laughs too cheaply. He would have a wonderful catalogue of moves and entrances and exits and comic techniques that he'd gleamed from watching the greats and he loved all that. He loved the shtick of comedy and how comedy works. How to exit and get a laugh.[17]

An example of his being admonished for cheap laughs stuck with Simon for the rest of his days. Many of the productions at the Old Vic would require the leading performers to additionally play some of the walk on parts that in bigger companies might otherwise be left to extras or stand-ins. During one particular performance when Simon was engaged in one of these roles, Nat Brenner was busy dishing out his advice to the leading actors.

After reminding them of their motivation and directing them with their movements, he spared one last thought. He looked across at Simon, who had been hamming up his non-speaking role and said simply, 'oh, spear carrier on the end—play it straight.'[18]

It was a line that Simon held dear and he actually pondered that had he been able to afford the luxury of ever writing his autobiography, it might have made a reasonable title. It was certainly advice that he retained, as evidenced in his most successful role as Jeffrey Fairbrother, where he claimed the lion's share of the laughs with barely a single punchline in his entire stay on the show.

The advice was also something he imparted on his sister. 'He had a marvellous phrase, which I have often used,' says Selina. 'He'd say, "Yes, it's quite good. I think you should dry it up more." What that means is that you should take the comedy down a bit as though you don't know it's funny. That's the key to comedy I think.'[19]

Although Simon was happy to take the criticism, the apparent overplaying may well have been attributable to the naughtiness in him rather than a lack of awareness of the comedic line over which one should not cross. 'He would giggle at what he was achieving in comic terms, but he was always quite happy to be brought down a peg or two,' says Caird. 'He wasn't precious or grand about himself. He would say, "Yes, I knew that was too much. Sorry."'[20]

Simon may have been a remarkable comedy performer, even in those early days learning his craft, but he was also a talent in all other departments. For him, everything about the theatre carried an interest. With the family background he had been exposed not just to the performers but also to the whole theatrical world and that meant that he knew the business and technical sides as well.

To his new classmates, Simon's skills were baffling to exist in one so young. Tim Pigott-Smith recounted:

> He knew about the business, but I was hopelessly green about it. He just seemed to be on another planet in terms of professional awareness and in terms of the basic skills. It was the first time I had encountered a really, really proper actor. I just thought 'Oh my God, this boy's really got it together.' When we were doing *Love's Labour's Lost* and Simon was playing Berowne, you just sat there and thought, 'Oh boy, this chap's on another planet. He's way, way ahead of the rest of us.' He was completely brilliant.[21]

The skills were everything to Simon, and he engaged in many debates with Pigott-Smith during their two years together. 'We used to argue about craft and art all the time and of course, Simon was right. You'll get much further with a bit of craft than you will with some poncey idea about the spirit of the thing.'[22]

Simon even developed a near encyclopaedic knowledge of the theatre in general. Joanna Lumley, who Simon would become firm friends with years later, remarked, 'He loved to know who had played the parts before, where it had been, how it was done, how long it ran, which languages it had played in. He knew everything, and it wasn't his duty, it was his pleasure.'[23]

When meeting up again a few years after leaving the Old Vic, John Caird and Simon were comparing stories of their first experience of the theatre. Caird's first recollection was of a production of *Toad of Toad Hall* on the West End. So mesmerised was Caird, a seven-year-old at the time, that he highlighted this production as being the reason he chose to go into the theatre.

Simon pounced. 'What year?' he asked. When the reply of 1955 came back, he rattled off the details. 'That would have been the Shaftesbury Theatre,' he began, before reeling off a perfect listing of the casting details. It was an attention to every aspect of the theatre that followed Simon throughout his life.

Caird believes that it was simply another example of Simon's devotion to something that interested him and proof that his lack of success in education was not representative of anything more than this, commenting that, 'He was incredibly bright, had a very high IQ, just not in the things that didn't interest him or things that he couldn't do anything about. He knew his sphere of interest and influence and he inhabited it with enormous relish and fondness and sweetness.'[24]

Time at the school during the day was of course primarily centred on the acting process itself, yet this was an immersive experience for most. Christopher Biggins felt that there were a few different sects—the serious professionals, a group into which Pigott-Smith and Simon, among others, fell—and those such as himself who fell less for the profession and more for the lifestyle and camaraderie that surrounded it.

While it is understandable that Biggins should place Simon in the serious actors group—he was, after all, deeply devoted to his craft—it would be wrong to suggest that he was forsaking drama school life to discuss motivation and Shakespeare.

Caird, Irons, and Pigott-Smith would spend many long evenings dragging on into the early hours discussing acting theory, politics, and world events; this was not for Simon. If it was something that he had no influence over or interest in, he became easily bored and looked for ways out of the conversation.

Despite his talents being recognised so early, Simon brought with him some inevitable baggage from his troubled education. His undiagnosed dyslexia and his nervous disposition were both issues that needed a vent.

For his dyslexia, Simon was able to rely on his colleagues for support. For somebody who had achieved so little in the ways of formal education, he was a fiercely intelligent man. With the group of peers being so small in number, it's of no surprise that he found assistance easy to come by. Caird remembers Simon's problems, and how he simply found a way around them:

> I remember helping him with the text of some of the plays that we did, helping him understand the text. He couldn't get his eyes around the words—reading was always a bit of a torture for him. He loved to study slowly and learn and get things learnt very early.[25]

Nerves, however, began to manifest themselves in other ways. As a child at Bedales, and indeed at The Hall School before that, Simon had achieved mixed success when dealing with his compatriots. It's perhaps unsurprising that by the time theatre school arrived, the nervous disposition had grown somewhat. Thumb-sucking, a trait that had been prevalent at school, came with him to the Old Vic, but once again, no one really cared—it was just a quirk of Simon's character that further endeared him to his circle of friends.

'He would suck his thumb and stroke his nose while he was concentrating on something,' says Caird. 'He wasn't even aware that he was doing it. It became an endearing idiosyncrasy and people didn't mention it after a while. You could tell it was something he had been doing since he was a little child, but he did it as a sort of automatic reaction to tension or extreme concentration. He did it all through the two years at drama school.'[26] In later years, this nervous tic would be replaced by a stroking of the ball of his hand by his third and fourth fingers.

Nervousness was something Simon kept a fairly tight lid on until performances came around, almost like a cork in a champagne bottle. Tim Pigott-Smith remembered:

You were never hugely aware of Simon's nerves when you were working with him, except when it got nearer the time and then you realised that he was really tightly wound. You'd see it on him—his breathing would become different, he'd become agitated in the wings. Then as soon as he went on he was in complete command. Very strange. It's all in the mind. He used to wrap himself up and you'd see him pacing and you'd think, 'I'd better leave him alone.' He used to clear his throat very loudly in the wings too, sometimes you'd have to say, 'Si, Si,'—and then we had the three S's—shit, shower and shave—and the last thing was check your flies before you went on![27]

Simon's loud clearing of the throat was a Ralph Richardson-esque eccentricity that would continue well beyond theatre school. Selina Cadell remembered fondly her brother's habit of waiting in the wings prior to his first stage entrance, clearing his throat numerous times before announcing 'fuck 'em' rather over zealously before striding on to the stage.[28]

Socially, Simon was flitting between London and Bristol. His colleagues remember no particular sexual targets from his time to keep him in Bristol for any longer than was necessary, not of any seriousness at least. Of course, there was a significant imbalance between male and female students, so the pairing off that did take place left plenty of unattached males.

It was an easy journey to return to London by train and for Simon, this was a must. He needed to be back home where he could access the West End and immerse himself once more in the theatrical environment for which he longed.

When Simon had first told his parents that he wanted to pursue an acting career, they had been supportive of his desires but had warned him that it would most likely be a financial struggle. The Cadell family were not exactly on the breadline, but they had instilled in their children the value of financial management and the need for them to be self-sustaining. For Simon, that was not always so easy to put into practice.

As almost anybody involved in some kind of further education will know, the struggle to pay one's way can be never-ending. For Simon, whose generosity knew no material bounds, that struggle began at theatre school and continued until well into the success of *Hi-de-Hi!*.

One of Simon's issues financially was that he had a slightly distorted view of what constituted the bare essentials necessary for a decent standard of living. He believed that even if you might not be working now, you would be one day. As such, the cigarettes, cigars, and wines that would be seen by others as unnecessary expenses remained in his budget.

This approach during theatre school was not a particularly prudent one. Michael Hadley remembers that many of the group were gaining their daily caloric intake by drinking Guinness instead of wasting money on food.

Simon's preference was for a good wine, which served neither the calorific purpose nor a reduction in his outgoings.

Equally damaging to Simon's financial situation was his generosity. Money was to be enjoyed and despite suggesting to the press in later years that he was not prone to grand gestures, he was actually a very generous man who took great delight in sharing his earnings with his friends. Indeed, Selina recalls that, 'When he earned money, he spent it on all of us all the time. I don't think I've ever met anyone who was as generous as he was.'[29]

One typical example occurred some years later during the filming of *Enemy at the Door*. Radio producer Jane Morgan, with whom Simon developed a life-long friendship through numerous Radio Four plays, had parted company with her husband, who had subsequently remarried. She was then invited to a party by their mutual friend Michael Bakewell. Jane knew that the party had the potential to be thoroughly miserable for her, being unattached at the time and witnessing her ex-husband with his new bride. Her friends suggested casting an eligible companion to attend with her, and Simon's name was mentioned.

'I called Simon and said "Simon, there's this situation ...",' remembers Jane. 'I'd barely got two words out before he said, "Jane, do you think Michael Bakewell would invite me to his party?"'[30]

Location filming for *Enemy at the Door* took place on the Channel Islands. For Bakewell's event, Simon flew back home, collected Jane Morgan, and glued himself to her side for the entire event before returning to his location shoot. When recounting that story during the research for this book to Stephanie Turner, Simon's partner during that time, she was unsurprised.

'That is Simon ... really kind, well intentioned,' she reflected. 'Big gestures, but properly meant and ones that nobody would know about. If it cost money or not wouldn't make any difference. If he needed money for that flight it wouldn't make any difference because that's what he'd decided to do.'[31]

With such extravagance in his nature, it was perhaps inevitable that Simon's money ran out, and he looked at other options. Earning a paltry £11 a week as an acting ASM, he and his chums would often head to a small club near the Theatre Royal in Bristol. Here, Simon would more often than not head for the blackjack tables. Tim Pigott-Smith was among his party when they visited the clubs, and he remembered the nature of Simon's spending:

> We were getting so little money—we were of a very different nature in that respect. We tended to save, but if Simon had money in his pocket he used to enjoy it. At the end of the week when we got our pay packet, we'd go up there and Simon would quite often go onto the gambling tables. I wouldn't say he got addicted, but he got worryingly involved in it.[32]

Simon himself, however, did believe he got addicted and would often find himself out of cash. He was reliant on a little inside help, finding a female croupier who became used to her regular visitor. When Simon was desperately short of funds, she would give him some unofficial assistance. This particular approach did not last for long. As he later recalled, 'I discovered myself being thrown out of the casino. I can't remember anything between the two pairs of strong hands grabbing me at the table and landing in the street!'[33]

The forced removal from the Bristol casino may have prevented further debts at that time, but it didn't cure Simon from his love of blackjack. An addictive personality is not so easily swayed. Years later, when his partner and future wife Beckie Croft accompanied him to a casino, the only time she did so, she could see the traits of Simon's love of gambling in full swing:

At that stage we had no money—we were sleeping on a mattress on the floor. Even though we had carpets on the floor, it was pretty basic. He would enjoy losing as much as winning. He put on £50 and won £100. I took back the stake money so that we'd come out quits. After about two more hands, he wanted the £50 back. He said, 'well I need it to win back the money.' I said, 'No, no … that's gambling—that's losing. It's not good for you.' He wasn't pleased at all and he never took me gambling again. He used to love it though. He didn't bet on horses or anything else, he just liked blackjack.[34]

For the crucial second year of theatre school, Simon and Michael Hadley moved on from the Waverley Road B&B. Tim Pigott-Smith rented an enormous house in Clifton at £39 a month. Christopher Biggins, Tony Falkingham, and Hadley joined him there. Such was the vastness of the property that they could easily take in more *ad hoc* boarders, which from time to time included both Simon and his uncle, Peter Howell, when he had business at The Old Vic.

The completion of the year had the potential to make or break a career. The performance of *The Alchemist* in June 1969 was effectively an advertisement of the talents as the group prepared to move into the real world of theatre, one where they needed to be earning money to pay their way.

This was the production to which all kinds of talent-spotters were invited. Agents would be watching, looking to sign up the best of the year's influx into the industry. Irons, Pigott-Smith, Hadley, Biggins, and Caird—the full year— were about to take their bow and place themselves in the shop window.

For Simon and Hadley, this pivotal production did not quite carry the make-or-break status that it did for their many friends. Having come from the National Youth Theatre, the pair already had agents on their side, so they at least had somebody to fight their corner should work not be forthcoming upon their release. Of *The Alchemist*, Hadley remembers:

I was Face and he was Subtle. We were very worried about it as we were rehearsing. Simon to his credit never showed any inkling of the fear of what we were about to do and what hung on the final shows. It was only afterwards that he admitted that he was as scared as hell, as scared as any of us. A lot of people had a lot resting on that performance.

We couldn't believe that it went so well, though Simon was utterly confident that we would get all the laughs. Nat Brenner [director] came round at the interval and broke the rule of coming to people's dressing rooms—he was just so delighted with what was happening. I was stunned by the audience reaction to what was going on. We worried so much about whether we were going to pull it off, but we did, no small thanks to Simon being at the centre with a cool head—apparently the cool head, but chaos inside.[35]

As the group bade farewell to their theatre school, perhaps Tim Pigott-Smith's recollection of that production of *The Alchemist* sums up Simon's stay at The Bristol Old Vic Theatre School best: 'I played Subtle in 1995 and I used to think, "What on earth did Simon do with this part?" I just couldn't crack it. I used to think back and think "I wish I could see his performance again, it might help me." He was completely brilliant.'[36]

5

And Now for Pleasure

Graduation from the Old Vic Theatre School in Bristol was never a guarantee of success in the acting profession but for Simon Cadell and a number of his colleagues, that production of *The Alchemist* had sealed his future.

Patricia Lord had taken up responsibility for Simon within the profession as his first agent, a role that cemented a friendship for the rest of his days. 'If they were good enough, they could be really difficult and I'd put up with it,' she reflects. 'Simon could have his moments, but it was only moments and it was usually from worry. But he was an absolute joy to look after.'[1]

The combination of agent and friend meant that Simon respected Patricia's opinion above most others. Beckie Croft remembers, 'She was so naughty, she used to keep him dangling on a string. He couldn't settle, he couldn't rest, until he heard what Patricia thought of the performance.'[2]

He would join some of his friends in the Old Vic's own repertory company within weeks of the end of the school year. Among them was Tim Pigott-Smith, who lamented how times have changed:

> Loads of young actors from our year at theatre school went off into rep. They can't do it now, it's not there. There was a feeling in a funny kind of way that as a young actor you had to work your apprenticeship. You'd spend a few years in rep and then you might end up in a really good rep - we were lucky that we'd started in a really good rep—and then with a bit of luck you might get your claws on the bottom rung of the Royal Shakespeare Company or National Theatre. That was the trajectory that we all aspired to.[3]

Departure into rep left a gap in Simon's schedule, a five-week break that would allow him a first well-timed foray into television. Although armed with an agent, it was a former National Youth Theatre colleague that helped Simon not only gain his first made-for-television role, but also to obtain his coveted Equity card in the nick of time.

Esta Charkham had moved on from performing in theatre since Simon first worked with her on *Zigger Zagger*. By the summer of 1969, Charkham was now secretary to a casting director working with Yorkshire Television on a new television show, *Hadleigh*. Gerald Harper played the title role in a production that would run for four series through to 1976.

'I was cast in the role of a friend of Hadleigh's girlfriend,' recalled Simon in an interview for *TV Times* years later. 'At that time, the programme makers, Yorkshire Television, were experimenting with colour. The episode I was in was one of the first to be recorded in colour with new super-sensitive cameras. At one point, the air-conditioning system broke down and the cameras became overheated. As a result, we went into overtime.'[4]

As an actor fresh from drama school, the opportunity to earn extra money was always welcome. 'I was absolutely delighted,' he continued. 'The overtime payment was more than my pay. I couldn't understand why the other actors were so fed up about it all.'[5]

Although Simon's one-episode role on *Hadleigh* was his first in a television series, he had in fact been seen on the small screen during the run of *Zigger Zagger*. The BBC had decided to bring the National Youth Theatre production into their studios for a one-off performance filmed for airing in September 1967 and directed by John Glenister.

Co-star Michael Hadley recalls Simon's delight at his first venture into the new medium:

> Simon was fascinated by it and relished it. Most of the rest of us were just drifting around in a daze. I remember we saw Derek Nimmo being dragged around supported on both arms and I remember feeling 'I hope I never get like that.' He was just overworked. He was doing a television series and a radio series and in the West End doing *Charlie Girl* at night and he was just out on his feet. And you just thought, 'Is that what this industry is about?'[6]

It clearly was not an experience to dissuade Simon, and he recalled how his debut small-screen role enabled him to gain his Equity card: 'In those days you used to be able to get a card just by getting a part on television. The day my contract ended was actually the day they changed the rules, so I got my card only by the skin of my teeth.'[7]

Simon's first television role was a satisfying experience. One can only imagine the excitement that it brought him, especially given the timing of his ten days of filming, coinciding as they did with the moon landings. He later recalled: 'The morning after the event everyone arrived late for rehearsals because the landing was supposed to be at one o'clock in the morning but was delayed and happened three and a half hours late. London was full of people falling asleep that day—the cast of *Hadleigh* was among them.'[8]

Appearing on television for the first time was a double-edged sword. A jobbing theatre actor whose career was in its infancy was unlikely to bring in much of a wage, but television offered far greater fiscal opportunities. Yet there was another issue that Simon would have to overcome—his self-loathing of his gently lopsided face. 'I did watch that episode [of *Hadleigh*]—and hated myself in it,' he later recalled.[9]

Years later, with *Hi-de-Hi!* at its peak, he still recalled his horror at seeing his own face on his television debut. 'I could hardly believe it was me,' he said. 'It was rather like a dreadful moving passport photograph, endlessly showing oneself at one's worst. I've hardly watched myself since.'[10]

Self-image was a constant doubt raging in Simon's mind. The gentle curves of his face would eventually be part of the charm that made the British public fall in love with Jeffrey Fairbrother, but in those early years, the fear that his looks might hold him back caused a great deal of inner turmoil. It was a recurring theme across interviews for many years and the depth of feeling ranged from mild irritation to hatred.

'He couldn't bear the fact that his face was wonky,' remembers Beckie. 'That's why he never really wanted to go into films, because of the idea of seeing his face that big. He did have quite a thing about it, that he'd never be a proper leading man because he didn't look like Jeremy Irons, who was proper pin-up stuff.'[11]

Patricia Lord recalls conversations regarding Simon's facial shape: 'Once or twice we talked about it and he did say to me, "Do you think I should have something done about it?" and I said, "Absolutely not."'[12] Nonetheless, it was a demon that would never fully be buried until the popularity of *Hi-de-Hi!* was gaining momentum.

Joanna Lumley recalls a scathing review during their run in *Noël and Gertie* several years into Simon's successful ascension to leading man in a successful television show, remembering that a particular critic went after his crooked jawline:

> What kind of critic goes after those sorts of human criticisms? It was somebody in a good paper who ought to have known better. There was an operation you could have had which was to take a bit out of your face and pull your jaw around. But then you'd have to have your teeth re-set and everything re-done. Simon talked about it, but we all said don't do it.[13]

Simon's concerns over his appearance did not stop with the shape of his face. David McKail shared a dressing room with him in 1975 when appearing together in *The Case in Question*; ironically, it was the same dressing room shared by Simon's father John and his god-father, Donald Sinden, when they were first treading the boards. McKail recalls that Simon's vanity was an endearing one that encompassed other elements of his appearance:

> He had sessions twice a week with his trichologist, who massaged his scalp and prescribed a daily kelp tablet to stop his receding hairline. He had a horror of going bald. He was very aware that he was not a conventional leading man, what with inheriting the Cadell twisted lip.[14]

For all his concerns over his facial appearance, only the odd isolated vindictive critic would ever judge Simon so superficially. Only adding to his unique character, stage performances never suffered and once *Hi-de-Hi!* had made him a headline name to place on the billboard, doubts about leading man status would ease.

Gyles Brandreth felt that although Simon knew he would never be a traditional romantic lead, 'as the years went by he realised that every part is a character part, and it's all about characters. It would have mattered less and less.'[15]

'Certainly in performances you forgot it,' reflects director and friend Nick Renton. 'With that concern of the outside, you have to produce an inner light of some sort, which he always found. That was always the most astonishing thing, seeing what he did on stage. You just didn't notice it.'[16]

Looking back, Beckie believes that Simon's dislike of his appearance contributed to the 'inner light' to which Renton refers, which in turn had other advantages:

> Because he was not particularly beautiful, he had to work at getting the ladies and therefore he worked very hard. In all these surveys they say how to get a woman is to be funny. Well it was absolutely true. He was a wow with the women, which technically he shouldn't have been. He was incredibly charismatic, he had the most hilarious wit—so sharp. It was genuine charm, not smarmy. You can usually see if someone's just trying to be charming, but he genuinely was … and hilariously funny, which was very appealing.[17]

The concerns about his screen appearance had to be buried, although there would be only one other minor television role in those early days for Simon— in ATV's *Hine*, a Barrie Ingham vehicle about the dubious dealings of a British arms salesman. This aside, he would have to wait a good many years before television success would come his way; this was no matter for the teenager as he now had his Bristol repertory season to throw himself into.

After a final performance of *As You Like It*, which closed the then Theatre Royal at Bristol because it had to be closed for repairs, Simon then went on a tour of the West Country for about three weeks. Michael Hadley had left, but Jeremy Irons and Tim Pigott-Smith were among his Old Vic chums to continue with the run.

The tour consisted of two plays, *The School for Scandal* and *A Delicate Balance*, the latter of which did not involve Simon. 'We had played it at the Little Theatre, but it then went on to do the tour which is quite unusual,' remembered Pigott-Smith. 'Simon played Snake extremely well. Again, the technical ability he had—he was able to fall into the style of it very readily.'[18]

There followed another dual production tour in 1970, with Simon alternating as Lane in *The Importance of Being Earnest* and Nicola in *Arms and The Man*. It was an end for Simon's particular Old Vic colleagues, with Jeremy Irons and Tim Pigott-Smith moving away from the Bristol company and upon conclusion of the tour, Simon himself would bring his much-valued association with the Old Vic to a close.

With no significant break into television on the horizon, Simon continued to work his apprenticeship within repertory theatre, joining the Nottingham Playhouse Company during the summer of 1971. There he would join a company with the likes of Michael Elphick and Delia Lindsay in productions of *A Close Shave*, *Antigone*, and *The Balcony*.

During this time, Simon shared a flat with two of his fellow cast members, Charles Waite and David Schofield. Money was of course still short, hence the sharing of the apartment. The three enjoyed each other's company and got up to all the things one would expect of young stars in the making sharing digs.

Schofield remembered the difference between styles of the three. Celebrating his twenty-first birthday in Nottingham, Simon sought some advice from his friend. Schofield recalls: 'Donald Sinden told him that for his birthday he could have either a Cartier watch or the cash equivalent into his bank account. Most of us impoverished actors would have welcomed the filthy lucre ... dear Simon plumped for the watch!'[19]

It was indeed quite a choice from Simon, given that he was rarely in possession of any funds. However, with his fondness of the finer things, in retrospect one can see the thought process behind his choice.

He was also opting for a slightly different choice of alcohol. His penchant for fine wines came at a price, so he had to cut his cloth accordingly when looking for alcoholic beverages. Charlie Waite remembered: 'On some evenings, he would shout out from the bathroom to be brought another "Vera". We would smile and comply. He never took himself too seriously and was wonderfully camp and extrovert.'[20]

In 1972, Simon landed the role of Simon Green in the William Douglas-Home black comedy *Lloyd George Knew My Father*. While he had been in almost constant employment since departing theatre school, and had performed in productions of some of the greatest playwrights, this part was undoubtedly the most desirable of all the roles he had tackled to date.

The new play was about an elderly couple facing the prospect of their country home being demolished to make way for a new bypass. Lady Boothroyd announces to her disbelieving husband, General William Boothroyd, that should the bulldozers move in on the Monday morning, she will not be there. She will in fact be taking her own life in protest.

The central characters of the production were an eccentric couple reaching their twilight years after a marriage containing '40,000 boiled eggs', only for the bypass (approved by their own son-in-law) to end up taking any hopes of a contented retirement away from them. While Simon's role, that of the boyfriend of the Boothroyds' daughter, was comparatively minor, it mattered not.

Chosen for the leads were future Dame Peggy Ashcroft and future knight Ralph Richardson, themselves a delightfully eccentric pairing and also symbolic of the acting heights to which Simon aspired. Not only that, but being close friends of the Cadell family, they had both been chosen by Gillian and John to carry godparent responsibilities. Peggy Ashcroft was Patrick's godmother while Ralph Richardson was chosen as Selina's godfather.

Of all the theatrical stars of the time, Richardson was undoubtedly one of the brightest and to appear alongside him on the West End would be seen as the pinnacle of one's achievements. 'You wanted to be Olivier, Richardson or Gielgud ... somebody who had worked in the theatre all their lives,' recalled Tim Pigott-Smith of the drama school's aspiring thespians. 'They didn't have the same level of competition from television then—that all began to grow through the late 1970s. It was a different world.'[21]

They were in a different world to most maybe, but one that Simon had already seen via his parents' theatrical dealings. This was where he wanted and indeed needed to be. Richardson was by now into his seventies and displaying all the eccentricities that only endeared him to Simon further. Yet as full of admiration as Simon was, he retained a desire to carve out his own eccentricities rather than simply be Ralph Richardson or John Gielgud.

John Caird remembers his friend's desire to scale the theatrical heights of his heroes, while retaining his own identity:

He could do Donald Sinden, John Gielgud and Ralph Richardson to a tee because that was part of his sense of self—that he knew these great actors and aspired to be like them. He wasn't ever self-deceiving. He wasn't one of those actors who wanted to be John Gielgud or Laurence Olivier, he was still very much himself. But Simon was in love with the glamour of the theatre and the West End. He adored the idea of being part of that history when theatre was at its most glamorous in the twenties, thirties and forties—Novello, Coward, Rattigan—and I think he saw himself in that tradition.[22]

So it was then that a twenty-two-year-old Simon took his place alongside acting royalty and after pre-West End previews at Oxford and Leeds, the Ray Cooney and John Gale production descended upon the Savoy Theatre for Simon's first experience of being in a West End success. One can only speculate on his own feelings on reaching such heights so early in his career. He would undoubtedly have experienced first night nerves, something he never conquered, but he was in good company.

Years later, he recalled the occasion: 'I remember watching Ralph Richardson and Peggy Ashcroft on stage before the first night of *Lloyd George Knew My Father*, and I've never seen two such frightened people. They were holding hands for reassurance. It told me that everyone is mortal and it doesn't necessarily get easier as you go on.'[23]

Co-star Janet Henfrey, who played the eccentric pairing's daughter Maud, remembers the younger cast members being in awe of Richardson and Ashcroft: 'I owed my part in great measure to Peggy and was close to her in that production, at a time when my mother was critically ill.'[24]

As Janet had sought comfort with leading lady Ashcroft, Richardson took Simon under his wing. Aside from feeling a family responsibility, he clearly saw something in this youngster that made him feel he was worthy of his time and his wisdom and a young Simon was more than happy to absorb anything offered in his direction—including alcohol. Simon recalled in his wine book, *Right Vintage*:

When we'd settled into our run at the Savoy Theatre, Ralph invited me to have a drink with him after the show. This became a fairly regular occurrence, so in the year I was in the show with Ralph, I must have been to his dressing-room thirty or forty times.

The opening routine was always exactly the same. I'd knock at the door, which would be quickly opened by Hal, Ralph's dresser. Hal was barely five feet tall, very dapper, with a smiling but somehow scrunched-up face, a tan (more Max Factor than Mother Nature) and a curious arrangement of red-coloured hair. He always reminded me of a hamster.

Ralph would be sitting at his dressing-table in a white towelling dressing-gown with the initials RR embroidered in blue on the left-hand side. As he saw me he'd say, 'Ah, it's the Boy.' (Ralph gave me the name very early on in rehearsals. I was only twenty-two!) The dialogue would then proceed as follows:

Ralph: Gin?

Me: Yes, please.

Ralph: Hal, gin for the Boy.

Hal would scurry over with two huge and beautiful crystal tumblers (Ralph lived in some opulence, there was a Turner hanging in his dressing-room) and a bottle of Gordon's. Ralph would pour a vast amount of gin into each glass.

Ralph: Tonic?

Me: Yes, please.

Ralph: Hal, tonic for the Boy.

Hal would bring the opened bottle of tonic. Ralph would take it and splash the tiniest amount of tonic into each glass. He'd hand me my glass and then without a word drain his. Hal quickly refilled it with the same proportions, four-fifths gin to one-fifth tonic, and as Ralph lifted it to his lips to take a sip he would say, 'And now for pleasure.'[25]

Simon's recollection of Richardson's lovable eccentricity was certainly not an isolated incident, such was the character of the man. The doddery and aged appearance was belittled by the fact that he would arrive to each rehearsal on a motorbike he would then store at the Savoy's garage. Richardson also gave Simon a tip on how to shave fifteen minutes off the matinee performance by simply cutting out chunks of the play. 'I don't think anybody notices, do you cocky?' he would tell his young protégé.[26]

'Wonderful, wonderful people to work with,' remembers Patricia Lord. 'Enormously generous—Richardson was mad as a bat, but absolutely superb.'[27] Richardson's eccentricities were never more evident than within his curtain call. According to Simon, after each Wednesday matinee, he would have bangers and mash sent to his dressing room. Whether in demand or anticipation we will never know, but while taking the matinee curtain call he could be heard to be chanting 'sausages, sausages!'[28]

'He adored Richardson,' remembers Nick Renton. 'Totally his kind of actor in his head, because of the eccentricity. And precision ... it was like a machine tool. I think Simon wanted to be as naughty as Richardson, but he wasn't quite like that. His head was different.'[29]

The production of *Lloyd George Knew My Father* consisted not just of two acting royalty co-stars. It contained everything Simon loved about the theatre—the quirks of its stars, the ageing but characterful theatre and the grand formal feel that Simon adored.

Chris Ellis, himself a fledgling lighting designer at the time with Robin Midgley's theatre in Leicester, recalls the pomp of the occasion:

The Savoy Theatre was quite old-fashioned at the time. The pre-war lighting control was a bank of old 1930s wire-wound resistance dimmers in the basement that sometimes 'stuck' and had to be hit with a stick to get them to fade to black out or the next cue. The control desk looked like a Compton Organ console. Everyone, including the console operator and the 'man with the stick' all wore evening dress. On matinees, a lady would appear in the orchestra pit and play show tunes for the old ladies.

The audience would take tea and cakes in the stalls and circle bars. My wife thinks that the more infirm ladies may have been served at their stalls seat as well. At each performance, David Fleming [the company manager], would greet the audience in immaculate evening dress in the front foyer. Everything was very genteel. Simon was, of course, the perfect gentleman and quite charming.[30]

Lloyd George Knew My Father was not a complete success with the critics. *The Stage* review, written by R. B. Marriott, described the play as 'exceptionally thin on invention and comic forcefulness.' However, most of his criticisms were laid firmly at the door of William Douglas-Home, citing Richardson and Ashcroft for their 'superb performances.' Simon was of course a new talent at this stage in his career, but did enough with Suzan Farmer for the pair to be described as 'appealing and amusing as the young things.'[31]

Despite his lack of experience, Simon's abilities, charm, and willingness to learn endeared himself to his colleagues. 'He was a delightful chap to have in the company,' recalls co-producer Ray Cooney. 'He was a real team player and everybody in the company admired him.'[32] This was no small measure of Simon's talents, given the quality of the cast alongside him.

It is not inconceivable that some of Simon's charms and gentlemanly ways were if not initiated, certainly fine-tuned while working alongside Richardson. Selina remembers:

He did adore Ralph. I remember Simon saying that he always wore a suit to rehearsal, it didn't matter what he was playing. Simon did that quite a lot and that was the kind of thing he would pick up from Ralph. You would say Ralph perhaps personified the English gentleman ... his manners, his speech, his charm. Even though he wasn't backwards in coming forwards, he was so charming, and I think Simon was influenced by that charm in a rehearsal room.[33]

Never one to rest on his laurels, Simon continued to learn from all around him. Nick Renton remembers one of his friend's favourite stories from the Savoy production, which demonstrates that however highly regarded his work was considered to be, Simon was always looking to better himself and the production:

He had a scene that used to get a laugh on a particular line. He thought it was going very well but gradually it all went away. He worked at re-investigating the scene in his head and the motivation of the character, whether he was turning or moving. 'If I'm playing the scene wrong maybe the whole character's wrong.' So this great disaster was looming.

He became aware that Richardson, who'd left the stage and would normally go off to the dressing room and tot up for the next one, was standing in the wings watching him. After a day or two, Richardson said, 'About that line. Before you say the line, take a deep breath and put your weight on your back foot, look up to the gods and then say the line.' He went and tried it and of course the house fell down.

He was an actor who could take that technique and make it his own and then glue it with something else. Not all modern actors can do that. The moral of that story to me is that you can solve it completely technically and you don't give up anything, you just go forward. He was like that. He disguised being a technical actor—that was what was so beautiful. The use of technique you can see in some actors as being there, you can see the wheels turning. But he could float it back another way which is to do with surprising yourself and the audience. That sense of just holding a pause and then something happening which would get the laugh.[34]

Simon himself remembered learning about the actor's bubble from Richardson:

When I got too close to him on the stage, he said, 'Oh no. No. No, too close, you're in my bubble.' I understand it totally now. He knew that, unless one was playing an intimate scene with somebody, space on the stage is terribly important; and, if two characters who are not being passionately intimate get too close, the audience definition between the two disintegrates, and he called it his 'bubble'. It was in no sense ungenerous.[35]

Simon was not just developing his acting skills. Always one to have a devilish twinkle in his eyes, he fell victim to Peggy Ashcroft's fits of giggles. Around thirty seconds before the end of a particular scene, the great actress would begin to corpse. With her laughter infecting the other performers, Simon recalled how Richardson would take command of the situation, remembering: 'He used to come on and say everybody's lines and get everybody together and bring the curtain down. We always used to have to go and apologise to him at the interval.'[36]

Reviews and ticket sales are not always reflective of one another, and so it proved with *Lloyd George Knew My Father*. Sir Ralph Richardson and Dame Peggy Ashcroft had only signed for six months. Ray Cooney remembers, 'Ralph Richardson couldn't believe it when he agreed to extend his contract for a further six months (because of the huge success) and Dame Peggy wouldn't. So he got Celia Johnson [another of Simon's theatrical favourites] to take it over and it ran for a further year!'[37] It may not have been a particularly well-paid time in Simon's life—certainly not well enough to pay off his debts at least—but it was certainly a golden time in terms of the company that Simon was now able to keep on stage.

Best friend Gyles Brandreth was juggling a number of projects at the time, roping Simon in on each. *The East Blows Cold* was a *son et lumière* at Temple Newsam House in Leeds. Sandwiched between this and a subsequent *son et lumière* at Royal Greenwich was a golden gala event for the benefit of the Oxford Playhouse. Among the theatrical glitterati were Peggy Ashcroft, Alec Guinness, Michael Redgrave, John Gielgud, Cyril Fletcher, and Sir John Clements—a veritable who's who of the theatre scene in the early seventies.

Brandreth remembers these productions fondly although ever the perfectionist, he felt that both *son et lumières* could have been better. Of the Leeds production, he was scathing in his own assessment. 'The truth is: it's a bit of a disaster,' he wrote into his diaries. 'The building is dull; the lighting is unadventurous; the script is plodding; the performances are fine, but *we can't hear them* ... we have a corrugated iron roof over the seating and the rumble of the rain makes it impossible to hear the soundtrack.'[38]

The second of the *son et lumière* at the Royal Greenwich saw an even more distinguished cast list contribute their vocal talents, and once again this was largely thanks to the clientele of John Cadell. Simon weighed in too, but this one fared little better. 'Here, we put up a tarpaulin,' says Brandreth. 'We didn't want the noise issues as we had with the hailstones. But there was wind. The first night, the wind was so great that the tarpaulin roof was lifted off and landed on Edward Heath, who was then Prime Minister and was there with the Prime Minister of Portugal! We're the people who killed *son et lumière*. It was quite popular until I came along!'[39]

Despite having a long West End run to boost his reputation, Simon chose to go back into rep, this time at the Belgrade Theatre, Coventry. Here, he would form a lifelong friendship with director Nick Renton, who would take the helm of three productions during his tenure at the Belgrade.

'The first thing I did was try and recruit a company and one of them was Simon,' recalls Renton, whose first effort was *Romeo and Juliet* starring John Hurt and Lisa Harrow as the doomed young lovers. He continues:

He did a Mercutio in a bizarre wig. He loved that ... the reason for the wig was that we got talking about speech patterns and the way Mercutio used words a little bit like the Marx Brothers. Somewhere within that, the Harpo Marx effect came out and out came the wig. His mother came and after the first night said 'Take the wig off!'[40]

After tackling Shakespeare, Renton rifled through a stockpile of scripts for something appropriate for a small-scale studio theatre. He eventually stumbled upon a script by Trevor Baxter entitled *Edith Grove*. 'Edith Grove just kind of fitted him,' recalls the director. 'It was a very, very English play about madness, roots ... there was a central Jewish character in it, set just before the oncoming war, with guilt. That was very much up the tree of what he liked playing a lot.'[41]

Simon was given further positive reviews to add to his growing portfolio, cited as having played Justin Jackson with 'a seething anger' in *The Stage* review. That same piece commented on the performance of Sheila Brownrigg in the title role, remarking that she performed 'with a style and inventiveness which would be difficult to better.'[42] Brownrigg was quick to acknowledge Simon's contribution to her own performance. Writing to Simon shortly after the brief run, she thanked him for being 'a rock of strength when I was nervous,' who 'gave and gave to me in so many scenes.'[43]

The performances and direction earned more plaudits than the play itself, but it was sufficient for an option to be taken to transfer to the West End under a new title of *Lies*. Sheila Brownrigg was replaced for the run at the Albery, but she knew that Simon would go with the production. 'I foresee that they will not recast you,' she wrote. 'They would be mad if they did because it would be very hard to find another actor so young but so enlightened and able and strong in an extremely difficult part.'[44] Brownrigg's thoughts were another endorsement of Simon's advanced wisdom and knowledge of the industry and she hoped that the play would give him a 'further step up the theatrical ladder.'

Despite also saying that the new production should keep Nick Renton—'he understood the play'—no one else survived the transfer. Renton remembers: 'Simon was very sweet. He said, "I think I only got it because Jean [his grandmother] was a great mate of Wendy Hiller's so she knew who I was."'[45]

Dame Wendy Hiller took over the Edith role from Sheila Brownrigg, with Michael Aldridge, Sandor Eles and Joyce Donaldson completing the company under the watchful eye of David Giles. Reviews were generally not dissimilar to the Renton production that went before it, with the acting talent given extensive praise for their interpretation of a troubling script. Charles Lewson's review in *The Times* referred to Simon's reprisal of the Justin Jackson role as 'remarkably effective' and 'a performance of the kind that made Owen Nares so popular.'[46] Of this, Simon would have been particularly proud, as would his mother Gillian.

A brief and at first seemingly insignificant entry on Simon's CV at that time came during his spell in rep at Birmingham. He performed in two productions at the Brum Studio. One was the bizarrely titled *The Thing-Ummy-Bob (That's Going to Win the War)*, and the other was *How the Other Half Loves*. The significance would increase, however, as the latter of these would set him up for a whirlwind tour of South America and introduce him to the most significant young lady of his life thus far.

Don't Let's Be Beastly to the Germans

By the mid-seventies, Simon Cadell was consistently performing on stage, but had yet to find a breakthrough television role. Offers for work on the small screen were coming in but only in dribs and drabs. A role in *The Love School*, starring Ben Kingsley, was followed by a pair of well-received television plays from the pen of Simon Gray—*Plaintiffs and Defendants* and *Two Sundays*. The lack of television work did not particularly bother Simon from a creative standpoint though as theatre was his main passion, just as long as he continued to work and the pleasures in life were still affordable.

He had completed his time in rep at Birmingham, and at that point there were no further thoughts afforded to *How the Other Half Loves*. His focus now moved onto a return to the West End, appearing in *The Case in Question* at the Theatre Royal, Haymarket in the spring of 1975.

The Case In Question is a largely courtroom-focused play based on the C. P. Snow novel, *In Their Wisdom*. A wealthy tycoon has passed away and rather than leave his fortune to his spurned wife of some years before and their social worker daughter, he has instead left it to the son of the woman who cared for him in his later years. What follows is mostly a battle of morals that seems to paint no one in an especially positive light, except maybe the cut-off daughter, who is only persuaded to contest the will under the advice of her employer.

The play was directed by and starred Sir John Clements, another dramatic heavyweight that Simon was delighted to be working with. He was always content to be lower down the cast list if it meant that he was working with a leading actor that he could learn from.

One particular piece of advice that Clements imparted on Simon was during a visit from Gyles Brandreth. Clements and Simon had no problems enjoying their alcohol, most notably during a stay at an Oxford hotel when Brandreth was putting on a production of *St Joan*. The pair had no trouble polishing off a couple of bottles of port as they sought to outdo each other with their repertoire of magic tricks.

Clements, however, knew where the line had to be drawn. While at the Haymarket, Simon and Gyles invited Sir John to join them for lunch ahead of one of the week's matinee performances. Simon rather assumed that they would be ordering some wine to accompany their meal, but Sir John reprimanded his admiring young co-star.

'We're doing a matinee', said Sir John.

'One glass sir?' was the response from the youngster.

'Oh no,' said Sir John as he explained his reticence. 'Remember there will be people out there who have never seen you before. They will be seeing you for the first time. They should always see you at your best.'[1]

Simon had never been one for drinking for the sole purposes of getting drunk. He liked wine, but he liked to enjoy the quality of the wine as opposed to the act of drinking. From this point on, Simon never cared for drinking before a performance. Future wife Beckie concurred, saying that in all the time she knew Simon, he absolutely, religiously would not drink until after a show.[2] Years later, he explained that this was also partly due to his addictive personality, saying: 'There are people who can smoke one cigar a day, or two cigarettes a week, but I'm not one of those people any more than I can have one glass of wine. I don't drink until I've finished work because I know that I'd rather have three glasses of wine or none.'[3]

The Case in Question earned a mixed bag of reviews. It was a difficult play in which to find any character to particularly care for, with the possible exception of the disinherited daughter, but Simon did earn special mention from Irving Wardle, who recognised his performance as being 'subtly sympathetic', expanding that, 'if that supplies a meaning, we have the actor to thank for it.'[4]

Towards the end of 1975, Simon made his first venture into the medium of radio drama. With his silky, polished vocals and his fine mimicking skills, this would be a welcome diversion from theatre and television for the rest of his working life. Despite their challenges, the two *son et lumière* performances had given him his first real taste of audio narratives and it became clear that there would be a huge demand for his vocal talents.

When Simon had been appearing on stage in *Lloyd George Knew My Father* at the Savoy, among the audience one evening had been radio producer Jane Morgan. Morgan had a friend who was in the supporting cast and had come simply to enjoy the production. Her impression of Simon stuck with her.

In 1975, casting was being considered for a radio version of George Meredith's *Evan Harrington*. Up against his old pal from theatre school, Tim Pigott-Smith, Simon was given the title role. 'I got him to audition for *Evan Harrington* because he hadn't ever done any radio,' remembers Morgan. 'I was wavering between him and Tim Pigott-Smith. But then, there are some people that you immediately love working with, and Simon I immediately loved working with.'[5]

Simon seemed perfectly suited as Harrington, a man in love with the daughter of a wealthy baronet and whose standing as a gentleman is jeopardised when he inherits not only his father's tailoring business, but all of the accompanying debts.

Although missing out on the lead role, Pigott-Smith was still cast in the production and he recalled the fun of working again with his old friend. 'We were like naughty boys,' he remembered of the venture. 'Acting has to be fun. If you're playing, your imagination works very easily even if it's a really serious play. I think we played billiards in one scene. We decided to bring in a prop billiards table, which you don't do on radio. So we played billiards with scripts in our hands, which was huge fun.'[6]

The show was well received and indicative of the many successful plays that Morgan would go on to produce. Simon was always a welcome and willing contributor and continued working with Morgan on radio across the next twenty years. It was also the beginning of a devoted friendship, one that somehow typified Simon in many ways in terms of his loyalty, generosity, and love of the good life.

'We became such very good friends,' explained Morgan as we shared a chat over a cup of tea. 'I can see him sitting at this very kitchen table on Christmas Eve having great arguments with my mother about why she read the *Daily Mail*. She was thrilled to be here with a television star, she thought he was wonderful. But of course, she went back to her friends and said, "Well, yes, a very nice young man but very opinionated!"'[7]

A few times a year, Simon would take his friend out for extravagant meals in Hampstead. Morgan recalls how prior to one particular occasion, she had put her back out. She had heard that one way to ease the pain of such a situation was to stand back to back and be bounced by somebody. When Simon arrived, they tried this and it seemed to provide some respite and so off they went for their meal. She continued:

> We'd had a wonderful dinner and I got up to go and could hardly move. The restaurant had been all over us because we'd been terribly extravagant with the finest wines of course. Anyway, Simon bounced me up on his back in the restaurant and they were furious and threw us out! We were just opposite another restaurant, so Simon said, 'right, we'll go there.' They took one look at us and said no, so I crawled home and went to an osteopath the next day![8]

As good a pair of friends as they became, the familiarity did not jeopardise Simon's work, nor irritate other members of the cast. 'He was great fun to work with, but he was also a hard worker,' Morgan continued. 'He'd challenge you, he'd have ideas and if you didn't match him he probably wouldn't want to work with you again, so I always felt excited that I was going to work with Simon. It's a great joy when someone you're working with can be your friend as well and it not get in the way of the other actors.'[9]

There were a number of highlights within Simon's radio work. He notably appeared in the many Charles Dickens productions that the BBC commissioned with Morgan, each time taking on the role of Dickens himself narrating. As ever, Simon was devoted to the craft and was keen to ensure that the production received the best of him.

Morgan recalls: 'He'd never do narration unless he'd heard the scene it came out of or the scene that it was going into, so that he was a linker, not dictating to the actors how the scene was going to be played.'[10]

One other significant radio success was a pair of Rosamond Lehmann stories, *Invitation to the Waltz* and *The Weather in the Streets*. The glowing testament of Simon's performance as Rollo Spencer, the debonair man that leading lady Olivia first encounters at a society ball, came from the author herself, who had based Olivia on her own life. 'Rosamond Lehmann had very definite views,' says Morgan. 'She was utterly thrilled with Simon's performance. She said, "Where did you find him? He *was* Rollo." Rollo was supposed to be the person that Rosamond herself had been in love with.'[11]

The working relationship between Morgan and Simon concluded with *The Diary of Samuel Pepys* in 1995, just months before Simon's death and which also marked Morgan's final play on the staff at the BBC. She reflected on their final foray together:

> It was during Pepys that I remember him smoking in the canteen. It was a time when smoking was getting forbidden everywhere, and it was a cigar of course. The manager came over and said 'I'm terribly sorry sir, you're not allowed to smoke anywhere now.' Simon replied, 'I'm terribly sorry—it's alright if I finish it though isn't it?' The manager agreed—he was so charming about it, there was no way the manager could actually say no![12]

In 1976, Simon joined a theatre company known as The Actors Company. Sir Ian McKellen and Edward Petherbridge had created the company in 1972, with the intention that this would be a self-governing collective who would carry out all of the management duties, casting decisions, etc. among themselves. The group's first production had been *Ruling the Roost*, adapted and directed by Richard Cottrell.

Simon joined the group in time to appear in a pair of shows, Shaw's *Widowers' Houses* and Sir Alan Ayckbourn's *How the Other Half Loves*, in which he had appeared only a few years previous. He was to reprise his role as William Featherstone in the Ayckbourn play, something which pleased the playwright considerably.

How the Other Half Loves had enjoyed a significant run on the West End, starring Robert Morley among others. Reviews had not been especially kind to the show, with Morley coming in for particular criticism. What had started life as an ensemble piece had been mauled by Morley. He and Sir Alan had clashed over changes to the script, and when changes could not be agreed upon, Morley proceeded to make them anyway. The resultant run in the West End was a financial success but to many, it was at the expense of the play and damaged the work of Sir Alan.

The Actors Company production saw Moray Watson take the Morley role. Watson was the senior figurehead of the group, even though no single performer was expected to be of any more importance than any other. Neil Stacy, another new member of the company, remembers Watson as being very patient with the many discussions, contributing no more than raised eyebrows and the odd sigh. In the Morley role, he was quite brilliant.

This new incarnation of *How the Other Half Loves* pleased its creator no end. Sir Alan reflects on the production with pleasure:

> I saw Simon in this production and remember it well. It did a great deal to restore the original play's reputation, having been somewhat pulled out of shape by Robert Morley during its successful West End run. The gist of many of the reviews for the revival read along the lines of, 'oh, it really wasn't a bad play after all!'[13]

Certainly for a collective democracy of actors, taking on a play that had been so mercilessly turned into a star vehicle was quite an ambitious task. The original intent was for the play to have been an ensemble piece about three adulterous couples, based in a set that alternates between two separate living rooms. It was a brave move to try and return it back into this format from the production that Morley had tailored to his own liking, *The Times* having described Morley as, 'a star capable of turning *Bartholomew Fair* into a one-man show.'[14]

Regardless of their critical reception, the two shows, along with some infrequent performances of Harold Pinter's *Landscape and Silence*, completed their brief run in the UK in preparation for a British Council-funded tour of Central and South America.

Between opening in February 1976 and the commencement of the overseas tour, political troubles that had been brewing in Argentina for some time finally came to a head. Since the death of President Juan Peron in 1974, the country's future had been becoming ever more uncertain. In the early hours of 24 March 1976, President Maria Estela Martinez de Peron, wife of the former president, was detained and the cities were placed under martial law. It did not seem a particularly appropriate time for a group of actors to be dropping in on a pre-funded tour of the neighbourhood theatres with British plays, especially one such as *Widowers' Houses*, which had been originally written with social problems high on its agenda.

As a young man in his mid-twenties, for Simon, it was a tricky balance to navigate between his career, which was undoubtedly going to benefit from the tour, and his political beliefs. He had been on breaks before, holidaying in the more stable environment of Venice and visiting the South of France with the entire family and that of great family friend Donald Sinden, but a tour of Jamaica, Mexico, Brazil, and Argentina was an entirely different prospect.

With his theatrical background, his love of the finer things in life, his obsession with the golden age of Coward and Rattigan, and his remarkably well-spoken persona, it was all too easy to believe that Simon's political beliefs would have had no room for such things as socialism. Such an understanding was far from the truth.

Outwardly, Simon gave the impression of somebody more accustomed to employing staff to uncork the wine and serve the caviar, and be disconnected with the outside world. Those who knew him better, however, knew that Simon was a man who hated class divisions and had a deep sense of moral obligation and a revulsion of injustice.

Politically, he was very much of socialist leanings, even getting involved in some publicity for the Social Democratic Party with Shirley Williams in the new party's early days. Yet while steadfast in his beliefs, work was Simon's priority so theatre surpassed any political discussions; indeed, Gyles Brandreth, who would become a Conservative MP for Chester in 1992, cannot recall a single political discussion with his friend despite their obvious differences in viewpoints.

The company flew out from Heathrow in April 1976, destined for their overseas adventure. It was to begin with a week of performing in Kingston, Jamaica, another destination in turmoil. Ahead of planned elections in the country, political violence was at its height in the early months of the year and the company would leave Jamaica just a few weeks before a state of emergency would be declared. Neil Stacy recalls Jamaica as being the most unnerving stop on the tour:

> The politics then were really quite dangerous. There was a lot of gunfire. We couldn't act in the main theatre in downtown Kingston because nobody would go to it. People just didn't dare go into the centre of Kingston at night because of the crime and the political violence. That was all exciting because of course at that age, you're excited by it rather than repelled by these scenes.[15]

Escaping the perils of Jamaica, the group headed to Mexico for several weeks for a rather more bizarre stay. As the tour was funded by the British Council, the members were treated remarkably well given the chaos around them. They were greeted at the British Embassies and placed in separate suites at the hotels. The relative luxury of those diggings changed somewhat at one of the Mexican venues. Stacy remembers of one particular town:

> We were put up in the dormitory of a school. It was next door to a nunnery and the belfry of the nunnery was outside the window of the dormitory all the fellas were in. I do remember us all being woken at some unearthly hour by nuns apparently flying through the air. They were pulling on the ropes in the belfry and swinging with them. It was the most bizarre sight. I looked out of the window and there were these nuns, swinging in the air hanging off the bell ropes.[16]

The bizarre view of apparently leaping nuns was not the only contrast to the dangers they had left behind in Jamaica. In a place called San Miguel de Allende, the group found themselves performing to a theatre full of dogs, which had been allowed into the auditorium with their owners. 'Being English, we found ourselves playing to the dogs, trying to get their attention,' says Stacy. 'That was a very local audience, Simon was quite bemused by it all.'[17]

After a brief spell in Rio, on 31 May 1976, the company landed in Buenos Aires for a nine-day stay as the last leg of their tour. This was certainly not the ideal time to have been booked into Argentina. Since the military coup, more and more left-wing activists were disappearing from the streets. In what was dubbed the 'Dirty War', it was estimated that as many as 30,000 socialist figures vanished in the years between the death of Juan Peron and the eventual restoration of democracy in 1983.

In theory, these had been people highlighted as some kind of terror threat from the left-wing, but along the way, members of the church, students, unions, media, and artists were all targeted. It is understandable then that it was with some relief that Simon was not as vocal with his socialist principals as a twenty-five-year old with firm beliefs could have been. Neil Stacy remembers that Simon was very reticent about being in Buenos Aires, recalling:

> He was very political then. He was very concerned that we were visiting in the year that the generals had just taken over. One had to take with you, whether you smoked or not, packets of cigarettes in your pockets to bribe soldiers to let you walk down streets, which had suddenly become no-go areas. Even if they hadn't, soldiers would just stop you and demand cigarettes. One had a feeling of being in a new world, with all the gunfire at night.[18]

One such occasion where these issues were brought to light was an evening when Simon and co-star Stephanie Turner went to the theatre themselves. Stephanie remembers uneasily:

> We met a rather left-wing theatre director. We saw a production of *The Kitchen*, by Arnold Wesker, at some little theatre outside of Buenos Aires. We got quite friendly with this guy and both gave him our telephone numbers. We told him that if he were ever in England, to get in touch. He never did, and we did wonder afterwards whether something terrible had happened to him. People were disappearing and he was very left-wing.[19]

The plays themselves were remarkably well received. Stacy felt that the Latin Americans had a greater tolerance for the long speeches of the Shaw play than the English. Expats were of course a significant presence in the audience, and despite concerns that the plays would be a little too English for anybody else, audiences loved them. However, a number of other problems befell the company on their travels.

With the tour in full flow, two of the group who were handling the company management discovered that an administrator turned out to be cheating with the finances—public money at that. Midway through the tour, the group of actors, so inexperienced at such things, had to appoint somebody else to get to the bottom of the irregularities.

On another evening, during the stay in Rio, several of the group were injured and had to return home. They had been hurt in a car crash after a party. Jonathan Adams and Barbara Murray, who had broken her jaw, were flown home. In keeping with the all-for-one, one-for-all ethos of The Actors Company, each of the players understudied one another. With two absentees for the remainder of the tour, that meant that Simon stepped into the Pinter play, learning it almost overnight. There were only a handful of performances of *Landscape and Silence*, so Simon's fine performances were all the more creditable given the lack of opportunity to hone it.

Having survived South America, Simon did not immediately leave The Actors Company, playing with them once more in a production of *The Amazons* in early 1977. However, The Actors Company itself did not last much longer.

Simon was reflective of his time with the group. He felt that having come into the company three years into its existence, he had made some enemies in attempting to ensure that Edward Petherbridge have control of the next season. In reality, one cannot help but feel that conflict was always going to be an issue. Neil Stacy remembers:

> There were some pretty acrimonious meetings. I found the whole thing deeply tedious. Doing plays is not a democratic exercise. It needs a dictator,

and that's the director, someone whose judgement you've got to accept. If actors were any good at running anything, they wouldn't become actors. One would spend endless meetings discussing who should be playing what part, what play one should be doing next. I remember absurd meetings proposing to do Othello and offering it to Sidney Poitier.[20]

As Simon was soon to leave the company, he helped engineer Nick Renton's arrival into it. Simon was appearing in *The Amazons*, and although not involved in Renton's production of *The Entertainer*, it did afford Renton the chance to see first-hand the problems within The Actors Company. Reflecting on his arrival in the group, he explained:

The Actors Company was odd because they cast each other. They'd all sit and cast each other and directors weren't meant to be part of that process. It really only worked when Petherbridge and McKellen did it. I do remember one conversation where I said 'why not go and get Jacques Tati?' and Simon thought it was a brilliant idea, but half the people thought, 'who's he?'[21]

Years later, despite feeling that there were still people that would not talk to him because of feathers that he had ruffled, Simon was quite proud of all that had been achieved at The Actors Company, remembering:

It was a remarkable experience. With an Arts Council grant of barely £50,000 we managed to tour two full-length plays, an Ayckbourn and a Shaw, plus two Pinter one-acts all around England and South America plus a London season for which there was no funding at all.[22]

One particular member of the touring company Simon had gotten to know well was the young actress Stephanie Turner. She had a similar situation to Simon in terms of work, taking a few television roles in such programmes as *The Sweeney* and *Whatever Happened to the Likely Lads?*, but mostly working in the theatre.

Simon had been somewhat nomadic in terms of both his romantic life and his physical location, with no one captivating his interest for long and living mostly with fellow actors on a temporary basis. Of course, with his lack of a particularly sound approach to finances, the latter was no great surprise.

In Turner, something different tweaked his interest. Here was a delightful, intelligent woman, but one from a completely different background who challenged him. For her, stories of Noël Coward and the latest eccentricities of Sir Ralph Richardson were amusing, but they were not what she lived for.

At the time, Stephanie was in another relationship but touring one of the most unsettled areas together for two months had made Simon more aware of her. Stephanie also got to see the other side of Simon—the more political Simon with the unexpected views.

'Privately, there was this other side that was serious, committed and hated injustice,' remembers Stephanie. 'There was no doubting his political convictions ... and to feminism too, which in 1976 was fairly early.'[23]

Simon rarely spoke publicly about his political convictions. As such, the expectation remained that having come from a seemingly privileged background that consisted of boarding schools and the theatrical glitterati, Simon would be somewhat disconnected from the problems of the ordinary man on the street. Indeed, Simon went to great pains to keep himself out of the tabloid press on pretty much any subject.

However, once in a while he would let things slip. In 1989, he told the *Radio Times*: 'There is a proportion of this country which thinks that because it speaks what is called Queen's English it is better than anyone who speaks with a West Indian or Liverpudlian accent. I find it quite appalling and it appears to be getting no better.'[24]

Being someone who was making a career from speaking so well, it was refreshing to hear that Simon railed against the idea that this somehow made him superior. 'He had an amazing accent but had a total lack of snobbery,' reflected Stephanie.[25]

'There can be so much artistic snobbery in this business,' Simon told the *Daily Express* in 1985. 'The silliest thing in our society is the inability of people from opposite backgrounds to talk and communicate with each other. Class division in this country is something which has made it almost medieval. I would fight against that to my dying breath.'[26]

The seeds were there for more than a friendship, and upon return to the UK, Simon would pursue a relationship with Stephanie, and he was a very focused man when it came to getting what he wanted.

Professionally however, Simon's first screen work when he returned was a seemingly insignificant piece. Anglia Television were producing a television movie that would be aired over the festive period of 1976. It was a Celia Johnson vehicle, *Dame of Sark*, in which she appeared as the governess of the island of Sark when the Nazis arrived in 1940.

An adaptation of a William Douglas-Home story, a number of the leading players had appeared in the stage version a few years previously. In isolation, *Dame of Sark* is a very small entry in Simon's vast body of work, but looking back, it is a curious pointer to the breakthrough role that was to follow.

In 1977, Simon was still without permanent digs. On the hunt for somewhere to stay, he was fortunate enough to run into Richard Heffer. The pair had been in the same collective in Bristol, but were in separate companies. They had struck up a friendship as they were not in the same plays as one another, meaning they had time to chat.

As they became reacquainted, Heffer had found himself a flat in Notting Hill. It was a fine property with communal gardens, but the area was not terribly desirable in the seventies. However, given its size, Heffer was going to need to rent out a room and so Simon took up the offer. He packed up his belongings into his little white Mini and headed for Ladbroke Gardens.

The pair rekindled a good friendship at a time when finances continued to be stretched. Simon was still in the red, with only infrequent one-off roles in television, which he knew was where the real money was. Ironically, the scene Heffer found when he went to the Cadell family home in Highgate would in different times have been a goldmine.

Heffer was very keen on art and when he would arrive for tea, Simon would clear a space for his friend as he said, 'I'm sorry about the mess, all these wretched pictures', shifting FCBC originals to make room.[27] The Scottish colourists took a long time to find their value in modern times.

So the pair occupying the Notting Hill flat had reached a point where neither was working and therefore neither was earning. Ten years on from entering The Old Vic Theatre School, John Cadell's warning that acting would be a financial struggle was still very accurate.

'We'd completely run out of money,' remembers Heffer. 'We had this sort of system whereby we said, "What have you got left?" and we said, "Right, we'll pool all our resources and just have a meal and that will be it. Let's have a glass of wine, a meal and we'll go off and become dustmen or something."'[28] The pair did as Heffer suggested and after piling their coins together, they went to a restaurant in Ladbroke Grove and had the acting equivalent of a last supper together.

The next morning, a call came through to the flat. It was Heffer's agent, telling him that he had been successful in his audition for the part of Peter Porteous, a principal character in a new London Weekend Television drama about the Nazi occupation of Guernsey during the Second World War. It was one of the principal roles and would ease the financial situation at home for Heffer. In typically charming fashion, Simon expressed his delight for his flatmate, who felt that the programme itself would have been just the sort of thing to suit Simon.

Rehearsal day came and off went Heffer to the Duke of York barracks to begin preparation for his new role. As the new group sat around rummaging through scripts and introducing themselves to one another, it became clear that there was a problem as the beginning of rehearsals was delayed.

Heffer asked what was happening and received a response from one of the production crew. 'The chap that's going to play the frightening part of the German Officer hasn't turned up,' was the gist of the response.[29] As it turned out, the actor chosen had found himself a movie role.

An administrative member of the crew was tracked down by Heffer, and he grilled him for updates. 'I need to know what's happening,' he said, trying to convey the impression that he himself might be able to do that part. 'I really need to know, it's really important to me.'

'We've got a slight problem at the moment because he can't do it,' came the reply, trying to play down the significance of a lead actor not showing up. 'He's got a film. He wants to do the film, so he can't commit for this long TV series.'

'That's all I need to know,' replied Heffer, who promptly rushed out of the building to find the nearest phone box.

When Simon answered, Heffer implored him to take immediate action: 'Simon, Simon—ring your agent. The guy hasn't turned up for the part of the officer, so for Christ's sake get onto your agent.'[30] Get onto his agent he did, and Simon was awarded the most significant role of his career to date in a primetime commercial television series, *Hauptsturmführer* Klaus Reinicke in *Enemy at the Door*.

'We came back and had another meal,' remembers Heffer of their joint success. 'By God we hammered it. It was a good two years' work. We danced around and had hangovers for days!'[31]

Simon's new role was as a Nazi SS officer. He was a thoroughly repulsive character, with no apparent redeeming features masked by his allegiance to his superiors. Simon later reflected of his breakthrough role:

> He was a thoroughly evil man. I was determined to play him like that, too. The SS was a criminal organisation, and I have seen lots of films and TV series where a sheen of glamour was attached to the SS or Gestapo. That's rather disgusting I think.
>
> I was determined that this man should be played without humour, glamour or any other saving grace. He was a child of his generation. It probably wasn't his fault that he was like he was, but that was what Hitler and his infernal cronies did: they brainwashed a generation.
>
> I did enjoy playing him, despite everything, although it's pretty difficult to play something like that without cliché. I hope I succeeded. Certainly when you put on that Nazi uniform, which is a breath-taking piece of design, you understand why they felt invincible. I wasn't particularly jolly to know at the time![32]

Enemy at the Door was very well received by both viewers and critics, and Simon received particular plaudits for his sheer nastiness. In April 1978, LWT announced a second series and he was getting something now that he had not previously been exposed to—he was getting recognised in the street.

Recognition was something Simon would have to get used to once he landed the part of Jeffrey Fairbrother in *Hi-de-Hi!*, but this initial foray into celebrity was of course entirely related to a nasty piece of work, remembering that, 'one friend said it's unbelievable you could be so vile.'[33]

'People's reactions astound me,' he told the press shortly after the end of the programme's two year run. 'I got one fan letter from a lady saying she was pleased I was in the area. She said it put her in a position to spit in my face, knock me down and kick me in a place that really hurt.'[34]

A further incident he remembered was when a 'nicely-dressed middle-aged man' came up to him in the street and said, 'Haven't I seen you on television as an SS officer?' When Simon responded in the affirmative, the man simply shouted, 'I hate you!'

In a typically calm and charming manner, Simon explained to the man that, 'I wasn't meant to be loved. The SS was a criminal organisation.'[35]

Despite the curious encounters, Simon was quietly delighted with his success. It meant that he was doing a convincing job. Television success had been secured at last, but it was nothing compared to the career-defining role that was just around the corner.

Pies, Pies, Who Wants a Custard Pie?

The success of *Enemy at the Door* coincided with a change in Simon's personal life. He had never given up on the idea that he and Stephanie Turner should be together since their time in South America.

There had been an attraction that developed during The Actors Company tour, but Stephanie was already in a relationship. Simon represented a polar opposite to the person Stephanie was involved with at the time. He pursued the relationship and Stephanie found it endearing that the Simon she saw was revealing more of himself than the one most people encountered.

'I'm a stubborn devil,' Simon said of his pursuit of Stephanie. 'Once I want something badly enough I don't let go. I've never been through one of those complicated love triangles before and I wouldn't like to do it again. It was an experience the two of us want to put well behind us.'[1]

She decided to end her existing relationship and she and Simon moved in together in January 1978. Simon's mother was particularly pleased that he was starting to put down some roots. 'At last I know where he is,' announced the protective Gillian Cadell, and Stephanie remains friends with the Cadell family to this day.[2]

With *Enemy at the Door* under his belt, Simon was starting to get more work than before, and it was as diverse as one could imagine. Among his busy schedule were roles on television in *Edward and Mrs Simpson*, a narration role in a film about Dada and Surrealism, *Europe After the Rain*, and the voice of Blackberry in the animated movie hit, *Watership Down*.

At the same time as *Enemy at the Door* was thriving, Stephanie was successful in auditioning for the role of Inspector Jean Darblay, the lead in a new BBC police drama, *Juliet Bravo*.

Unfortunately for Simon, the success of *Enemy at the Door* was about to come to an abrupt end. Unexpectedly, the head of LWT at the time, Michael Grade, wielded the axe and the programme was cancelled at the end of its second series.

The demise of the show was a big surprise. Popular with viewers, a third series had seemed inevitable. Grade's decision to end the production was believed to be a commercial one. 'As far as I know, they ran out of money,' recalls Richard Heffer. 'It's always the trouble when you have commercial TV because it had to fight its own way. It was very successful. I think they spent too much money trying to film over there in the second series in Jersey and Guernsey, so I think they thought well we've done two, let's call it a day.'[3]

The phrase 'when one door closes another opens' has never been more apt than for the situation now facing Simon. *Enemy at the Door* had been his real breakthrough role, both reputationally in terms of having a recurring television role that elevated his career, and also financially.

Over at the BBC, the corporation's hit comedy writing team of David Croft and Jimmy Perry were busy casting a pilot for what they hoped would be their latest sitcom success. By 1979, *Dad's Army* had found its place in the hearts of the British viewing public and in so doing had earned Croft and Perry a privileged position within the BBC's writing staff. Their successful follow-up project, the since much-maligned *It Ain't Half Hot Mum* was still going strong but would soon start to become less palatable for a modern audience. Looking upon history with glasses tinted by modern political correctness, the show is harshly treated and kept away from repeat schedules, but its success was phenomenal and it topped viewing figures throughout most of its time on screen until 1981.

David Croft had of course struck up an additional writing partnership with Jeremy Lloyd, and *Are You Being Served?* was still going from strength to strength. Croft liked to write from experience and he had already used that to great effect, with his Home Guard and department store days bringing huge success. It was perhaps inevitable then that he would link up with Perry again and turn to their separate experiences working for Butlins in the 1950s in search of a further comedy vehicle.

Jimmy Perry had just seen a new project of his own, *Room Service*, bomb beyond measure at ITV. This, along with a later comedy entitled *High Street Blues*, were recalled by Perry when talking to *Hi-de-Hi! Companion* writer Rob Cope, as being terrible shows: 'They were so bad, even the cameramen walked out. People are kind and they often say "Oh they couldn't have been as bad as all that." Believe me, they were as bad as all that.'[4] Perry was kind enough to admit that these failings never occurred when working in tandem with David Croft.

Perry had himself been a Redcoat at Pwllheli Butlins a few years after the end of the Second World War. A RADA student in search of some income, he had decided to raise some funds by approaching Wally Goodman, head of the entertainment staff at Butlins, for a job at the camp. Looking beyond his concerns over Perry's perceived posh accent, Goodman agreed to give the aspiring actor a job as a sports organiser in return for digs, cakes, and £8 a week.

By the time Perry came to take up his role, his employers had realised that he was actually a drama student and subsequently changed his responsibilities. Under threat of dismissal due to his inadequacies as a sports organiser, he was given the task of hosting the competitions now synonymous with the holiday camp experiences of the mid-twentieth century—knobbly knees, glamorous grandma, and ugly face.

Perry was a natural and kept his role at Butlins until leaving at the end of the summer season to resume his RADA training. He had thoroughly enjoyed compering the numerous talent shows, competitions, and revues and would use all of his experiences when the time came to create *Hi-de-Hi!*, a wartime phrase he himself had shouted to the holidaymakers of South Wales as he tried to bring smiles to their faces.

Although also employed by Butlins, David Croft's experience was in a different sphere. Like Perry, Croft had been a budding actor with aspirations of making it on the big screen, but it was his writing skills that he developed under the guidance of the holiday camp giants. While also penning musicals and television pilots, he found himself compiling scripts for the in-house Butlins reviews, along with tackling the production duties.

With nearly all of the cast in place for their fledgling television project, the crucial centrepiece of the show still eluded the creative partnership. They needed a fish-out-of-water type to tackle the role of the entertainments manager. They thought they had found their man in John Quayle, a fine comedic actor who could boast a CV that included some of the most successful products that seventies television comedy had to offer. However, he had commitments at the National Theatre that would prevent him from taking on a full series should the pilot episode prove successful. With Quayle now out of the picture and the rest of the cast in place, David Croft began calling around agencies for a possible replacement.

During the autumn of 1979, Simon Cadell walked into BBC Television Centre's room 301 to audition for the part of Jeffrey Fairbrother. The scene chosen by Perry and Croft to assess the young actor was the one that would open the pilot episode. Jeffrey was facing the wrath of his mother as he explained in a heated discussion why he was turning his back on a career as a professor at Cambridge University in pursuit of more excitement as the new entertainments manager at Maplins Holiday Camp.

In the eventual pilot, the role of Mrs Maud Fairbrother, Jeffrey's mother, would be taken by former Old Vic player Joyce Grant. In the audition, however, Jimmy Perry would play the outraged matriarch. Perry was suitably impressed with Simon, recalling that, 'before he'd said more than the first few lines, we knew he was the one.'[5]

Simon returned to Stephanie in buoyant mood. 'How did it go?' she asked.

'Fine,' replied Simon. 'They wanted someone who was at least thirty-six years old.'

'What did you do?'

'I told them I was thirty-six of course.'[6]

Simon was still in his twenties at the time. Once again, his ability to appear old beyond his years had worked in his favour. The phone call came within twenty minutes of setting foot in his Notting Hill home that Simon had been given the part that would change his life in every way imaginable.

On 10 October 1979, location filming began on the pilot episode of *Hi-de-Hi!* before culminating in a live studio recording on the 26th. When recounting tales of the filming in his autobiography, David Croft recalled the instant success of the opening show. 'We made a great pilot programme and the studio audience lapped it up. It was one of the happiest shows we ever produced. The presence of Simon Cadell in the company made everyone try to perform up to his standards.'[7]

The collection of actors assembled was an eclectic mix to say the least, much like the characters they were to portray. The people Simon would spend most of his screen time with were Ruth Madoc, Paul Shane, Su Pollard, and Jeffrey Holland. It was a new experience for Simon, a side of the business he had not yet seen.

'They were all the "turns",' he later reflected. 'People like Felix [Bowness], who is basically a stand-up comic and a warm-up man; Paul Shane, who is a genius stand-up comic; Su, who is almost a law unto herself ... so we were an odd mixture of people but we very quickly worked very well together.'[8]

Despite their outward differences, Simon struck up firm friendships among the cast. Paul Shane had been a stand-up comic in the working men's clubs in the North, and he and drunken Punch and Judy grouch Leslie Dwyer were particular favourites. He later recalled the pair with admiration:

I saw him [Shane] do his club act in Sheffield once and he was like a tiger. I think the most extraordinary one of all was Leslie Dwyer. He had spent his entire life in the business of making people laugh or getting the most out of the tiniest opportunity. We used to watch him work with a simple prop or just making the most out of one line or one look. He knew how television worked better than the rest of us put together, it was magical to watch.[9]

Of course, as Jeffrey became such a popular character on Britain's television screens, Simon became synonymous with those very talents that he so admired in Dwyer's acerbic delivery.

Such was the affinity with Shane that when the pair were called upon to do interviews in the early days of the show's success, the two leading men of *Hi-de-Hi!* would trade career histories at the expense of any uninformed interviewer. Shane would answer questions regarding his theatrical training at the Bristol Old Vic Theatre School while Simon would recount stories of belting out Tom Jones numbers during his nightclub comic career having started his working life down the mines at fourteen. It was a routine that Simon enjoyed so much that he repeated it years later with Michael Gambon, notorious himself for playful games of one-upmanship.

Hi-de-Hi! was an instant success. Viewing figures were regularly topping the 15 million mark. Croft and Perry had found a gentle blend of knockabout comedy and warm nostalgia, helped by the fact that the holiday camps of the seventies had not really lost their appeal just yet. Notices of 'baby crying in chalet sixty-one' did not seem as unthinkable then as they would now. Simon remembered of the success:

> I always thought that this is good stuff. I thought if we all do our jobs properly this will be a success. We were absolutely blown away by how quickly it became an enormous hit. David's series beforehand, *Dad's Army*, nearly didn't make a third series before it took off and became the institution it is now. With *Hi-de-Hi!*, by the end of the first six episodes we were a big hit. It astonished us how quickly it was welcomed.[10]

Key to Simon's approach to Jeffrey was the same lesson that he had been learned at the Old Vic Theatre School—playing it straight. Stephanie Turner remembers Simon's intent with the part:

> He knew what he wanted to do with it. Simon was determined that he wasn't just going to be a feed, he was going to have his own laughs. He wasn't just going to be a recipient for all these deep eccentrics around him who were of course all delightful and charming. But he really worked very hard indeed not to just be a cypher for the eccentricities, he was going to be his own actor and be very funny too. The only one who could not have been an eccentric was Simon's character.[11]

Simon was keen to draw his laughs from his mannerisms, delivery, and reactions more than the lines themselves. Jeffrey Holland recalls how Simon's acting background gave him more opportunity to expand on the scripted lines:

> He was an absolute asset to the show. He gave the most immediately truthful, real performance and he was the only one that David Croft allowed to expand on the script. When he was reading out the letters from Joe Maplin in the staff room, which suited his voice so well, he would actually

add things. 'Listen here you lot—that's him talking, not me,' was added by Simon, and David loved the way he did it. He really knew the character.

A wonderful bit of business that he did regularly was when he had to go onto the mic to do an announcement. He'd blow on it and tap it to make sure it was working. He made a running gag out of that one.

There was a wonderful scene where he was in a chalet and was half dressed. Gladys knocks on the door and just comes in and he's standing with his trousers off and he's holding them in front of him. When she looks down at them, Simon looks down and sees the fly is open so he just zips the fly up slowly. It was so lovely the way he did that, an immaculate piece of business.[12]

Simon's influence and the respect in which his opinions were held were evidenced further by the fact that he managed to talk Jimmy Perry out of giving Jeffrey Fairbrother glasses, believing that there was no need for an obvious prop to emphasise the professor status.

Key to Simon's performance was his deadpan and rather bemused facial expressions, except of course when Joe Maplin demanded more smiles from his staff. He later revealed:

That po-faced expression just happened. Things like that you don't actually think about when you're rehearsing a new character: it just happens if you're playing the part correctly. Actually, he [Jeffrey] does have a sense of humour, though his sense of humour is totally different from anybody else's. He likes to make jokes about Oxford and Cambridge. Well, Oxford and Cambridge might as well be Mars and Pluto to the people there. His appreciation of humour is a donnish sort, and he really has no place in Maplins Holiday Camp.[13]

Location shoots took place at Dovercourt Bay Holiday Camp. This was a camp owned by Warner Holidays that had been providing holiday fun to the British public since 1937. Filming there for *Hi-de-Hi!* took place out of season in October, explaining the comparative lack of sunshine during many of the outdoor scenes, and of course the pained expression on Jeffrey Holland's face following numerous dunks in the unheated swimming pool.

During filming for the first series, members of the public had yet to really discover the comedy in having an entertainments manager who had little rapport with the holiday camp's customers. One instance saw a critical lady walk away, believing Simon to be a terrible actor.

In the pilot episode, Jeffrey is to be introduced to the first batch of holidaymakers of the 1959 season. Uncertain of his role, resident comedian Ted Bovis (Paul Shane) simply informs Fairbrother that he should take to the outdoor stage carrying a tray of custard pies and wearing a chef's hat, and say his one line: 'Pies, pies, who wants a custard pie?' The inevitable exchange would follow whereby Bovis would eventually let Fairbrother have one of his own pies square in the face.

Fairbrother is of course a fish out of water, uncomfortable in front of people and not prone to overly exaggerated expressions of humour or emotion. He ambles onto the stage and mumbles his line into the microphone, barely audible, before being cajoled by Bovis into repeating the line with more gusto.

While this scene, which neatly encapsulated Simon's entire time as Jeffrey Fairbrother, was being filmed, Jeffrey Holland, who played Bovis's protégé Spike Dixon, was at the back of the pool watching, and recalls:

> I was standing on the perimeter with a few punters who had wandered in off the street. He mumbled his 'Pies, pies … who wants a custard pie?' and before that he'd done his softly spoken 'Hi-de-Hi' and they all offered a groaning 'Ho-de-ho'. This one woman turned to her friend next to me and said 'he's bloomin' terrible' and walked off. She just walked away thinking that he was a terrible actor, she'd missed the point completely, but it made me laugh for days.[14]

Such a verdict would have pleased Simon. As with his street encounters after *Enemy at the Door*, it proved that he was getting the part perfectly. That being said, nerves were still a major influence on him. Despite all of his stage experience and the suggestion, albeit an unwelcome one to him, that he was an expert comedy actor, the world of popular sitcom was still a new one to the fledgling television star. Paul Shane told the press that while the rest of the cast were busy wishing each other well, Simon was too nervous even to reciprocate.

'We all trembled in one big group,' he told reporter Colin Wills. 'All except Simon Cadell. He was so nervous, he couldn't bear to be near anyone. He couldn't even speak or wish you good luck. He'd just look into your eyes and grip your arm before going on. We knew what he meant.'[15]

Simon had always considered comedy the more difficult kind of acting to achieve any level of success with. He always felt that it was an awful lot easier to have people stay silent in their seats with dramatic acting than to pull laughs from them. Jeffrey Holland admits that Simon was terribly nervous, but eventually, the audience pulled them through: 'It was a marvellous thing because we could use that laughter to try and do our comedy properly. Although we were working to the cameras, we were listening to the audience.'[16]

Simon himself was never snobbish about Fairbrother and was a huge fan of David Croft's writing. As such, he was never dismissive of the humour he was asked to convey to the public. He later reflected that although he had started his career believing that he aspired to be an amalgamation of Rex Harrison, Jack Buchanan, and Noël Coward, none of whom would have been seen dead in a holiday camp, he was very grateful to both the show and the actors and the scripts that created it.[17]

Hi-de-Hi! went from strength to strength, although not without its hiccups. One such moment came during the filming of an episode entitled 'Carnival Time', guest starring another Perry and Croft favourite, John Le Mesurier as the Dean of Cambridge University attempting to convince Fairbrother to return to teaching.

The episode's storyline involves a demand from Joe Maplin that the entertainments staff get involved in the local carnival, entering a float in which Gladys Pugh would be tied to a post as The White Virgin, surrounded by a curious mix of cowboys and Indians. The climax of the scene was that Ted Bovis tried to make things more convincing by lighting a fire near the post to which Gladys is tied. The float catches fire and the staff eventually drag it into the pool, Jeffrey Fairbrother reinforcing the knight-in-shining-armour obsession always emanating from Gladys.

David Webb, one of the Webb twins involved in the supporting cast of the Yellowcoats staff, remembers the day very well as things swiftly took a turn for the worse:

There was Tony [his twin], myself, Chris Andrews [another Yellowcoat] and Barry Howard [the sneering male half of the resident ballroom champions, Yvonne and Barry Stuart-Hargreaves]. We were dressed up as cavalry with these fibreglass horses, like Bernie Clifton's ostrich. We hadn't rehearsed going into the water so nobody had calculated the effect that running into the water with these fibreglass horses would have.

So we bundled into the water, and the drag on these horses pulled us under. I just about managed to stay up with Barry on our side, but on the other side of the cart was my brother and Chris Andrews. They went under and it was a very, very frightening moment.

Simon was at the front of the cart and he jumped off there to save Chris Andrews, and Jeff Holland grabbed my brother. David Croft later said that in all the shows he did, that was the closest he'd come to a tragedy.

There was a restraining wire for the cart coming down and it had snapped into the swimming pool. When you were in the pool looking up at the cart it looked massive and frightening really. The restraining wire on the cart when they checked it at the end was down to one single little thread. It was a frightening moment, and Simon was a bit of a hero that day.[18]

The instant success of *Hi-de-Hi!* very quickly secured a renewal from the BBC for a second series, and after spending the entire time in the 1970s in the red, Simon finally began to see a positive in his bank balance. He did admit, however, that the money was second fiddle: 'Money isn't the prime motive for doing the show—you just don't buy a Rolls-Royce on BBC salaries.'[19]

Work was now beginning to flood in. Simon still had his staple diet from radio plays, most notably as Celeborn in the twenty-six-part adaptation of *The Lord of the Rings*. Yet television roles were beginning to pop up, with appearances in some of the most popular shows of the day, among them *Bergerac*, *When The Boat Comes In*, and two episodes of *Tales Of The Unexpected*.

One rather more bizarre appearance was as host of *Miss Europe 1981*. The international beauty show was still considered worthy of a primetime BBC 1 slot then, and Simon was chosen as host of the live event. It was an unusual choice, and one that on this occasion he admitted that he did for the money. He voiced disapproval, saying, 'All these rich middle-aged European gentlemen and their protégés. It was all pretty sordid, I can tell you.'[20]

'The truth is, I was terrified out of my wits,' he told the *Daily Mail*. 'The fact that I may not have seemed it is all to do with being an actor. I had always promised myself that I would try to avoid live TV because it is so frightening.'[21]

Interestingly, Simon rarely joined his new colleagues in guest appearances as *Hi-de-Hi!* gained momentum. As others appeared on *Blankety Blank*, *It's A Knockout*, and a variety of other popular celebrity television shows of the time, Simon limited his extra-curricular *Hi-de-Hi!* excursions to granting one child's desire to be a Yellowcoat via *Jim'll Fix It*.

'I did the *Royal Variety Performance*, but I wouldn't do anything else,' he told Rob Cope for the *Hi-de-Hi!* fan magazine, *Hello Campers*. 'I think that actors are best at acting and I didn't then—and don't now—want to become a television personality. That side of things just doesn't interest me, although I don't deride people who want to do it. I find that I just don't enjoy it.'[22]

For all the success that *Hi-de-Hi!* was finally bringing him, domestically, Simon and Stephanie Turner's relationship had run its course. The pair were enjoying the biggest successes of their careers, with *Juliet Bravo* a runaway hit with Turner in the starring role. Stephanie reflects:

> We had fallen madly in love. But it didn't work out. All the things we'd hoped for didn't happen. We had some very good times, but it was very difficult because I'd come out of a relationship and was guilt ridden and it didn't work. The relationship with Simon was doomed from the start really. It was rebound in the biggest letters.
>
> He had pursued me and when I think back he probably stayed longer than he wanted to or should have done, but he was deeply honourable and must have felt a huge responsibility I think. We parted sweetly and we always spoke—there was a tremendous sweetness about his personality, real sweetness.[23]

·THEATRE·ROYAL·
·HAYMARKET·

Licensed by the Lord Chamberlain to Mr. Bancroft, 18, Berkeley Square.

FAREWELL ✦ PROGRAMME

ON THE OCCASION OF

Mr. & Mrs. BANCROFT'S

RETIREMENT

FROM

MANAGEMENT.

✳ ✳ ✳ ✳ ✳ ✳ ✳ ✳

MONDAY, JULY 20th, 1885.

✳ ✳ ✳ ✳ ✳ ✳ ✳ ✳

Bancroft, Photo.   Oxford Street.

THEIR ROYAL HIGHNESSES
THE PRINCE AND PRINCESS OF WALES
Having Graciously Signified their Intention to be Present.

The handbill cover for *Masks and Faces* at the Haymarket Theatre signifying the retirement of Mr and Mrs Bancroft.

MR. and MRS. BANCROFT, with Members of their present Company
will Play the Second and Third Acts of

ASKS & FACES

An Original Comedy,

WRITTEN BY CHARLES READE AND TOM TAYLOR.

ACT II.—A Room in Mr. Vane's House, ACT III.—Triplet's Home.

ARTIST - - MR. WALTER JOHNSTONE.

SIR CHARLES POMANDER	MR. FORBES-ROBERTSON
ERNEST VANE	MR. BARRYMORE
JAMES QUIN	MR. E. MAURICE.
COLLEY CIBBER	MR. C. BROOKFIELD
MR. SOAPER	MR. ELLIOT
MR. SNARL	MR. KEMBLE
TRIPLET	MR BANCROFT
LYSIMACHUS	MISS KATE GRATTAN
JAMES BURDOCK	MR. PERCEVAL-CLARK
COLANDER	MR. C. EATON
HUNDSDON	MR. YORK
PEG WOFFINGTON	MRS. BANCROFT
MABEL VANE	MISS CALHOUN
KITTY CLIVE	MISS MAUD WILLIAMSON
MRS. TRIPLET	MRS. CANNINGE
ROXALANA	MISS MABEL GRATTAN

MR. HENRY IRVING

will speak a few parting words, written in verse by Mr. Clement Scott,

AND

MR. J. L. TOOLE will appear.

Mr. BANCROFT will bid farewell.

It also showed the arrival of Simon's great-grandfather, Perceval Clark as he was known
to this point in 1885.

Above left: Simon's great-grandmother, Mary Hamilton Boileau.

Above right: Simon's grandfather Perceval Perceval-Clark at a young age, dressed for a performance.

Below left: Perceval Perceval-Clark around the beginning of his theatrical career. Programmes and reviews would continue to list him with variations of Percival Clark, Perceval Clark, and Percival Perceval-Clark.

Below right: A youthful Jean Cadell, Simon's grandmother, whose career would blossom after joining George Alexander's company.

Above left: Grandmother Jean at the peak of her acting career.

Above right: Jean Cadell with her only son, John Cadell Perceval-Clark, *c.* 1919.

Left: Jean Cadell continued acting until 1961, her final appearance coming in *A Very Important Person.*

Above: Francis Campbell Boileau Cadell, widely known as Bunty, with nephew John.

Below: Bunty's paintings took many years to reach their present value. This one of Simon's father, John, in Loretto colours on Iona remains in the Cadell family's possession today.

Above left: John Cadell Perceval-Clark was an avid sportsmen in his youth, achieving particular success at rugby, but was equally adept at cricket and even trying boxing.

Above right: Gillian Howell was a successful actress in her own right; working in the same company as Jean Cadell would see her united with John Cadell Perceval-Clark.

Below: Gillian Howell (left) with Peggy Ashcroft in *The Heiress*, 1947.

Above left: John Cadell in his RAF uniform. John disposed of the Perceval-Clark from his name in 1939.

Above right: John Cadell continued his brief acting career after the war, also trying his hand at broadcasting before becoming a very successful theatrical agent.

Below left: After a difficult birth that threatened both of their lives, Gillian shows off her new baby, Simon John Cadell, May 1950.

Below right: Infant Simon Cadell *c*. 1950.

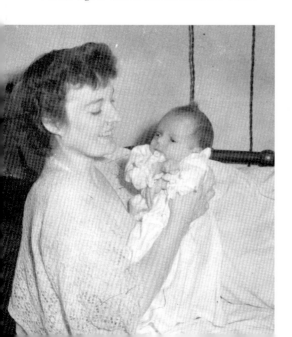 

Above left: Toddler Simon.

Above right and below: Simon was always keen to perform if there was an available audience, even as a child.

Above: Simon relaxing on a boat in the South of France *c.* 1962. The Cadells regularly took holidays with the Sinden family, the South of France becoming a favourite of Simon's.

Below: Patrick, Selina, and Simon relaxing in the safe confines of home, where theatrical comings and goings were commonplace.

Above: Already seeming older than his age, Simon appearing as Pompey in *Measure for Measure*, with Andrew Cahn, 1964.

Below: As Sherlock Holmes (seated) in the Bedales production of *A Study in Sherlock*, 1964. It was Gyles Brandreth's first encounter with Simon and the beginning of a lifelong friendship.

Above: Portraying an actor in a monkey suit (second from right), Simon in his second Bedales production with Gyles Brandreth, *Thirty Minutes in the Street*, 1965.

Below left: A debonair, almost Oscar Wilde-like pose, typifying Simon's theatrical leanings.

Below right: A wistful look from a teenage Simon, looking to escape the confines of formal education and begin his theatrical career in earnest.

Above: Simon (left) as Subtle, Michael Scholes as Abel Drugger, and Michael Hadley as Face in *The Alchemist*, 1969.

Left: Simon as Subtle (centre) in *The Alchemist*, with Hazel Clyne and Jonathan Bury, 1969. The show was career defining for many of the cast and was a huge success.

Above: Simon at the window as Subtle with, from left, John Caird, Roger Ball, Tony Falkingham, Peter Godwin, and Tim Kightley, *The Alchemist*, 1969.

Right: In the brief gap between theatre school and his first repertory tour, Simon made his small screen debut in *Hadleigh*, pictured here with Elaine Donnelly and director Peter Cregeen, 1969.

Above: Simon (right) in *Oh, What A Lovely War*, 1969.

Below left: An early publicity shot as Simon prepared for his acting career. Television stardom would elude him until the late 1970s.

Below right: The many faces of a young Simon Cadell.

Above: Simon with mother Gillian and Sir John Gielgud at Gyles Brandreth's Oxford Playhouse benefit, May 1973.

Right: Simon as the best man at the wedding of Gyles Brandreth and his bride Michèle, 8 June 1973. Gyles would return the compliment at Simon's own wedding.

Left: Simon with sister, Selina, and mother, Gillian.

Below: The Actors Company touring South America in 1976, including senior figure Moray Watson, Neil Stacy, and future girlfriend Stephanie Turner.

Above left: A menacing pose from the mid-1970s.

Above right: On horseback filming *Enemy at the Door* in 1978. The role of the loathsome Nazi officer would be a breakthrough one for Simon. (*Courtesy Richard Heffer*)

Right: Between takes filming *Enemy at the Door*, cigarette in hand of course. At one point, Simon was smoking up to eighty Gitanes a day. (*Courtesy Richard Heffer*)

Above: The role that made Simon a household name, as Jeffrey Fairbrother in *Hi-de-Hi!*, with Ruth Madoc and Felix Bowness looking on during one of their infamous staff meetings.

Below: The full cast of *Hi-de-Hi!*. The show would regularly attract viewing figures around the 15 million mark.

Right: The cast and crew of *Hi-de-Hi!* in less formal mood. Future father-in-law David Croft (top left) became close friends with Simon.

Below: Simon as Bill Bain opposite Elizabeth Sladen in *Name for the Day*, 1980.

Left: Hosting the 1981 Miss Europe competition. Simon hated doing live television, rarely getting involved in the celebrity chat show circuit.

Below: Appearing as a destitute Prince Philip opposite Kenny Everett's Queen Elizabeth II in a sketch from *The Kenny Everett Television Show*, 1981

Above: With Joanna Lumley publicising *Private Lives*, 1981. It was a last-minute role for Simon and established a lifelong friendship with Lumley.

Below: Reunited with director Peter Cregeen, Simon as Mr Murkitt opposite Carole Hayman in *Where Is Betty Buchus?*, a *Saturday Night Thriller* for LWT, 1982.

Above left: With Ruth Madoc in the hugely successful but exhausting stage version of *Hi-de-Hi!*. Simon would leave the show, and the television series, in 1983.

Above right: Simon in relaxed mood aboard the Orient Express, well away from his relentless workload.

Below: Relaxing in the cafes of Venice with Beckie, though even aboard a gondola, he received the cry of 'Hi-de-hi' from passers-by.

Right: With Alan Dobie, Simon as the debonair cad A. J. Raffles, 1984.

Below: Simon Cadell in a nutshell, pre-political correctness, holding godson Oliver Farago and a glass of wine, and enjoying a fine cigar—all in a hospital room, 1984.

Above left: 'How nice to see you with your clothes on,' HRH The Queen Mother allegedly once commented in reference to Simon's naked escapades in *Blott on the Landscape*.

Above right: A relaxed John Cadell in later life, a gentleman in all aspects of life.

Below: Backstage during one of Simon's most challenging roles, Archie Jumper, with Timothy Bateson and Andrew Sachs in *Jumpers*, 1985.

Above: The marriage of Simon Cadell and Rebecca Croft, 9 March 1986.

Below left: Reunited with Joanna Lumley, starring as Charles Condomine in *Blithe Spirit*, 1985–86.

Below right: One of Simon's biggest comedic influences, Donald Sinden, looks on during the wedding celebrations. Simon left to fulfil his obligations in *Blithe Spirit* before returning to the festivities.

Above: The cast of Jane Morgan's radio production of *Martin Chuzzlewit*, 1987. The producer would utilise Simon's skills in her plays for nearly twenty years, establishing a firm friendship.

Below left: In costume backstage at the National Theatre. Simon earned rave reviews as the repugnant Inspector Benedict Hough in Sir Alan Ayckbourn's *A Small Family Business*, 1987.

Below right: Simon achieved his most successful post-*Hi-de-Hi!* television success in 1987 as the loveable estate agent Larry Wade opposite Carol Royle in *Life Without George*, which courted controversy upon release, 1987.

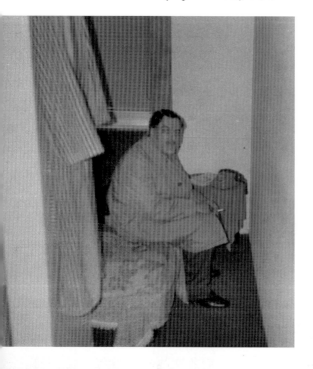

Above: A final season cast shot for *Life Without George*, including Michael Thomas (far left), Simon's brother-in-law, 1989.

Below: Simon performing as one of his idols, Noël Coward, opposite Patricia Hodge in the successful 1989 production of Sheridan Morley's *Noël and Gertie*. (*Courtesy Tristram Kenton*)

Above: Simon was among a number of celebrities photographed by Mohamad Ansar for display in the National Portrait Gallery in 1990. (*Courtesy Mohamad Ansar*)

Below: The cast of *Singles*, 1991. Simon joined Eamon Bolan, Susie Blake, and Judy Loe for the third series. Despite excelling as the egotistical Dennis Duval, the show was not renewed.

Above: Reunited with Su Pollard in *Don't Dress for Dinner*, with Briony Glassco, John Quayle, and Jane How, 1991. Simon once affectionately asked Pollard to lower her voice to a scream.

Below left: Simon relaxing at the house in France. The Cadell family would escape many times to their French property, but never did get around to the renovation project they had intended.

Below right: After Simon's heart operation, the Cadells retreated to the Caribbean for his recuperation where he decided to reduce his theatrical workload to aid his recovery.

Above: Relaxing with elder son Patrick in Barbados.

Below: Looking out to sea from the shores of Barbados, with Alec and Patrick.

Above: Simon in his final role as Vladimir Kozant, a serial child murderer in the disturbing thriller movie, *The Cold Light of Day*, released in 1996.

Below left: 'Our revels now are ended.' He is also remembered on the Cadell family tombstone in Edinburgh with his father and grandmother.

Below right: Simon's final resting place, the peaceful churchyard of Honington.

Simon Cadell as his fans best remember him.

Simon had always treated the media with caution. His was never the sort of personality that courted press coverage so when his relationship with Stephanie came to an end, he did his utmost to keep it from the tabloids, especially as the pair were starring in two of the BBC's biggest hit shows at the time. With that in mind, his sudden availability was little known and to his eternal credit, the break-up with Stephanie never generated the headlines that it might otherwise have done.

Simon's friendship with writer David Croft had blossomed. Most of the cast would stay in The Cliff Hotel in Dovercourt while filming on location, but Simon spent more of his time with the show's writer. There was no doubting that his acting experience made him a particular favourite.

Then, one day, two of David's daughters appeared on set for a visit. They were fascinated to see the show being filmed. Beckie Croft was carving out a career as a model, and her natural beauty did not go unnoticed. Off camera, Jeffrey Holland pointed out the attractive girl to Simon. In response, he simply emitted a 'hmmm' in a manner befitting Terry-Thomas, either in acknowledgement or in a knowing way that hid the fact that he already had designs on the boss's daughter.[24]

Beckie remembers well the first time she met Simon: 'We were coming back from a holiday and we went in to see John Kilby. Penny [Croft] was seeing John, and Pen and I had been in France together. We decided that rather than go straight home, we'd drop in on Dad and see the filming.'[25]

The two sisters were equally impressed by their first encounter. 'He was just the most charming man of all time,' Beckie fondly recalls. 'And so funny. Very few resisted Simon's charms. He was one of the few actors who didn't talk to you and turn his eyes over your shoulder to see if someone more important has come in.'[26]

Elder sister Penny concurs: 'It's that gift that some people have. That when they are talking to you, you absolutely believe that you are the only person in the room, the most important person.'[27]

Beckie could not resist his charms and he and Beckie became an item. The pair were subjected to one of the more bizarre incidents in Simon's life shortly afterwards, and one of those moments where his attempts to keep his private life from the media were doomed to failure. The duo had been invited, along with a number of other people to dinner at the home of Rikki Howard, who had played Betty Whistler in *Hi-de-Hi!*, one of the Maplins Yellowcoats. Howard lived at a crescent address, and Beckie and producer John Kilby were following Simon, who was driving himself in his Mini.

As he neared a parking space, a Bentley appeared from the opposite direction, so Simon ducked into the space to allow the oncoming car to get past. Instead of going past, the Bentley pulled up alongside the Mini blocking Simon in, and two men got out. As the events played out Beckie watched in horror:

Simon went to get out of his car to say, 'Sorry, were you trying to park here? I was just trying to get out of the way.' One of them grabbed him literally by the collar and threw him against the car, shouting something we couldn't quite hear. Me being really stupid, I got out of the car to see what the problem was.[28]

Simon tried to talk to his assailants who either did not understand, or did not want to comply with his peaceful requests and promptly pulled an aerosol can from their person and sprayed it directly into Simon's face. As her partner fell to the floor in agony, Beckie challenged the pair and received the same treatment. John Kilby's attempt to intervene met the same response, but he was able to see through the blur to get the registration of the Bentley as it pulled away.

'You are blinded completely,' recalls Beckie. 'It's really weird—you drop to the floor because it takes away your oxygen.'[29]

The trio of victims stumbled their way to Howard's home, and their intended host called the police. At the authority's request, they were all sent to Moorfield Eye Hospital. While there, the police received a call to say that two men had handed themselves in and that they needed to go to Chelsea Police Station to identify them. Such was the chaos of the unexpected events that Beckie struggled to identify the pair involved, especially with impaired vision.

The following morning, Beckie and Simon returned to Rikki Howard's home, where it was suggested that given the nature of the two attackers it might be prudent not to press charges. These were gentlemen of dubious moral character exiled from Italy, and such a move was not recommended. However, because the men had given themselves up, it was the police who decided that charges should be brought.

When it came to court, the men, despite having handed themselves in, planned to plead not guilty. Their defence was that they had believed themselves to be under attack, something which Beckie found quite absurd. She remembers:

I was wearing a boob tube, bright blue fluorescent skin-tight trousers. John was not exactly a threatening looking chap—small and greying with a little moustache. We had to go through the courts and go through the whole court process. We got to the Old Bailey and the morning they were due to be tried for it, they changed their plea to guilty.[30]

Beckie's recollections of the events are understandably tinged with horror. As it turned out, the attackers were actually destined for the same party as she and Simon had been invited to attend and were known to their hosts, hence the warning that prosecution might not be a wise move.

Simon's wounds ensured that he was unable to be made up for filming for some days, but it was not the only time he suffered injury when out and about. He and David Croft had once been leaving a restaurant in Soho when they were accosted by a drunken man who demanded they hand over cash. The man later claimed that not only was he drunk, but he was also unaware of who his potential victims were, as if that would excuse him. On this occasion, Simon's hospitalisation came from the lump of concrete hurled at him, and once again he found himself plastered across the tabloids.

One further such tabloid fodder caused Simon more private embarrassment than anything at a time when his popularity was at its height. One morning, the alarm was raised when a fire took hold at the residence of the Croft family at Honington Hall in Suffolk. The papers picked up the drama and told how Simon 'braved flames and smoke in a frantic bid to save valuables.'[31]

Simon was not someone who really did frantic, his being more of a calm, measured approach. On this occasion, he was indeed on site as neighbouring fire brigades joined forces to try and contain the blaze. Yet he actually stood at the front of Honington Hall with the Croft daughters, watching the devastation and just said, 'Fuck!' as he chomped away on his cigar.[32] Being a man of great charm and honour, the day after the story appeared in the tabloids, Simon took himself on a quick tour of the local fire stations to thank them for their efforts and to apologise for how the story had been manipulated in the press.

Hi-de-Hi! had made Simon a tabloid regular. It had brought him a positive bank balance, power at the theatre box office, and most significantly of all, a charming young lady who would go on to become his bride. Yet consistent with the entirety of his career, Simon was restless. It was time for a change.

Jeffrey Fairbrother Wheeze in the Pool

With three series of *Hi-de-Hi!* completed, Simon's success was escalating. Work offers were plentiful going into 1983. His relationship with Beckie was a contented one and for the first time since leaving theatre school, he had a bank account that was in the black. Life was good.

Filming for the fourth series of *Hi-de-Hi!* had ended just before Christmas and the show was still a regular fixture within the top ten viewing figures. The final episode of that series fell just short of 14 million viewers, one of its best efforts yet, so there were no signs of a fall in popularity, except with its leading man.

One of the most common problems that a star of a sitcom can suffer is when a catchphrase takes hold. It is a double-edged sword as on the one hand, if everybody on the street is yelling it at you, your show must be popular. On the other hand, however, it can be a thorn in your side if everywhere you go you are bothered by it and every job you audition for is clouded by your most popular success.

Simon was not remotely interested in actors who complained about their success, but in the case of *Hi-de-Hi!*, the issue of being yelled at when in public was magnified. The show's title was also the catchphrase, itself a bit of a problem—'nobody ever yelled out *Life Without George*', he later reflected, even though the shows' viewing figures were almost on a par with one another.[1] Yet the yelling of 'Hi-de-Hi' was seen almost as a call to arms, with each member of the public expecting to hear a jolly 'Ho-de-ho' when they had initiated the exchange of perceived pleasantries.

At the height of the show's success, cries of 'Hi-de-Hi' were aimed at Simon almost everywhere. He tried his best to respond appropriately, but it was inevitably a drain for somebody who wanted to be an actor more than a celebrity. Of recognition, he once said: 'You can't be blasé about that kind of thing, and anybody who tells you otherwise is talking a load of rot. Okay, when it happens the 150th time, it might be slightly boring for you. But one must never be rude and always be tolerant, and one must keep it firmly in one's head that there are thousands of actors who will never get to that stage.'[2]

Brother-in-law Peter Farago remembered a time at a takeaway when they encountered a group of around twenty-five Dutch children, who all started yelling 'Hi-de-Hi'; even overseas, he would receive the same greeting. 'We were on a gondola going down the Grand Canal and somebody was going the other way and shouted "Hi-de-Hi!"' remembers Beckie Croft. 'He was very pleasant though, he never gave them anything other than nice reactions.'[3]

Simon had a healthy relationship with his fans and inevitably received a significant amount of fan mail when *Hi-de-Hi!* was at its peak. One particular fan has indirectly assisted with the writing of this biography.

'There was this lovely policewoman called Kate,' remembers Beckie. 'She was Simon's biggest fan ever and she went to see every single thing that he did. She did these two scrapbooks, which she gave to me after Simon's memorial. Her real interest was in Simon. He was very fond of her as well, he was very touched.'[4] Those two scrapbooks were a goldmine of information.

Simon had initially believed that he would only do three series of the holiday comedy. It was undeniable that playing Jeffrey Fairbrother had brought him fame and a moderate fortune and doors were opening in the theatre, now that his name in the programme was becoming an advert for the shows in its own right. Yet he was very wary of typecasting. Towards the end of his run in *Hi-de-Hi!*, he commented that, 'After I had played a Nazi in *Enemy at the Door* I lost a few parts because people thought I was too sinister. Now I have lost some parts because I'm considered too light.'[5]

He had baulked before doing a fourth series, already outstaying his plans by an additional eight episodes, such was his affection for David Croft. Yet whereas trying to avoid being permanently thought of as Jeffrey Fairbrother had been paramount in his mind when determining to leave after three series, he now had another reason for leaving. After twenty-six episodes, Jeffrey was beginning to bore him.

After much consideration, he did decide to film a fifth series, confessing that: 'I'm exploiting the situation. I know I may have to sit out TV-wise for a time so I'm getting money in the kitty.'[6] Yet the decision was only a temporary reprieve for the professor. Simon was finally ready to say goodbye to Jeffrey.

Before Jeffrey was to say 'Goodnight Campers', Simon had the opportunity to live out one of his long-held fantasies. There are many theatrical heavyweight roles that he could have been born to play, but when the call came to line-up at the King's Head in Islington in *Noël and Gertie*, there would not have been enough wine in the cellar to dissuade him from taking up the role of a man that he was surely destined to portray— Noël Coward.

Sheridan Morley had devised a production based on the vast array of letters, songs, diaries, poems, and films of Noël Coward, most specifically regarding Coward's relationship with Gertrude Lawrence. Coward's relationship with Lawrence was of huge significance and she became an integral part of both his professional and personal lives.

The show Morley originally conceived had been for two actors, two singers, a narrator, and a pianist. The words for Coward were all from characters he wrote for himself or from his musings, poems, or lyrics. This appealing aspect only enhanced Simon's desire to play the role.

Opposite Simon's Coward was his great chum, Joanna Lumley in the role of Gertie. The pair had first met in 1981 in the most unusual of circumstances. One Friday evening, Simon had been having dinner at the home of Gyles Brandreth when the phone rang. James Villiers, playing the lead role of Elyot Chase in Noël Coward's *Private Lives*, had suffered an injury and was unable to continue in the role. They wanted Simon to take his place.

'He broke his Achilles tendon on stage, or the tendon snapped,' remembers Joanna Lumley, who was playing Amanda opposite Villiers. 'He went as lame as anything. Jimmy said, "Did you kick me?" and I said, "No, I didn't touch you." He was completely crippled by it and we had to go on with the stage manager playing the part of Elyot the next night.'[7]

Simon immediately left the Brandreth house and headed home, ready for a journey north. With the stage manager playing the role on the Saturday night, Simon had the two days to prepare for role. Joanna continues:

> We travelled up by train together having only met on the platform. We sat in the first-class carriage doing our lines. He was a really quick study and got it in no time at all. We were doing the argument scene and people thought we were having a real row. It was Elyot and Amanda shouting at each other in the middle act.
>
> When we went on that first night it was a packed theatre, and he got a standing ovation at the end because he didn't put a foot wrong. He was dazzlingly good, and glamorous, suave, funny and his timing was matchless.[8]

Simon and Joanna were a tried and tested partnership, perfect for *Noël and Gertie*. They would take the acting side of the production while the songs would be performed by David McAlister and Gillian Bevan. Morley himself would narrate, with William Blezzard as the musical accompaniment. Blezzard had been the musical director for Joyce Grenfell and was a direct link to that golden era. Gillian Bevan recalls of the production:

> There was something utterly charming about all this thirties glamour being portrayed on this tiny stage in this rather grimy and eccentric pub. Backstage

was something else. It was pretty grim, basically a corridor which I think we all shared—and Lum' and I were always in early pretty much cleaning the loo and wiping down surfaces before we started putting on make-up and false eyelashes and getting into our frocks.[9]

On the day of dress rehearsals, Joanna Lumley was thrown from a horse while filming a commercial. Ever the trooper, Joanna refused to forego her role. Kenn Oldfield, who as Gillian puts it 'managed to get some choreography on that tiny little stage,' remembers Joanna being desperate for some pain relief before going on stage.[10]

> Literally twenty minutes before the curtain went up, Jo said to me, 'darling, darling, my back's gone. Jo got on the floor, just removed every strip of clothing and just lay on her stomach going 'darling, darling, do something,' so I massaged her back for her. We got her on that night, but she was in real pain.[11]

Lumley's desire to get on and complete the whole month's run in considerable pain was typical of the spirit that Simon and his colleagues felt. They were all aware of both the quality of the work they were appearing in and the era that it represented.

'None of us were doing it for the money,' says Bevan. 'I remember Jo and I laughing our heads off when Dan Crawford [founder of the King's Head] came in and shoved fifty extra pounds in our pockets as business and advance bookings had gone through the roof.'[12]

With Morley and his four stars remaining on stage for the duration, the cramped stage did little to enhance the show and reviews were decidedly mixed, though it should be said that the bulk of those who criticised went after the production's creator. The general feeling was that with Coward and Lawrence having only actually appeared together in *Private Lives* and *Tonight at 8.30*, the knitting together of other songs and material for purposes other than those for which they were created did not fully convince people of the importance of the pair's relationship.

One review from Steve Grant in *Time Out* decided that while he felt the show would be a 'treat for all confirmed *Noël and Gertie* fans everywhere— alas for the rest of us, the show has problems.'[13] His criticisms were not aimed at Simon, but the suggestion that, 'there is a sensitive portrayal of Coward by Simon "*Hi-de-Hi!*" Cadell' would not have sat well with the actor.[14] It was an ominous link to the perils of Jeffrey Fairbrother, forcibly reminding the *Time Out* readers of where they may have known the name from.

For all the revulsion Simon may have felt at this reference, the counter side was the success of the show. In his autobiography, Morley commented that the press night contained no more than sixty occupants in the venue. The next day, queues were lined-up at the box office and Morley reminded Crawford of the reason why:

> If every member of our audience had gone home, rung three friends each and told them not just that they had to buy tickets to see our show, but that they had to turn up this very morning at the box office, you would still not end up with a queue like that. It's called television. You don't watch it, I don't watch it, but millions of others do.[15]

Morley had bought a copy of the current *Radio Times* and showed it to the King's Head's theatrical maestro. The television pages revealed that both *Hi-de-Hi!* and a rerun of *The New Avengers*, starring Joanna Lumley, were included in the previous evening's schedules. Jeffrey Fairbrother may have been a frustrating persona to carry around, but to some degree, he was a necessary one.

As for Simon's interpretation of Coward, other members of the press were kinder, with Christopher Hudson writing in the *Evening Standard* that, 'Cadell has Coward's inflections, his timing, his dragonfly wit, his self-deprecating clarity off to perfection. It is a vivid and debonair performance.'[16]

His Gertie was equally impressed, with Joanna Lumley remarking that, 'He channelled Coward somehow because he could turn on a sixpence, but it's quite difficult to play, which I think Simon quite liked. It's very deep, there's all sorts of poignancies in Coward. Coward would have adored him.'[17]

Clearly the public were quite content with the offering and *Noël and Gertie* sold out for the remainder of its run, closing only due to other commitments for its stars. Bizarrely for Simon, that meant a reprisal of both Jeffrey Fairbrother and Noël Coward all rolled into one.

David Croft and Jimmy Perry had always been quick to see the opportunity to expand on the success of their television programmes. *Dad's Army* and *It Ain't Half Hot Mum* had both been made into successful stage shows, with the former also spawning a feature-length film, so it was perhaps inevitable that the pair would decide to take *Hi-de-Hi!* on the road.

On 7 June 1983 at the Alexandra Theatre in Birmingham, a stage version of *Hi-de-Hi!* opened for a five-day run before transferring to the Pavilion Theatre, Bournemouth for a full three-month summer season, finishing shortly before filming would begin on a fifth series for the BBC.

The format of the stage version was a bit of a mixture. The first half was very much a recap of how Jeffrey Fairbrother had come to find himself as an entertainments manager at Maplins Holiday Camp. Jeffrey remained woefully inappropriate in an entertainments role—'on its own, forty-one,' he would call when hosting bingo. Even now, as the cast prepared to say goodbye to Jeffrey, Simon was still finding ways to improve things:

> Ruth Madoc was being a damsel in distress in a jungle, and there was a big Tarzan cry on tape, so the audience were expecting me to swing in on a rope and save her. I was supposed to jump in on a trampoline, then onto the rope and swing onto the stage. I thought, 'I can't do this, I'll break my back.' So on the first night, the Tarzan call went out and I just walked on and looked at the audience as if to say, 'Do you really think I was going to swing in on a rope?' It worked like a gem and got a huge round of applause.[18]

The second half was a little more indulgent for the cast. It had been well-documented that the characters in the television show were primarily all failures in their chosen fields. In the stage show, we would see what the characters had really wanted from their lives.

This novel approach would give a bit of licence for the performers. Jeffrey Holland and Paul Shane combined to play Laurel and Hardy (Holland has since toured to much critical acclaim in a one-man show about his comedy hero, Stan Laurel); Su Pollard would give vent to her ample singing talents with her rendition of 'Look for the Silver Lining'; Ruth Madoc performed *Madam Butterfly*; and Simon went back into the Noël Coward character to give a rendition of 'Mad Dogs and Englishmen'. It was a version that Simon had perfected many years before at the Bristol Old Vic alongside John Caird, who remembers:

> We did a sort of end of term cabaret at one point. Simon decided to do 'Mad Dogs and Englishmen' and I played the piano for him. So we spent hours and hours and hours rehearsing it because Simon was meticulous about getting the exact rhythm and tempo and rubato, and the exact number of beats at the end. We spent hours getting that right and he was so proud of being able to sing the song and do the Coward voice in exactly the right way.[19]

The show was a roaring success, although hugely demanding on its actors. Unsurprisingly, Leslie Dwyer and Diane Holland were not healthy enough to be involved in a production that had twice-nightly performances throughout its run.

'It was absolutely knackering,' remembers Jeffrey Holland. 'We were all being paid fairly well, so they had to do twice nightly in order to make the money to pay us. At the end of the week, we were on our knees. We just couldn't wait to get back to the studios for a series because it was much lighter work.'[20]

Such was the success of the stage show that a decision was taken to move it onto the West End where it would play at the Victoria Palace. The theatre was no stranger to stage versions of successful celluloid franchises, having played host to Sid James, Barbara Windsor, Peter Butterworth *et al.* in the successful *Carry On London* run of the mid-1970s.

Simon had already made clear his plans to quit the TV show. 'It was tough deciding to quit, but I knew I was running the risk of being Mr *Hi-de-Hi!* forever,' he explained. 'We've seen what happens to some actors who stick with a TV show year after year. When it comes to making a break, other producers don't want to know them.'[21]

As disappointing as it was to lose the show's figurehead, the Croft family knew in advance that Simon's decision was final and they made no attempt to talk him out of it. It was a time in Simon's life that had brought him a new level of fame and financial reward, and in some ways, he would struggle to ever shake being known as Jeffrey, but he adored his time working on the programme. He later reflected:

> I have no regrets and I think it did the series some good. How many times could Jeffrey innocently keep turning down Gladys? Also, I felt as an actor that Jeffrey was becoming too easy to do. But they were enchanting people to work with. We became very good friends and I have had a sort of withdrawal symptom from not seeing Paul or Su Pollard or Ruth Madoc every day.[22]

Simon was quick to acknowledge to Sheridan Morley in *The Stage* the positive side of Jeffrey in terms of theatrical roles. 'These last four years have been extremely happy,' he told him. 'There's no doubt about it, a hit comedy series on television moves you further forward in the theatre than a hit drama series. Look at what happened to Penelope Keith, Richard Briers, and Paul Eddington. They all now lead the West End because of their television-comedy background.'[23]

Simon bowed out of *Hi-de-Hi!* on screen on 22 January 1984. There was no big final farewell, something that Simon slightly regretted, although his playful suggestion that Jeffrey could have been found hanging from one of the doors at the swimming pool was perhaps more than the viewing public could have taken.[24]

There was in fact no reference in Simon's final episode to any impending departure for the Maplins entertainments manager. It was only in the opening episode of the sixth series that we discover Jeffrey has taken up a post in Wisconsin and would not be returning for the 1960 holiday season.

Opinion is divided about the final four series of *Hi-de-Hi!*. To its creators' credit, viewing figures never really faltered after Simon's departure, despite the complete contrast in dynamic that took place for Gladys when David Griffin's Clive Dempster arrived and offered more advances in her direction than she was used to. There is little doubt, however, that some of the 'fish-out-of-water' charm was lost for the rest of the show's run.

While Simon never entertained the idea of returning for the final episode of the programme in 1987, he did nonetheless attend the final recording, sharing the emotional and poignant farewell as Maplins is closed down and sold off, leaving its ragtag collection of entertainers to face their unknown futures. It is difficult not to feel a lump in the throat when Spike is comforting a disconsolate Ted as they await their departure from the poolside at the end of the season.

When the *Hi-de-Hi!* stage show had its run at the Victoria Palace extended, it had to be without its leading man. He had already lined up further theatre work and so the show would go on with a new man in the role of Jeffrey Fairbrother. Michael Knowles, another from the Croft and Perry stable as Captain Ashwood in *It Ain't Half Hot Mum*, had on paper all the credentials to take on the role, but he was not Simon Cadell.

'The poor lad didn't stand a chance,' says Jeffrey Holland. 'He did really well, but it was unacceptable to the audience. I played Private Pike once on the [*Dad's Army*] stage show and I didn't get a single laugh. All the words came out in the right order, but I wasn't Ian Lavender.'[25]

For Simon though, it was time to move on and he found possibly the most un-Jeffrey of roles to tackle next—his first attempt at *Hamlet*.

Simon had actually agreed to appear in *Hamlet* a year before his departure from *Hi-de-Hi!*. With the success of the stage show of the comedy, his schedule had bunched up somewhat and as such, he found himself needing to rehearse for his Shakespearian role during the Victoria Palace run of *Hi-de-Hi!*. If the idea of playing Jeffrey Fairbrother and Noël Coward in the same show was not bizarre enough, he would now find himself preparing for *Hamlet* in the dressing rooms of the theatre before taking to the stage for his Fairbrother-Coward hybrid. Simon later recalled:

> During the last four weeks of the run, Peter [Farago, director for the *Hamlet* production] and I used to meet in the Number One meeting room at the Victoria Palace. We'd have a sandwich for lunch and continue until the 'half' was called. My dresser would come in, I'd start shaving and making up and we'd still be talking. Finally 'beginners' would be called and we'd be discussing interpretation of a passage in the text as we walked down the steps together. The entrance to the stage was right by the stage door through which Peter exited as I walked on stage to launch myself immediately into my part ... by then it was fairly automatic, I'm ashamed to say.[26]

Simon's recollection of his preparation for Hamlet reminded him all too well of the need to escape Jeffrey. It had indeed become routine, and while never compromising on his performance, it was evident that the decision to leave was the correct one.

The meeting room to which Simon referred was a bizarre one. It had not been redecorated since Elizabeth Taylor's stay there in a run of *Little Foxes*. The result of this meant that the backdrop to the curious combination of characters and routine was one of violet walls, purple banquettes, and a fluffy white carpet, which Simon described as having 'ominous white stains' from Taylor's dogs.[27]

Director Peter Farago described the scene as 'extraordinary'.[28] The pair sat around a stained fluffy rug discussing *Hamlet* in a smoke-filled rehearsal room before a hasty exit to the stage, cries of 'Hi-de-Hi' for Jeffrey Fairbrother's arrival, into his lightning-fast rendition of 'Mad Dogs and Englishmen' as Noël Coward, before starting the whole process again the next day.

Of course, the extraordinary leap between the two ends of the acting spectrum inevitably drew interest from the media and concern from Simon. There was no question that the name above the theatre apron was good for ticket sales, and the production was a commercial success.

Peter Farago, who would become good friends with Simon by virtue of them marrying two of the Croft sisters, remembers the impact of Simon's involvement:

> I thought that in a way, his fame from *Hi-de-Hi!* helped bring audiences in. But there was this slight element of the people who wanted to see *Hamlet* thinking, 'What's this guy from *Hi-de-Hi!* doing here?' Then of course there were some people who had come to see Jeffrey from *Hi-de-Hi!* and it took a while to pull them round into one audience.[29]

It was inevitable that after becoming part of popular culture via screen comedy, Simon would have levels of nervousness about the new venture. It did not help when the concrete-throwing incident happened one week into his rehearsals.

'I wouldn't mind being extremely bad, and I hope to be extremely good,' he told Sheridan Morley. 'What I couldn't bear was the idea of being alright in the role. It's not that sort of role is it?'[30]

There was of course the fear that the dreaded cry of 'Hi-de-Hi' might appear from the audience, not helped by the tabloid press forewarning of the possibility and leading with such headlines as 'Enter Hi-de-Hamlet.'[31] It was not something new and Simon was aware that as long as his performance was good enough, the likelihood of cries from the darkness would be fairly slim. 'If it happens in the first scene it will be silly,' he said at the time. 'But if it happens in the fifth act then I'll know I've lost and I might as well go home.'[32]

The cry never came, which was some testament to the production and performance. Old friend Nick Renton went to see the play, and while there were no chants from the audience, he does recall Simon having to diplomatically deal with a disruptive element:

> There was a rather wonderful moment in it. I went to see a matinee, and being a matinee all the school kids were in. He was in the middle of it and electrifying in the role and then just stopped and said to them, 'Now if you're going to behave like that, you'd better get out.' But it was Hamlet coming to talk to them, kind of the equivalent of Richardson kicking someone's foot off the stage, which he did once when someone put their foot on the stage and he kicked them off![33]

Simon was fixated upon achieving all that he could with *Hamlet*, despite admitting that, 'I had never been one of those actors who had always wanted to play the part.' He devoted himself to the role, saying, 'It's very important to find a line through the text that you think works. You can't think about other Hamlets.'[34]

The combination of the workload and the stress of the leap from sitcom to Shakespeare did take a toll on Simon's health. Beckie was away on a modelling assignment and so one of his safety nets was gone. 'Rebecca has a clear intelligence about this business. She knows when to encourage me and when to pat me on the head,' he said.[35]

He felt the role of Hamlet made him rather depressive. As a result, he was losing sleep, and obtained some sleeping pills from his doctor, who warned him about the dangers of becoming addicted. 'I started off taking one a night and ended up taking three. I had to wean myself off them afterwards,' Simon said, relieved that Beckie's absence did not expose her to his grouchiness.[36]

Swiftly, he realised that the support of medication was a mug's game. He later reflected: 'I decided it was silly to carry on. I don't want to become reliant on drugs as it would be very easy to have a prop which you'd use unnecessarily. Besides, I didn't think it was the greatest thing since pop-up toasters.'[37]

Simon's nerves may have been more intense than usual, but reviews were mostly positive and highlighted his triumphant return to the bard for the first time since his Mercutio ten years prior. Martin Hoyle in the *Financial Times* hailed the interpretation, saying that, 'he speaks the verse better than anyone else on stage, with relish and understanding,' adding that, 'Mr Cadell keeps the Osrie scene buoyant single-handed.'[38]

In *The Guardian*, Robin Thornber's praise was gushing, proclaiming that, 'Simon Cadell's Hamlet brilliantly straddles the line between the modern, knowing, nudging style of acting and the powered performances of the Grand Manner.'[39] Perhaps most positive though was Eric Shorter's belief in the *Daily*

Telegraph that, 'no Hamlet was ever saner or more devoid of mirth. If that isn't a measure of this light comedian's achievements, I don't know what is.'[40] It is doubtful, however, that Simon would have appreciated being classed as a light comedian, but such was the power of the *Hi-de-Hi!* success to create a profile for the uninitiated.

The press would forever associate Simon with *Hi-de-Hi!* before anything else, despite the subsequent television successes and award-winning theatrical roles, but in terms of Simon's ability to move on from the kind but dull entertainments manager, it was safe to say that he had already begun to lay Jeffrey Fairbrother to rest.

With Fortune and Men's Eyes

When *Hamlet* finished its run, Simon had reassured himself that he was eminently employable after the departure from *Hi-de-Hi!*. Stage work was still his first love and with that in mind, alongside the continuing run of radio parts, he found himself back in the theatre at the Palace Theatre, Watford. Here he would take the lead role of *Raffles*, a man who was suave, gentleman cricketer by day and burglar by night.

This was Leon Rubin's revival of a play and character created back in 1903 by E. W. Hornung and Eugene Presbrey, updated for a more modern audience by the director himself. The lead character of A. J. Raffles, known as The Amateur Cracksman, was a public schoolboy gone bad. George Orwell once wrote of the character that, 'his remorse, when he feels any, is almost purely social: he has disgraced the "old school", he has lost his right to "decent society", he has forfeited his amateur status and become a cad.'[1] This combination of the smooth, elegant sophisticate countered by the devilish twinkle and bad deeds made him an appealing role for Simon, who admitted that his new stage persona was, 'not much of a gentleman.'[2]

One of Simon's co-stars in the show, Sarah Berger, recalls how Raffles would ordinarily have been played by a more classically handsome leading man:

He had talent, a beautiful voice and a sort of twinkle. But he didn't look like a classical leading man. He wasn't physically what you would expect Raffles to be, he wasn't glamorous in that respect. But he could act it. You're actually better off if you can act glamour because your shelf life is longer.[3]

Reviews for *Raffles* were a mixed bag. The updating of the show was very tricky, and reflecting on this, Peter Hepple's assessment was that, 'Despite the cool urbanity of Simon Cadell as Raffles and the blustering determination of Alan Dobie, the cat and mouse game does not entirely hold our interest and one suspects that its initial success was due to that great matinee idol Gerald du Maurier, not because of the merits of the play.'[4]

Simon himself conceded that, 'I think the secret of most plays is to treat them like new plays, but *Raffles* is very difficult to treat as new because it's set so rigidly within the Edwardian era with its unusual social behaviour patterns. Unless you are going to have a punk version you have to adhere to that.'[5]

Sarah Berger concurred, admitting that with a play that simply couldn't be fully updated to a modern audience, 'it was probably just a step too far.'[6]

Around the same time as *Raffles*, Simon was also taking on a rather dramatic change of role on television. His appearances on TV had been largely one-offs since *Hi-de-Hi!* and he was waiting for the right offer to come along.

Through the letter box one morning dropped a script for a series adapted by Malcolm Bradbury from the Tom Sharpe novel, *Blott on the Landscape*. The story of Blott is not dissimilar to that of *Lloyd George Knew My Father*, the show that had introduced Simon to the West End back in 1972.

The story is built around Sir Gyles Lynchwood and his wife Maud, who are residents of Handyman Hall in Cleene Gorge. Sir Gyles had initiated a plan to have a motorway constructed through his village, resulting in significant financial recompense. It is of course a plan that Lady Maud is initially unaware of and objects to fearsomely. The part offered to Simon was Dundridge, the planning official responsible for overseeing the construction of the motorway.

Starring *Minder*'s George Cole in the leading role, Simon was thrilled to be involved, even if producers' attempts to persuade John Gielgud to join the cast had failed. Simon had been starring in *Hamlet* in Birmingham when the script arrived, and he immediately cancelled his upcoming holiday plans to allow him to appear in *Blott*. 'Don't lose this one,' he told his agent.[7] Of the Dundridge role, Simon recalled:

> The character is such a strong part it is almost an Inspector Clouseau/Peter Sellers king of thing. The clown, the failure, the good-natured, averagely attractive man whom British women, and it seems their husbands, are most at home with as entertainment figures. The comedian is always the sexual loser. And it is very successful.[8]

When the show came to air, it provided the viewing public with a side of Simon that they had quite literally never seen before. Of the Bradbury adaptation, Tom Sharpe had said 'it's the best thing I've ever seen, although he has put a lot of sex in it.'[9] So it was that Simon came to reveal himself to the public for the first time.

One would assume that for somebody who had never liked the face he saw in the mirror, Simon might have similar misgivings about displaying the rest of him. He was actually surprisingly blasé about it. Perhaps it was the financial compensation that appealed to his fiduciary side.

He had performed his first nude scene back in the 1970s, when in a small role opposite Alan Bates, he had to lose his towel in a changing room. Due to this, his fee rose from £100 to £190. The scene was eventually cut and according to Simon, the BBC asked for their money back; they did not get it.[10]

When filming *Life Without George* a few years later, Penny Croft remembers a scene where she had to ask Simon to drop his trousers. 'I asked him if he was okay about it,' she recalls. 'He said "Totally. What underpants do you want me to wear? Or none in fact?"'[11]

In *Blott*, he was forced to bare almost all. This led to an amusing backstage moment after a Royal Gala for the Queen Mother, when Her Majesty met Simon in the post-show line-up. She allegedly said, 'It's nice to see you with your clothes on,' before moving on to the next participant.[12]

Blott was well received by the public and the critics, and certainly gave Simon a belief that there was television life after *Hi-de-Hi!*. His portrayal of 'a manic character, funny to the outsider but not to himself,' remains a popular choice among his fans as one of his most memorable roles, which makes it all the more disappointing that it was limited to one series.[13]

Reportedly, the cast used to sit around in the evenings when on location in Ludlow, and discuss where things might progress in a second series. Simon rather felt that Dundridge would make the natural progression from jailed civil servant to intelligence.[14] Sadly, despite the success, no second series was ever forthcoming.

Simon had two more theatrical ventures lined up for 1985, one very familiar territory, the other anything but.

That spring, Simon had joined an old friend in a production of Tom Stoppard's *Jumpers* in the form of fellow sitcom royalty, Paul Eddington. Looking back, it was actually a veritable who's who of the most successful sitcom talent of the previous ten years, with Felicity Kendall joining her *Good Life* co-star, along with Andrew Sachs, of *Fawlty Towers*' Manuel fame.

It seems a curious cast for a piece so difficult to tackle. Originally produced in 1972, director Peter Wood had been at the helm for the original and now for the revival. He came with a somewhat difficult reputation. Combine this with the complexity of the play itself and *Jumpers* doesn't look like a particularly comfortable home for Simon's talents, particularly as he had initial fears that he was too old for his particular role.

The dialogue was described by Paul Eddington in his autobiography, *So Far, So Good*, as, 'dense, in the sense that a Dundee cake is dense.'[15] Eddington, who played an aging professor delivering a lecture entitled 'is God?', admitted, 'I do not think any but a professional philosopher could follow the many arguments at the time.'[16]

Wood's reputation was a fearsome one. Eddington recalled that he, 'gives the air of someone in touch with darker powers ... the secret, I found, was to give as good as you got. If he swore at you, rather than submit blushingly it was best to swear back.'[17]

Nick Renton recalls a degree of reticence on Simon's part prior to the production:

> Peter had a reputation for stripping actors, stripping them all away and reducing them until they were gibbering wrecks. There were one or two who had gone through that and had to leave productions. I said 'Simon, how are you getting on? Do you think that'll be alright?' and he said, 'Oh yes, I know Peter, I know about his wiles.'
>
> Then came rehearsal, and Peter obviously realised that Simon knew about his wiles and he went at him. I remember after about five weeks of rehearsals he didn't know where he was. It was interesting that he felt he could have the measure of this guy, but he had a hard ride up to the first night there.[18]

Wood could be particularly harsh on new talent, something which did not sit well with Simon. Selina Cadell's theory was that: 'Dictatorships don't really work very well in the theatre and Peter was a dictator. Brilliant people—ideas were genius, but manners were appalling.'[19]

Simon was of course someone to whom manners mattered a great deal. For him, holding open doors and standing when a woman entered a room were things instilled into him by his impeccably mannered father and so were second nature to a man of chivalry and respect. Wood's bombastic approach was not one he was comfortable with. However, even Wood succumbed to Simon's charms.

'There was definitely a coming together, but a really nice reconciliation,' remembers Selina. 'Simon was delighted that he came out of it very well. I feel that they grew to like each other's company.'[20]

His subsequent dramatic role was a far more comfortable one and could not have been a more contrasting experience—back into the safe world of Noël Coward, starring with his firm friend Joanna Lumley in *Blithe Spirit*, directed by Peter Farago. For his latest dip in the Coward pool, Simon took on the role of Charles Condomine, whose second marriage suffers at the hands of the spirit of his deceased first wife, played by Lumley. *Blithe Spirit* received healthy reviews, the only real criticism aimed at it being that the eccentric medium (Marcia Warren) who brings Lumley's character into the story was in danger of unwittingly stealing the show.

Back on familiar ground, Simon found himself the recipient of positive reviews once more, Jeremy Kingston commenting that, 'Simon Cadell always looks funny when dejected,' while Peter Hepple's review in *The Stage* went as far as to say, 'Simon Cadell, with his harassed, slightly disconnected air, has stealthily developed into the best of the latter-day Coward interpreters.' [21, 22] Surely a review to gladden his heart, had he ever read them, which he did not.

Theatrically speaking, Simon's life may have reverted to tried and tested ground, but on a personal front he was about to enter into new territory. Beckie Croft's sister, Penny, had fallen pregnant towards the end of 1984. Previously sharing a flat together, Beckie now felt that with a baby added into the mix, living with her sister would no longer be ideal. Peter Farago, Penny's other half, moved in and Beckie moved out. Simon suggested that the pair get a flat together, which they did.

Simon had always made attempts to keep his private life from the media. When he and Stephanie Turner parted, he went to great lengths to keep the split from the tabloids, and so by the time the papers found out, the breakup had long become old news. 'My private life I try to keep, to the greatest possible extent, private,' he told Ian Woodward in 1983. 'It is mine, my friends are mine, and that's it. There must be some sanctuary.' [23]

Having begun the relationship with Beckie, the boss's daughter at the time no less, Simon also deflected questions about his romantic life, often telling the tabloids that there was no one special in his life at the time. As though to deflect the media further, he continued to suggest that as a busy actor, relationships were simply not something that ever crossed his mind for any length of time:

> I'm not being coy, but I just don't think of myself as a confirmed bachelor, or as somebody who is going to get married one day. If it happens, it happens. I get very involved in my work, very involved indeed. This sort of temperament makes me realise how difficult life could be if ever I should marry. I don't think, while rehearsing, I'd be very much fun to live with. And it wouldn't make any difference whether the woman was involved in the theatre or not, I'd be just the same. [24]

Simon was a generous man, almost to a fault. He loved spending money on other people, even if he had none. Yet being romantic, he said, was not his dominating trait. 'I think there is a streak of romance in all of us somewhere. But I'm a typical man, I'm afraid. I forget birthdays and anniversaries, and I never buy flowers or surprise gifts.' [25] Beckie was more than happy to put that particular self-assessment to rights, recalling:

> He was romantic, he was just very practical with it. He was very logical and practical. He was never one for arguing about unnecessary things. He was always saying, 'Don't sweat the small stuff, there's absolutely no point in getting pissed off.' I think I said something a bit inflammatory to him at the

dinner table once and Simon didn't react. Peter said to him, 'How come you let that go?' and he just said 'Because you don't sweat the small stuff. If you do that, then your whole life becomes bicker, bicker, bicker.' He just let it go, it wasn't important. But he did like big romantic gestures.[26]

When Beckie was in her early twenties, she had planned to go to Egypt. She knew that the cost of the trip would be expensive for an independent young woman with little money to her own name, and she spent a great deal of time trying to save for the break.

When the time came for the trip, Beckie had saved enough to go but that left next to nothing with which to enjoy the holiday. Simon collected her and drove her to the airport, handing her an envelope with a note. Within the envelope was around £500, a lot of money in the early 1980s. He could have just offered to help with the cost of the holiday, but instead he had wrapped the money in a note, in his own challenged handwriting.

When she opened the note, she made out the opening words of Shakespeare's Sonnet 29—'When, in disgrace with fortune and men's eyes.' Sonnet 29 bemoans the author's despair of yearning for greater popularity and disapproving when self-reflecting. All of his issues are brightened by the thought of his young love.

For a man who felt himself to be a gentleman of honour, but not of a romantic nature, it was quite the gesture and one that belies the image he portrayed to the media. In fact, he did buy flowers, frequently, taking the trouble to first discover the favourite varieties preferred by the recipient.

Beckie's trip to Egypt had nearly been a solo one. Her first boyfriend and his new lady came to Suffolk for a weekend so that he could introduce her to Simon. When the topic of Beckie's imminent trip arose, the girlfriend excitedly offered to fulfil a desire to visit Egypt and the pair became instant friends.

Unexpectedly, Simon managed to free up some time while Beckie was away, and so he visited his travel agent to get some advice on where to go in order to get some proper relaxation. The agent recommended the Jamaica Inn on the North Coast of Jamaica—a considerably different option to those of his previous trip ten years before, when relaxation had been a secondary concern to dodging bullets and gang warfare.

When Beckie and her friend returned from Egypt, Simon had arranged for a regular driver chum of his to meet them at the airport. After dropping her friend home, they continued to the flat in Notting Hill. The driver helped Beckie with her luggage and then loitered for a moment.

Simon had left another envelope. This time, instead of cash for a trip, the envelope contained a note saying, 'Come to Jamaica,' with a plane ticket attached. The lingering driver then informed her that he was under instruction to return the next day to take Beckie back to the airport in order to fly off to Jamaica for the remainder of Simon's Caribbean break—another grand romantic gesture.

Holidays for Simon had always been centred around the relaxation side of things. Adventurous voyages of discovery were not his cup of tea. He saw enough adventure in the dramatic arts; holidays were for taking time out. He and Beckie were frequent visitors to Venice and the pair even bought a house in the South of France with the intention of restoring it to former glories. Of course, with Simon's workload, any trips there led to inevitable firefighting of overgrown gardens and repair work, so the renovations never materialised.

When at the height of Jeffrey Fairbrother fame, Simon told *Titbits* magazine: 'I just love to escape to a friend's house in the French Alps. Last year, I crashed out for four glorious weeks just resting in his peaceful vineyards, drinking wine and eating toast and pate. I don't like crowds, and would rather be with people I know, getting brown beside a private pool rather than a public beach.'[27] It is an image very reflective of Simon and Gyles's poignant *Merry Evening* sketch from Bedales.

For two and a half weeks, Simon and Beckie enjoyed the sun and the romance of Jamaica before returning home to the life of a workaholic in the theatre.

About a month later, Beckie began to suffer from an ear infection. She went to her doctor, and after a variety of physical examinations and verbal exchanges, the physician questioned her patient: 'Are you aware that you're pregnant?' The answer was no, she was not aware. If it was a surprise to Beckie then it was doubly so to Simon. As much as he loved the idea of having an heir, finding the time to be a parent was not something that was going to be easy.

When lunching with Gyles and his wife Michèle at Le Manoir aux Quat'Saisons in Oxford, Raymond Blanc's first restaurant, Beckie and Simon were left to chat as the Brandreths went for a walk. The wanderers returned too early and received the 'hurry along' sign from Simon, so continued to tour the gardens.

Simon was a traditionalist and did not entertain the idea of having their first child out of wedlock, and so he was busy proposing to Beckie. He called Gillian after the proposal was accepted, announcing, 'Beckie's pregnant, we're going to get married. It's not because she's pregnant!'

Simon had long been welcomed into the Croft family courtesy of the mutual respect and friendship he had struck up with David Croft during their years together on *Hi-de-Hi!*. He once recalled his acceptance into the Croft inner circle, saying: 'When I first started going out with Beckie, her father checked me out on wine to see if I knew a good one. It was "Come into the cellar, my boy", and when I passed that test I was accepted.'[28]

'Dad absolutely adored him,' remembers Beckie. 'Even though they were a generation apart, I met Simon not only because he was in Dad's show but because he was Dad's friend.'[29] The Crofts were another family with tradition and acting as their cornerstones, and Simon fitted neatly into their way of life.

At the weekends, David Croft and Simon would sit at the dinner table and between lunch and the evening meal would just put the world to rights with their chat. That was something that had been part of the Croft children's upbringing.

'We did all sit and chat, even as kids,' remembers Beckie. 'We would always change for dinner ... not tiaras and dresses, but we'd put on nice clothes and they'd all go and have a drink in the long room. Simon of course loved all that. He could have his wine and chat, with lots and lots of anecdotes.'[30]

Simon enjoyed nothing more than holding court around a table with family and friends, fine wine in hand. However, he was not always in charge of such occasions. 'He had a fierce rival in my mother, who was the queen of holding court,' says Beckie. 'Nobody got to be above her. She was the queen, everyone else was the courtiers. Dad would just sit and listen and laugh a lot. He talked quite a bit to Simon, but he was quite a shy man.'[31]

With Simon's desire to be wed long before the arrival of the couple's firstborn, he and Beckie decided against a lavish wedding. He was not a religious person, and so they decided on a registry office ceremony in Chelsea, witnessed by Simon's choice of Gyles and Michèle, with Beckie's best friend Amanda Donohoe, most famously known for starring with Oliver Reed in *Castaway*, as her own witness.

Simon Cadell took his bride on 9 March 1986 and they returned to Le Manoir aux Quat'Saisons for a lavish meal. They went back to Manoir because they were regular visitors by now with Gyles and Michèle. 'We used to go up there and have the most ridiculous meals, seven courses of the most extraordinary food and wine,' says Beckie. 'We used to have a different wine with every course. When the food arrived, Simon would waft the scent of the food up his nose, he absolutely loved it, and of course Raymond Blanc was always very attentive.'[32]

Simon was still appearing in *Blithe Spirit* at the time, so after the ceremony, he had to travel back to the West End for the evening performance. At the end of the curtain call, Joanna Lumley called for the audience's attention and in a lovely gesture to her friend, told them, 'Just to let you know, he's not married to two women—he's now married a third!'[33] With that nice gesture received, Simon promptly got back into his car and returned to his wedding breakfast in Oxford.

Due to the clash with *Blithe Spirit*, there was no honeymoon; Jamaica had effectively been a pre-emptive honeymoon. That said, they had gate-crashed Beckie's sister's honeymoon, who on announcing that they were going to Venice managed to add the pair to their travel plans, Venice being one of Simon's favourite destinations.

The Cadell's first child was born on 15 August 1986. The birth was a far less difficult one to that which had brought Simon into the world. The biggest dilemma was the name of the baby boy, as the parents could not agree. Simon wanted to call his first-born son Piers. Beckie was having none of it. Living as they did in the Portobello Road area, which at the time was not known for being terribly welcoming, she did not particularly like the idea of calling 'Piers' across the local parks.

The next option pleased Beckie even less—Turkinal. Fearing that he would be stuck with the mocking name of Turkey, she argued Simon down to something more grounded, saying, 'Let's just give him a normal name, like John or David, that nobody is going to have an opinion about.'[34] In the end, they settled on Patrick. Gillian protested that it was a silly idea, having a prominent Patrick Cadell already in the family, but with the generation apart they felt that there would be no problem. Wary of Simon looking to use the name on any subsequent sibling, Beckie decided to take Piers off the table as an option for any future children by allowing it to be one of Patrick's middle names.

Parenthood was something new for Simon and something he did not take to terribly well from a practical perspective. He adored his children unconditionally. He just was not very good at being the practical hands-on father. Beckie can only recall him changing nappies two or three times during the early years of parenthood.

The reality was that being a constantly employed theatre performer did not lend itself to the routine of sleepless nights and dirty nappies. Simon was anything but chauvinistic, fully supportive of women's rights, but getting home from the theatre at one in the morning did not really mix well with a 6 a.m. feed for the youngster, or a school run trip for a toddler.

'He got away with it somehow,' remembers Beckie. 'He used to say, "oh darling, you're marvellous, I don't know how you cope." We would go up to Mum and Dad's pretty much every weekend. Then on Saturday mornings it would be me and Peter [Farago] at 6.30 in the morning spoon-feeding Ready Brek to these babies, while Penny and Simon were upstairs dead to the world until 10.30 when they'd come down for coffee.'[35]

The element of parenthood that Simon deplored was discipline. He was unsurprisingly more than happy to be the funny, jolly dad, walking into doors and generally entertaining his children. 'I remember him always being a bit of an entertainer,' remembers son Patrick. 'He had all these silly faces, voices, characters that he'd put on.'[36] Yet he simply could not do discipline.

'He just couldn't bare the idea of doing that, the thought of being horrible to the children in any way whatsoever,' remembers Beckie. 'He felt that telling them off was being horrible to them, so in terms of discipline? Absolutely not.'[37]

Beckie recalls one wonderful event reflecting Simon's parenting style one summer when visiting their property in the South of France. They had bought the aforementioned house in Toulouse and despite its run-down condition, Simon loved it. He was in theatre at the time so they decided that Beckie would go on ahead to the house and Simon would fly over later to join them.

So Beckie packed up the car with luggage, buggy, and by now two young boys. She drove to the cross-channel train, then bundled the three of them on and then off again. Driving across France was a new experience, and this she did with the two youngsters and eventually on to the airport where she awaited Simon.

Something both Stephanie Turner and Beckie recalled was that Simon considered flying to be an experience. One should always dress for it, never tracksuit bottoms or jeans, and it very often got him bumped up to first class. When Simon's flight touched down, he stepped out from the aircraft with his oversized cigar and a rolled up copy of *The Times* under his arm and that was the extent of his luggage.

'I'd had this horrid journey with two children and the luggage in the car,' Beckie remembers. 'I had everything, supplies for the house, car, kids, luggage and he arrived with one cigar and a paper and says, "Hello darling."'[38]

However amusing such stories are, they are told with humour and warmth and no dissatisfaction with Simon's involvement in parenting. Beckie says, 'I was never angry about it or felt he should have done more. He was doing other things, properly sharing the load … but the practical side of childcare was my load.'[39]

Simon's opinion on parenthood was unsurprisingly straightforward, saying, 'It suits me. I quite like the responsibility as well.' Most importantly, he added, 'I enjoy being a father.'[40]

Happy as Larry

While 1986 had brought a new son into his world, Simon showed no signs of trimming his exhausting workload to compensate. At the time of Patrick's arrival, rehearsals were already underway for Sir Alan Ayckbourn's production of *Tons of Money*, which would run at the Littleton Theatre from November the same year. Simon admitted that Patrick's arrival had been kept largely a secret, remarking on the early days of parenthood, 'It's wonderful … my son was born in August but we kept very quiet about it until now. He's a lovely boy, a very good baby.'[1]

Tons of Money was Simon's opportunity to fulfil one of his career goals, with the farce being one of three productions at the National Theatre to be directed by Sir Alan in that season, with Arthur Miller's *A View from the Bridge* playing at the Cottesloe and *A Small Family Business*, the playwright's own work, running at the Olivier from May 1987. Simon would have no role in the Miller play but would return in *A Small Family Business*.

Simon's long-held desire to appear in a National Theatre production was revealed to his sister in an aborted chat show appearance. He had been due to appear on Parkinson with Selina, but a late opportunity for the host to interview the Prince of Wales caused the appearance to be cancelled at the last minute. Selina recalls:

> The researcher came to talk to us. She said something like, 'Are you jealous of each other?' and I said, 'Well Simon's a star of course—I'm envious, but not jealous.' Simon was absolutely appalled. He turned to me and said, 'I don't know what you're talking about. You have the career that I want. I've never worked in the National Theatre.'[2]

Tons of Money was an aged play originally launched at a restaurant in Gerrard Street in 1922. After being touted to many agents, it was taken up by the partnership of Tom Walls and Leslie Henson. Such was the success of the original that after taking up a lease at the Aldwych Theatre, it would achieve fame as the first Aldwych farce. Subsequent efforts would be made to transfer the success to film with mixed results, most recently with a BBC production in 1954 starring a young Frankie Howerd.

Ayckbourn's production was described by the *London Standard* as more 'a renovation than a revival.'[3] Sir Alan admitted that some of the more risqué jokes and visual gags needed rewriting or updating to reflect the period, more than sixty years having passed from the original production.

Simon's role in the play, originally written by Will Evans and Arthur Valentine, was Aubrey Allington, a permanently monocled debt-ridden man who is left a sum of money. Seeing that the inheritance would do no more than cover his own existing debts, Aubrey and his wife Louise, played by Polly Adams, hatch a plan to fake Aubrey's death. Aubrey then impersonates the chief subsequent beneficiary in order to procure the pay-off from his own apparent death.

Problems ensue, however, when Aubrey returns as a long-lost cousin, George. Unbeknown to him, the genuine George has also surfaced, along with an additional George who is actually an actor employed by the unscrupulous butler, Michael Gambon, in an attempt to claim the fortune for himself. Simon was instantly smitten with the eccentric buffoonery of his new role. When questioned for *What's On*, he reflected of Aubrey:

> An upper class twit? I don't think Aubrey is quite that—he's more of a silly arse. Twit is a bit unkind. He is a man out of his depth, not very bright—Bertie Wooster was a genius by comparison—but really quite benign. He is lucky that he has a very quick-witted wife. He has quite a good outlook on life, but he doesn't like problems. He is always in debt, lives on credit, and when the chance of having literally oodles of money presents itself, they both grab for it.[4]

Tons of Money was not Simon's first venture into farce and would not be his last. Evidencing his ability to show extraordinary expertise at all levels of theatre, he would explain further:

> With farce of this kind it is very necessary to keep it fresh and polished, up to the mark. It's necessary to have more than two or three performances in a row, which is usually what happens at the National, so in this case they have done what they call a 'clumping process'. Sounds rather inelegant, but it means that the play will have slightly longer runs and therefore stay sharp.[5]

The part of Aubrey was played by Ralph Lynne in the 1922 production, but Tom Walls also took a role that continued in the run for two years. Simon's continued belief that staying in a role for too long was a bad idea for both actor and production was evident in his assessment of the part, admitting that: 'It's not a prospect I'd like myself—two years of the same play, eight performances a week! I find that you peak in a part after a time, and then it's very difficult to maintain the spontaneity. I think six months is about the maximum.'[6]

The production's reviews were mostly positive, if perhaps not as gushingly so as those for Sir Alan's subsequent productions for the National Theatre. However, Simon's own performance, along with that of Gambon who had reportedly chosen the farce with Sir Alan for the season, did draw attention.

In *Country Life*, Ian Stewart proclaimed that Simon had become 'one of our most accomplished practitioners of comedy with a manic edge'.[7] *The Daily Telegraph* salivated that he was 'excellent as Aubrey, whether in stuttering disguise, dropping his jaw in appalled surprise, or tumbling hazardously through the ceiling.'[8]

The physical demands of the role were significant, with Aubrey's potting shed destroyed in an explosion, and *The Month* bemoaned that 'Mr Cadell ran up a wall so efficiently that he could not make it down to take his applause. Sad: he earned it and so did his colleagues.'[9]

Co-star John Arthur remembers of Simon's devotion to the role:

> Simon did a stunt in *Tons of Money* and it struck me that he saw himself as a sort of comic tradition in clowning. He was always inventing bits of comedy business, the physical stuff. One of the things he had to do was come through the ceiling.
>
> What he had to do was to be standing outside of the audience above the ceiling as it were. On cue he would fall through a ceiling that was actually paper and drop onto the floor below. What was so terrifying was that you can't see where you are going. It was an extremely dangerous and brave thing to do.[10]

Tons of Money made way in spring 1987 for *A View from the Bridge*, the one production of the National Theatre season that Simon did not have a role in. It gave him a convenient break in his busy diary and although undertaking rehearsals for *A Small Family Business*, the next significant step in Simon's career was about to throw him back into the world of television sitcom, and in the most controversial of circumstances.

It was in the kitchen at the Honington residence of David and Anne Croft that Simon sat gently swaying in a rocking chair by the open fire. He and Beckie had made the weekly pilgrimage to the Croft family home to gather for Sunday lunch along with Penny Croft and Peter Farago, a ritual that Simon adored. Many times, he and David would sit around the rustic solid wood table chatting for hours over a bottle of fine wine.

On this particular Sunday, Penny surfaced to find Simon thoughtfully reading a manuscript that she recognised all too well. She had printed out her debut sitcom script, entitled *Life Without George*, from her new Amstrad and had left it neatly stacked in the kitchen. Simon had risen earlier than his sister-in-law and had read through it with enthusiasm. Penny recalls her embarrassment that the fledgling script had been absorbed by the leading man of one of the BBC's most recent sitcom successes, co-written by her own father to boot.

'It's good,' began Simon. 'Who's playing Larry?'

'I have absolutely no idea, Simon,' responded an off-guard Penny. 'We haven't got to casting yet.'

'Put me down for it, I want to do it,' said Simon, displaying his usual certainty in knowing what would work for him. 'It's modern, it's different, it's new—I want to do it.'[11]

Penny called the casting director to tell her the news and Simon's participation was sealed. Whether to avoid accusations of nepotism, or simply out of due respect for his sister-in-law, Simon would never reveal this in subsequent interviews regarding the role. Indeed, he told the *Radio Times* that: 'I knew Penny was writing the series, but I had not seen anything of the scripts until I came to audition—and lots of other actors were considered before me.'[12]

The approval of *Life Without George* by the BBC was a work of some ingenuity by its creator. Penny Croft was all too aware of the shadow of her father's immense success. *Dad's Army* may have gone from the screens, but its legacy was gathering momentum. *'Allo 'Allo!*, a lengthy success with David's other long-term writing partner, Jeremy Lloyd, was at the height of its powers, *Are You Being Served?* had only just drawn to a close, and a Simon-less *Hi-de-Hi!* was still commanding audiences in excess of 13 million with David Griffin as the leading man. Fearing a less than unbiased assessment of her work, Penny chose to take a different approach to getting her new project commissioned.

The BBC's Head of Comedy at the time, Gareth Gwenlan, received a script for a gentle, modern comedy from a university student based in Nottingham named Helen Garth. Gwenlan had a hand in many of the BBC's most successful comedy commissions, while also taking the production reigns of such BBC staples as *To the Manor Born*, *Butterflies*, and *Only Fools and Horses*. He was impressed. The BBC approach in those days was a simple read of the scripts: if they liked it, they went with it; if they did not, it was binned. Gwenlan was impressed that a debut writer of such tender years actually knew how to write a modern, relevant comedy and gave his approval.

By the time Penny went to the BBC to meet with the producers, contracts were signed and the wheels had been set in motion. Gwenlan ran into Penny in the fourth-floor corridors of Television Centre, suggesting that the two have a catch-up over a drink after his meeting with a new writer from Nottingham. Ten minutes later, Penny entered that very meeting revealing her hand to a furious Gwenlan. When he challenged her behaviour after the meeting, which he felt undermined him, she rightfully responded that: 'If you knew it was me you wouldn't have read it, you'd have said "it's not as good as your father" so you're stuck with me now.'[13]

So it was that on 11 January 1987, Simon arrived for filming what would be his most successful television comedy role after Jeffrey Fairbrother. In the programme, Simon played the part of a rather lost estate agent, Larry Wade, struggling to find his place in the yuppie era of Thatcher's Britain. Of his new persona, Simon said:

> Larry is very much a man of the eighties. He's concerned about the way he leads his life but not gregarious. He's a distillation of a certain sort of person who is about my age who is conditioned by the Labour Party in the 1960s and was then thrown by the obvious successes of Thatcherism in the 1980s. He's the one who has not become a yuppie.[14]

Despite the lasting fame of Jeffrey Fairbrother, Larry seemed to strike a greater chord with Simon. Perhaps it was the nervous obsessiveness, but where Simon turned to his cigarettes, Larry turned to endless bags of cheese and onion crisps and mugs of Marmite. Simon expanded on his new character:

> I'm very sympathetic towards Larry, but I do think he's probably more balanced than I am.[15]
>
> Jeffrey simply did not know how to act with women. He did not know how to treat Gladys. I'm much more in sympathy with Larry's caring 'New Man' attitude. I suppose I'm a fairly old 'New Man.'[16]
>
> Larry is an ordinary guy in his mid-thirties who is a bit obsessive about things. He's divorced, worried about his health, talks in clichés when he's nervous and loves a beautiful girl who doesn't feel the same way about him. It's a situation that many people will be able to relate to and is very much a comedy of the eighties. Everyone has a George or Georgina in their past. They're the dream lover, the one that got away, the one which represents the unattainable ideal which everybody yearns for at the expense of the perfectly good things that are attainable.
>
> I don't know why it should be, but men in particular tend to look back on their first love in this way. They always have a special place in their hearts.[17]

The anti-Larry alongside Simon's bemused character was Ben Morris, Larry's office partner at the estate agents of Morris, Morris and Wade and to whom all women were seen as playthings. While forever frowning on his young colleague's immoral stance, Larry was regularly turning to Ben for assistance in adapting to the expectations of the modern dating world. For this role, the casting director turned to Selina Cadell's other half, Michael Thomas. Penny Croft recalls:

> The casting woman called and said 'there is this guy in *Inside Out*' and I loved *Inside Out* and thought the guy in it was absolutely outstanding. He got cast and it was only when they were going to offer him the part that Beckie said 'you know he's going out with Selina?' Anyway, when I met him at the casting I absolutely loved him.[18]

For Thomas, it was a first acting venture into sitcom territory and not coming from a theatrical background either, he was grateful for Simon's guiding hand:

> It was terrific to work with him because he was so much more experienced— it was quite useful to tag on and pick up tips. I remember doing some filming with him on the south coast somewhere and he said, 'Look, let's just do it with a two shot.' Instead of doing it in two shots, one of each character in close-ups where you cut it afterwards, you just have the two characters walking up the street all in one shot and then you can really time it as actors. That was terrific because you knew you could just play off each other and the comedy came from that relationship rather than from an editor later putting it together.[19]

For the object of Larry's desires, casting turned to Carol Royle. The pair instantly struck up a respectful friendship, Royle describing Simon as, 'a marvellous actor and a marvellous human being.'[20]

However unconventional the approach to the commissioning may have been, it was nothing in comparison to the barrage of criticism that awaited the show when it first aired in spring 1987.

The opening episode was aired on 12 March 1987, less than a week after the end of AIDS Television Week. AIDS had become a hot topic in the media, and with the paranoid ignorance flying around at the time, the television companies took the unusual step of uniting in their attempts to educate the viewing public. The week had even been launched with a twelve-minute simulcast on both BBC channels entitled *AIDS—The Facts*. No fewer than twenty-six AIDS-related programmes were broadcast during the following ten days and the day after *Life Without George* first appeared on the screens, a five-week educational programme, *Facing Up to AIDS*, was aired on BBC2.

If the BBC had known that the opening scene of their new comedy would cause outrage, they would surely have taken an alternative view to the scheduling. Indeed, the review in *The Stage* at the time admitted doubt: 'whether the series would have got into production had the AIDS scare surfaced earlier.'[21] As it was, shortly after 9.30 p.m. on the first Thursday after AIDS Television Week, viewers welcomed Simon's new character into their homes via the bedroom of Carol Royle's Jenny. After what was clearly an unplanned sexual liaison, Jenny turns to Larry and says, 'I think you should go now Harry.'

'Actually, it's Larry,' responds Simon's affronted estate agent.

'Thank you for the sex,' says Jenny.

Delivered in Simon's unrivalled dry manner, Larry replies, 'You've made a wonderful experience something tacky.'

The scene was comparatively innocent and if a new comedy today opened with it, no one would bat their proverbial eye lids. However, this was hysterical 1980s Britain with a viewership that had just been subjected to multiple programmes that were either meant to educate, moralise, or provoke debate on AIDS and the methods of preventing a perceived impending epidemic. The fact that Jenny could not accurately recall her unplanned partner's first name was enough to send the media into a frenzy.

The BBC called Penny Croft the following morning in a panic. She recalls:

> I had to go on some programme live in Birmingham and defend it. The BBC press office rang me and said, 'You have to get on a train, you have to go … it's all gone mad, we knew this would happen.' The audience were saying it was irresponsible. I didn't know at the time as I was on the train, but one woman said 'It's been mentioned in parliament this morning.' The fact is it's a reality. People sleep with people they don't know. I said 'I didn't mean offence to anyone, I'm just trying to portray in comedy now a more modern life than *Terry and June* situations, which were not the life that I understood.' Then this one woman stood up and said 'Of course, you're an unmarried mother aren't you?' live on television. I said, 'I suppose that is correct,' and she replied, 'My case is made,' or something like that. It was ghastly.[22]

Simon was completely supportive of his writer and sister-in-law, who remembers: 'Simon wasn't scared of anything. I was saying "Oh God, we've got to go to a press conference" and he said "it's good, just stand by it." I knew everyone wanted us to fail, but Simon shrugged and said "Fuck 'em."'[23]

Those who could see beyond the paranoia of the media newsroom understood that *Life Without George* was actually a very modern, relevant comedy—well-written, expertly executed, and deserving of success. *The Stage* review summarised it expertly, realising that the lead characters were not representative of the kind of promiscuity coming under the media microscope at the time, saying: 'It has all the signs of being a winner—with a sharp and adult script by two new writers, a popular star in Simon Cadell, and some fleshed-out characters who are likely to be as real as the *Just Good Friends* pair or *The Mistress* trio.'[24]

It was very much a grown-up comedy, but elements of David Croft's humour were allowed to peak through. When Larry is discussing house sale criteria with the aging Mr Chambers, on hearing Chambers' middle names are David Copperfield, he quizzes, 'Your mother liked Dickens?' to which Chambers replies, 'Don't think so, I'm an only child.'

The Stage review continued: 'despite the nude-under-the-sheets opening they are not easy bed-hoppers and while she still pines for the perfect but departed George it is already apparent that an uneasy liaison with Cadell can be expected ... Cadell is a natural for the inept, blank faced and shy Larry.'[25] James Green's review astutely concludes: 'Not all the kind of behaviour our newly written health code preaches. But a smashing start nevertheless, and you can be sure that the word "condom" will emerge before long.'[26] In reality, the BBC had tried to encourage Penny Croft and co-writer Val Hudson to add a shot of a condom into the opening scene, but Penny rightly refused.

After an exhausting day of cross-examination defending her new creation, director general of the BBC, Michael Grade, called. To Penny's relief, she had another ally. 'Are you alright?' Grade said.

'Yes,' replied the beleaguered writer.

'I want to apologise for not sending someone from the BBC to back you up. I don't care what anybody says, I liked it and here's your commission for a second series.'[27]

Penny was shocked. After a very public mauling, irrespective of any reviews from the critics, Grade had taken the unprecedented step of granting a second series on the day after broadcasting the opening episode. 'He was very brave. But the people in the middle, they weren't keen on us at all,' recalled Penny.[28]

Having riled the establishment within the BBC, Penny decided to press further, insisting on women among the camera crew and better ethnic representation within the extras. 'I was hoisted by my own petard really. The little girl we got to work the cameras couldn't move the thing, so we had to employ a man to push it!'[29]

Life Without George did not encourage promiscuity with its leading characters. Larry was too out of touch with the modern dating world to play the field, nor did he agree with the morals of those that did. Jenny had just come out of a five-year relationship, which hardly suggested promiscuity. The show had simply suffered from the timing of its arrival. Penny reflects now:

> It's hard to remember now the culture as it was then. They gave us a tremendously hard time in the building. Susan Belbin was the director. That was radical, no woman had ever directed a comedy. Her and I would walk

into the BBC bar and the men would start humming the theme to *Cagney and Lacey* and say things like, 'Here come the dykes'. It was really tough there in the eighties.[30]

As the show found its audience, Simon's character began to strike a chord with the confused modern man. Larry was actually just a nice guy in an unfamiliar world and the writers began to get large amounts of fan mail, with much more pro-men than hate mail. On why the series was successful, Simon theorised:

> People recognize their own experiences in it. Larry is an ordinary fellow, a nice man who tries hard in life. Life isn't always kind to him, but it's probably no more unkind than it is to most people. He's jealous of George because George seems to be the 'ideal' man.
>
> The character I play is quite different from any other I've played. He's in the process of getting divorced from someone whom he regarded as a 'typical wife'. He thinks Jenny is very different and wonderful and beautiful, but he has difficulty in establishing the relationship he wants. The comedy lies in it all being so true to life. As an actor, you don't play a part for laughs. You speak the lines naturally, and if they're funny, it's comedy.[31]
>
> Larry's a romantic. He's head over heels in love with Jenny, but he was prepared to wait until he got her commitment. He tried to do the right thing, but that doesn't make him dull. Good heavens, he once got boozed out of his head and did a strip in a wine bar! I don't think Jenny would still be there if she found Larry exasperating.
>
> Funnily enough, it's only now as I talk about him that I realise how difficult it is to talk about him without thinking, 'this is sending me to sleep.' But that doesn't mean he's lacklustre. Only that Larry's a normal bloke with a bit of everything in him. You can't hang a label on him.
>
> There's a lot of me in the character. Like me, Larry's very much a man of the eighties. He's trying to be the entrepreneur, trying to run his business, trying to sort out his life.
>
> He's not a party-goer, but that doesn't mean he's shy. He realises he's probably a little self-centred and tries not to be. I suppose he's also a bit neurotic, but only in the sense that everybody is concerned with the way they organise their lives.
>
> The important thing for me is to care as much about playing Larry as I would about Hamlet. When you think that ten million people are seeing it—it's unbelievable really.[32]

Simon had great empathy for Larry, but there was too much on his plate to wallow in the aftermath of the furore surrounding his latest venture into television comedy.

Back at the National Theatre, Sir Alan Ayckbourn's deal included the requirement that he would produce a new work of his own creation and this took the form of *A Small Family Business*. Breaking with his normal routine of changing content right up until rehearsal, Sir Alan this time had his work complete a year ahead of its first airing, a result of the requirements of the National Theatre's Artistic Director, Sir Peter Hall.

Ayckbourn had agreed to take a sabbatical from the St Joseph Theatre in Scarborough, where he had premiered all of his work since becoming artistic director in 1972. The Olivier Theatre presented him with the opportunity to put on a larger production than those that his Scarborough residency permitted; with the stage design work of Alan Tagg, he took full advantage, creating a two-storey set that allowed the story to be told from a number of near identikit homes.

A Small Family Business was a morality tale suggesting that even the most innocently honest people can commit comparatively minor infractions, such as taking stationery supplies from the office, and take a journey down the moral slide into more depraved crimes. Despite suggestions from some media that the play was a political judgement on Thatcher's Britain, Sir Alan went to lengths to emphasise that it was a non-political piece aimed at the declining morals of society in general.

The honest individual in the play was Jack McCraken, played by Michael Gambon, who takes on his father-in-law's family-run furniture business. Hosting a party to celebrate his new career move, during which McCraken makes a speech to emphasise the need for honesty during his tenure, he is interrupted by the arrival of a sleazy detective, Inspector Benedict Hough. Hough was the role taken by Simon Cadell and one that became one of his most widely acclaimed successes on stage.

Hough was a huge step away from either Jeffrey Fairbrother or Larry Wade, his two eminently likable characters from the television schedules. Here, Simon went into depths of depravity, taking over a character at the very bottom of the moral code. It did not escape the attention of the critics who were united in their praise for such a believable and brave change of persona. *The Financial Times* was the most gushing, declaring that:

> The performance he [Ayckbourn] has elicited from Simon Cadell, as the hunched and sordid Hough, is not only extraordinary in itself, but a real advance for this talented but manneristic actor. You can smell Cadell's Hough at 50 metres … Cadell scrapes around in a moustache and oversized suit—trouser bottoms ignominiously obscuring his shoes—like a bestial pervert of a peculiarly English variety.[33]

Other descriptions of Simon's performance refer to him as 'magnificently vile', 'poisonously realistic' and 'unrecognizably twisted', with one reviewer suggesting that Simon played the part with 'hunched, insinuating relish.'[34, 35, 36, 37] Sir Alan recalls:

> He certainly did [relish the part]. Actors often welcome the chance to play
> a real out and out villain, which Hough undoubtedly is. Similarly, Clive
> Francis, who took over the role after Simon left and more recently, Matthew
> Cottle, in the RNT revival both approached the role with equal glee! Simon
> told me he had based his own characterization on a member of the current
> West End stage crew.[38]

True to his word meanwhile, Michael Grade approved the commission for a
second series of *Life Without George*, which went into production in October
1987. Simon was finding Larry more intriguing than Jeffrey Fairbrother. As
much as he enjoyed playing the entertainments manager, one of the core
elements of *Hi-de-Hi!* had been that the characters were largely losers in
their respective fields, and as such they rarely developed into anything more
than the people the viewing public first came to know; this was not so for
Larry Wade.

Larry was continuing his pursuit in the on-again, off-again relationship
with Jenny. Without the furore that accompanied the opening series, *Life
Without George* was garnering viewing figures that at times actually matched
Hi-de-Hi!, despite having a less primetime slot in the schedules and also
having more competition than just ITV and BBC2.

'We've done thirteen episodes and there's only one bedroom scene,' reflected
Simon on the alleged promiscuity. 'It's got this enormous reputation for being
risqué. It was great, a lovely group of people to work with and the writing
is excellent.'[39]

Domestically, Simon and Beckie were set to welcome their second son
into the world, with Alexander Peter being born on 8 September 1988. The
battle lines over baby names were a little less fraught this time. Beckie wanted
Alexander and Simon was accepting of that if he could shorten the name to
Alec, after one of his much-admired theatrical heroes, Sir Alec Guinness.

Simon was aware that his parenting was still not as hands-on as he would
like, and nothing would change in that respect with the addition of Alec to
the family. When talking about the upcoming third series of *Life Without
George*, when Larry is facing the prospect of parenthood, he responded in
a remarkably personal manner for somebody normally so reticent to reveal
much of himself to the media:

> He'll want to do his share at home. But like me, he'll probably discover that
> no matter how willing you are, if you lead a busy professional life the best
> you can hope to do is take part of the load off your partner.

But I think Larry will spend more time with his family than I am able to—
in that respect, he'll probably be slightly better as a father.[40]

The final series of *Life Without George* went into production in December
1988. The family links were enhanced further as Simon's sister Selina was
added to the cast. It was their first work together since performing pantomime
in *A Night in Old Peking* in 1981 and would remain their one and only
television venture together. Of that final series, Simon reflected:

> Larry has finally grown up. We're over his obsession and his desires. This is
> about his maturing attitude towards living with a woman and not making
> the same mistakes he made with his marriage. We seem to have touched a
> nerve with the public because they recognize the characters so well. There
> are plenty of Larry types, and Jennys around who have had problems in
> their relationship right from the start.[41]

Simon remained absorbed by Larry and as keen to see him progress as any
of the viewers, saying, 'You can't really call it a situation comedy because
the things that happen are not very extraordinary. The people involved
just do everyday things that are sometimes funny and sometimes sad. But
because you can identify with them you're intrigued to know what's going to
happen next.'[42]

Life Without George finished after three series. It was not planned to be
that way, and the BBC, Penny Croft and Simon were all expecting to make
a fourth series. It was to have been retitled as *Life Without George* was no
longer appropriate, given that the mysterious George was completely gone
from the storylines now, and it would have been set after a few more years had
passed. However, fate had other ideas.

Once More unto the Breach

After *A Small Family Business*, Simon had juggled the second and third series of *Life Without George* with a number of theatrical productions that had not replicated his previous successes. In 1988, he entered into another venture with Peter Farago—*Musical Comedy Murders of 1940*. Simon described the play with eagerness:

> It's a kind of pastiche of the comedy thriller genre of the 1940s, it's a very, very funny evening written by an American. It's about a group of people who go to an old dark house and are cut off by a snow drift ... very traditional stuff but what happens within that context is not and it's a riot—I mean there's secret passages and bodies falling out of the walls and a group of people who cannot cope with the situation at all.
>
> Although it's set in the 1940s, it was written by an American writer/director whose main fame is for really heavy, serious drama. He was asked by a producer to write a comedy thriller and he said no I can't write that sort of stuff at all, there's just no way ... he put down the phone, walked to the front door and there was a tax demand from the American tax authorities for $15,000. He didn't have the money so he rang the producer back up and he said listen, if you give me an advance of $15,000 I'll write it and so he wrote this. What's really interesting is that he's got a really clever theatre mind, this writer John [Bishop] and that's applied to something that's just a piece of froth not a soufflé.[1]

The production's casting seemed at first to be a stroke of genius, heavy as it was on big names in television, comedy, and music. *Doctor Who* star Tom Baker, up-and-coming singer Maria Friedman, comedy stalwart Sheila Steafel, and former RSC actress Margaret Courtenay seemed to be a talent pool that would surely make the production a success destined for transfer onto the West End from its opening in Greenwich.

Unfortunately, the strong cast was somewhat conflicted. As leading man and with a certain amount of financial investment in the production, Simon was keen that things should be a success, but with such strong personalities, it did not properly gel.

In the lead role, Baker played a villain whose evil was supposed to remain a surprise, but his exuberance at being bad left the audience in no doubt from an early stage as to the true nature of his character. Simon, meanwhile, tried his best to guide the young Friedman in her role, efforts not always appreciated, and with Steafel and Courtenay getting along poorly, the production did not achieve a West End transfer, perhaps justifiable given the cost of assembling such a high-profile cast.

Whether there was any real animosity among the group is questionable. Baker had definite ideas about how to play his role, but much like Simon, his own personality was charm personified. Simon Butteriss, who played Helsa Wenzel, remembered Baker as, 'completely charming. Never throws a diva strop or anything like that. The audience absolutely adored him in the piece.'[2]

Friedman had a great deal of stage time with Simon, almost to the point of being a double act within the play, but it simply did not work. Peter Farago remembers her as, 'an enormously talented woman and she has a wonderful voice. But, I don't know ... it wasn't quite right. There was no chemistry between Simon and Maria, and there should have been.'[3]

Farago rightly concedes that the reviews were not terrible, but they should have been better. Peter Hepple's *Stage* review praised every member of the cast, and noted Simon as being, 'in the front rank of our comedy players.'[4] Others were not so taken, saying that Simon's 'excellent performance isn't enough, by a long chalk, to save this short play.'[5]

Simon's own attempts to rally the cast did nothing to promote harmony off stage. A man about whom barely a single bad word was spoken in the theatrical trade could not get Courtenay and Steafel to get along, could not get Baker to conceal his villainy, nor could he generate the necessary chemistry with Friedman. 'Simon certainly wanted it to go the West End and he was trying to protect the piece,' recalls Butteriss. 'There was nothing other than goodwill in Simon putting his oar in.'[6]

Rightly or wrongly, the production did not move on to the West End. Having fought hard to get the rights to put it on, Farago breathed some sigh of relief that it would not transfer, wary as he was of the conflict within the cast continuing beyond the Greenwich run.

A few months after *Musical Comedy Murders* closed, Simon moved on to a two-hander play entitled *Double Act*. He admitted that the experience at Greenwich had left him expecting to take a break from the theatre for a while, simply reflecting that the Bishop play, 'hadn't quite worked somehow.'[7]

When Barry Creyton's new play found its way to his in tray, he was intrigued. After reading it several times, he admitted: 'I thought, "Well, Simon, you would regret it very much if you went to the theatre and saw somebody else playing that part so I think you'd better play it yourself."'[8]

Double Act was a depiction of a couple formerly married who meet five years after their split. Classified as a tragi-comedy, Simon reunited with Lisa Harrow, whom he had first encountered in *Romeo and Juliet* at Coventry, and director friend Nick Renton. *Double Act's* reviews scaled highs and lows, with *The Sunday Times* describing it as, 'hilarious', and its two stars as delivering, 'a pair of spitfire performances in what was undoubtedly a physical tour de force.'[9] This was not so for *The Stage's* Gerard Werson, who despite praising the acting talent described the play as 'a mixture of purient [*sic.*] smut and failed one-liners.'[10] Director Renton simply admitted that it was, 'just a very odd play.'[11]

There followed a five-week spell in *The Parasol* in Manchester, under the direction of Tim Luscombe. Simon's role as awkward middle-aged Alexei Laptev was described by Jeremy Kingston in *The Times* as, 'the best part Cadell has had in years.'[12]

Whether by careful planning or simple coincidence, it is curious that Simon, a gentle man uneasy with his physical features, would play a man described in *The Stage* as 'having everything except belief in himself.'[13] One of his character's lines, when referring to darkness, proclaims: 'I feel better in the dark. Women are less bored with me when they can't see me.'

Certainly, director Luscombe found Simon's involvement in the play an enjoyable one:

> I remember the work Simon and I did on the text of the play before we started on rehearsals and I was impressed with his energy and boundless ambition he had for the work. He taught me a lot about how much effort is required if you're to succeed and actually be good. He was painstaking and detailed to an extraordinary degree, but always light and fun with it, and never, ever the diva.
>
> I remember long conversations with him about how one might do comedy in the round. Neither of us ever had and for him it was a challenge, and a bit surreal because it broke so many conventions. But he mastered it in the end, brilliantly of course.[14]

Simon's appearance in *Noël and Gertie* in 1983 had been a success, but the play's creator, Sheridan Morley, had been dissatisfied with certain elements. The approach of having two Noëls and two Gerties to share singing and acting was not the right one, he felt.

Over the intervening years, Morley had ditched the additional singing roles, as well as the narration element that he himself had performed. He also decided to expand the dialogue for Gertrude Lawrence, moving away from the reliance of using solely Coward's writing, and creating what he estimated to be around thirty percent of new work of his own.

In 1989, Morley received a request to meet with Patricia Hodge. He assumed that Hodge had learned of the fact that the updated *Noël and Gertie* work was gathering dust and that she was keen to resurrect it. Morley's assumptions were correct, though he was initially reticent about getting involved. He had been given the opportunity to transfer the original piece several times and declined the offers each time, and now he was reluctant to go through the treadmill of securing funding and theatres. This was no matter for Hodge, who managed to secure everything a new production would need in a matter of weeks, in preparation for previews beginning at the Yvonne Arnaud in Guildford before settling in to a run at the West End's Comedy Theatre.

Among the secured talent was Simon. Indeed, his was the only involvement, beyond Morley, from the original King's Head production six years previous. Hodge shared Simon's passion for the Coward era, telling *The Times*: 'The show celebrates an era that is gone, when theatre supplied escapism, glamour and fun. It sprinkled a bit of stardust into people's lives.'[15]

For Simon, the altered format meant a return to singing. This was something he had done precious little of, save for his previous Coward interpretations and a short-lived foray into the vinyl format under the guise of Jeffrey Fairbrother. His exchange with Ruth Madoc on a version of 'Baby, It's Cold Outside' for the *Hi-de-Hi!* spin-off album is quite a fine comedy gem.

Simon's efforts in this comparatively untried element of his talent set were given similar reviews to most of his performances. Michael Billington gave a glowing assessment in *The Guardian*:

> He offers a brilliant rendering of 'Don't Put Your Daughter on the Stage, Mrs Worthington' rising to heights of boiling, brick-red rage on 'She's a vile girl and uglier than mortal sin.' He is mercurially skittish as the bell-bottomed tar in *Red Peppers* executing jaunty scissor-like leaps. And in a scene from *Blithe Spirit* he adopts a look of frozen outrage that renders a simple line like 'A woman in Cynthia Cheviot's position would hardly wear false pearls' inexplicably funny.[16]

Reviews for this incarnation of Morley's homage to Coward were mostly positive, nearly all noting that the change in format to a two-hander with no narrator was a step in the right direction. The ultimate accolade came at a first night supper party. In attendance was Graham Payn, life partner of Coward and by now the administrator of the Coward estate. Payn was delighted by the offering before him, saying, 'Noël and Gertie would have loved the show tonight.'[17]

Certainly, Morley was more than pleased with how his production had evolved. He later acknowledged in his autobiography that despite all subsequent productions based on his work, this would be his career-defining effort:

> I have seen countless others play Noëls and Gerties, some brilliantly, but inevitably none lingers in the memory with quite the magic of my first great West End team, and to this day I can never see or hear the show without thinking nostalgically of the way Patricia and Simon brought it so heartbreakingly to life. If I had done nothing else in the theatre as either writer or director or even … as an actor, that first *Noël and Gertie* would have been more than enough to take to my grave.[18]

The play was not without its complications. Hodge left the show for a brief spell when she became pregnant and Simon was showing signs of ill-health as well. It was noted in one review that they felt he was 'not, I think, fully recovered from his influenza.'[19] Another suggested that Simon had a tendency to 'shower the audience—and his leading lady—with saliva.'[20] Sheridan Morley himself admitted to seeing Simon suffer signs of declining health, but since a nationwide flu epidemic was noted in the press, Simon did what he did best and battled on regardless for the good of the show.[21]

The role in *Noël and Gertie* gained a nationwide television airing as he and Patricia Hodge performed a selection from the show at the London Palladium for the Queen Mother's ninetieth birthday Royal Gala. Despite revisiting the role of Coward at various times in his career, it is the only performance on television to remind us of just how perfect a fit Simon was in the role of his idol.

Simon's treadmill approach continued, moving onto his next project after finishing his time on *Noël and Gertie*, which was *High Flyers*, a Paul Kember comedy premiering in Bromley. Starring alongside James Hazeldine and a young Hugh Grant, the trio played husbands with wandering eyes. The three, friends from schooldays, stayed at a ski resort where they pursued the local ladies until their wives arrived.

Playing a man having a mid-life crisis, Simon was enthused for the role in a play he considered very much for the nineties. The play was deemed an adult comedy, and certainly Simon's description echoed that, saying that it was about, 'three couples and their emotional inhibitions and it highlights the immaturity of the upper classes.'[22]

Never a prude, Simon certainly had no issues with adult topics, bawdy humour, or colourful language if used in the right circumstances. However, he was not overly content with the marketing for his new venture. Publicity material described the show as raunchy, but Simon looked deeper and dismissed such a description: 'It's not raunchy in any sense at all,' he said. 'To have a picture of a pair of knickers on skis on the poster is appealing to the lowest common denominator, just like the gutter press. This play does not need it nor does the Churchill [Theatre in Bromley] and I think it's very dangerous to patronise people in this way.'[23]

Despite his outspoken views on the play's hook in the publicity department, Simon loved the script, describing Paul Kember as, 'very much an original playwright who lives, breathes and writes in the 1990's and he conveys the reality of the modern world brilliantly.'[24] All the more disappointing was that early positive reception did not result in a more commercially successful run.

Three series of *Life Without George* with viewing figures regularly above the 12 million mark had proven that the British television audiences were prepared to see beyond Jeffrey Fairbrother and accept Simon Cadell in other roles. A brief appearance in an episode of *About Face*, starring Maureen Lipman, kept Simon on our screens, playing Lipman's love interest in an office in Reading. Shortly afterwards, however, he made a more significant venture back into sitcom territory in a short-lived role that he relished.

Singles was already a successful comedy for Yorkshire Television penned by Eric Chappell and Jean Warr. It had debuted with a pilot episode for Thames in 1984, but had to wait a further four years before Yorkshire decided to commission a full series. Chappell was no stranger to writing successful comedy on commercial television, having scored major hits with *Rising Damp*, *Only When I Laugh*, and *Duty Free* among others.

As the title suggests, *Singles* had started life as a comedy about four unattached people down on their luck in their romantic entanglements. Starring Roger Rees, Judy Loe, Eamon Boland, and Susie Blake, the second series had culminated in the two lead characters, played by Rees and Loe, arriving at a registry office to get married.

Quite how the show would have continued under the guise of *Singles* with a married couple at the helm is unclear, but as it turned out this was not a hurdle Chappell and Warr would need to overcome. Roger Rees had been in America filming a part in the worldwide hit comedy *Cheers*, playing billionaire playboy Robin Colcord. Initially intended to be a brief role as an aristocratic and vain love interest for Kirstie Alley's Rebecca Howe, the character was a huge success. Rees was signed up by NBC to extend Colcord's existence in the show and he stayed in the States for another four years.

Rees's departure left a hole in the cast of *Singles* and the show took a year out as the writers pondered a new lead that could pick up where the Boston-bound actor had left off. It was decided that continuing in exactly the same spot as the second series ended, Malcolm, Rees's character, had gotten cold feet and jilted Judy Loe's Pamela at the last moment. Prior to this discovery, Pamela was searching for a second witness and made an approach to a mysterious character in dark glasses and a double-breasted cream suit. He was hiding from a media frenzy that he anticipated, but that would not materialise until he was caught escaping out of a side window.

Pamela would discover somebody she would deem the epitome of egotistical male chauvinism—actor Dennis Duval, himself awaiting a fiancé who would fail to arrive. Duval's role was Simon's latest venture into television comedy and a role where he felt he could really indulge himself. Unlike Jeffrey Fairbrother and Larry Wade, there was no call for underplaying for the laughs with Duval.

Duval was a failed actor, despite his protestations otherwise. His part in a soap opera ten years prior had been written out over a dispute about a restaurant bill, and further success had been limited to say the least. With three failed marriages already under his belt, each attributable in his eyes to the respective partners, his was an ego out of control. His expectation was that everything he did in life would and should be scrutinised by the public and press, if only for him to express revulsion that he could never lead a private life. In reality, no one ever noticed him, the press never followed him, and his only acting roles normally ended abruptly due to his personality flaws.

For Simon, this was a chance to flex his comedic muscles while indulging in some gentle payback for characters he had experienced in his career, telling the *Western Mail* that, 'Duval is a kind of vain, egotistical, flamboyant, pompous actor, and I shall have a lot of fun at my own and others' expense.'[25]

Simon recognised that actors rarely get to play actors, especially not ones that were unsuccessful and seemingly of limited talent, like Duval. 'I am taking the worst traits I can find and amalgamating them to produce something believable and funny, but not totally obnoxious,' he wisely told the *Radio Times*, recognising that a truly irredeemable character would have quickly repulsed the audience.[26]

Throughout the show, Duval continually lied about his fame, paid restaurant patrons to pretend to recognise him, sneaked his own 10 × 8 stills onto walls covered with genuine theatrical stars, all the while pursuing Loe's character in an attempt to overturn her initial impressions of him and maybe gain another wife.

Simon's abilities for accents, playing East End wide-boys and one-eyed retired war officers, brought a side of him to primetime comedy that the audience had not previously seen. Jeffrey and Larry had been timid creatures, giving little opportunity to break character, and he did get a bit of a surprise when searching within himself for inspiration: 'I was thinking of all the different types I have known, including myself. I never considered myself as being theatrical or over the top when speaking to people. Then I caught myself saying "darling" and "okay my old luv" when I called my bank!'[27]

'Dennis Duval is such a marvellous character I might be tempted to go totally over the top!' Simon told the *TV Times*. He was in some ways sympathetic to Duval's failings. 'When I contemplate Dennis's position, it really is a case of there but for the grace of God ... not that Dennis is actually conscious he's a failure—if he were, he wouldn't survive. He's good at self-delusion which makes him believe that his big break is just around the corner.'[28]

Despite critical success and the undoubted star quality that an unleashed Simon brought to the show, the third series of *Singles* was the last and we never got to see just how far Simon could push Duval in his mockery of both actors and their profession. Simon had clearly been happy to continue, confessing to suggesting Duval be cast in a television sitcom: 'If that happens, absolutely nothing could stop me going totally, sublimely, round the twist—absolutely mad!'[29]

The end of *Singles* would sadly be the last time Simon would be seen in a comedy series on television. His passion for acting had never been limited to the theatre. Always prepared to speak about the state of the industry that he loved so much, he bemoaned the demise of the television sitcom. Prior to appearing in *Singles*, he told the *Bromley and Croydon Advertiser*:

> The state of television is pretty bleak. The government seems to want to destroy the BBC or at least undermine it. The BBC produce some of the best TV in the world and for the government to try to undermine it because of in-house political problems is more typical of school fourth form behaviour. There are no risk-taking results in mediocrity and that is exactly what we are seeing now on our screens.[30]

Aside from narrating the children's animated television series *Bump*, a gentle story about a clumsy little elephant, Simon would not work on BBC television in the 1990s until a brief documentary about the Croft and Perry sitcoms in 1995, in very different circumstances.

With *Singles* having finished, Simon switched attention to his next venture on stage, and it was one in which he would find himself reunited with friends and family, as well as having more than a passing interest financially. Peter Farago had been asked by a producer friend of his to see a matinee of a new show entitled *Don't Dress for Dinner*. Farago knew something was not right with the production, but felt that with a lot of cutting and a change in approach it had the potential to work. He took the work back to Simon to show him. 'Yep, fine—let's do it,' was the positive response.[31]

Simon had always been a man who from an acting perspective, knew what he thought would work. Sister Selina found this a very helpful attribute if ever she called on her big brother for advice: 'He was a person who always seemed to be incredibly certain about things,' she reflects. 'He would speak to you very clearly. He never held back, he'd say, "don't be silly, of course it's right."[32]

That knowledge of comedy and timing was recognised by Farago as well, who says: 'You can never be sure in rehearsal of what will get a laugh and what won't. What got a laugh from the cast is very different from what laugh you might get from the public. He had an absolute knowledge of where the laughs would be. Sometimes I knew he was wrong—except he turned out to be right!'[33]

Simon's certainty that *Don't Dress for Dinner* was worth putting on was fully justified. He and Farago, along with David Suchet, had initially planned to put on a production of *Spellbound*, but the fundraising for the venture fell short of what was needed, so Simon and Farago instead decided to co-produce *Don't Dress*.

It was a story Simon loved, and as with *Hi-de-Hi!* before, the writing of the ludicrous scenes was what made it so appealing. He later told Rob Cope:

> I thought it was the most tightly written verbal farce I'd ever read. There is no point at which you think 'Oh come on, if she said that to him we could all go home,' which is usually what happens. It doesn't allow itself that option. What I loved about it is it isn't based on people running in and out of doors, but digging themselves into ever deeper holes by what they say. A brilliant piece of comic writing.[34]

It was a new step for Farago. While Simon had regularly stepped back into varying degrees of farce, it was not something the director had been involved with. Cast member Jane How remembered how Farago was an unlikely director for the genre: 'He did it very well, but it was a very unlikely choice. He didn't particularly know how comedy worked, but Simon did. He used to knock on the dressing room door and shout, "Hello, it's Peter, your director with no sense of humour!"'[35]

The co-producers briefly tried to persuade Simon's old pal from Bristol, Tim Pigott-Smith, to join the cast but he did not feel that a part in a West End farce was quite right for his career at the time. In a strange twist, Simon was joined in the cast by the man who had originally been lined up as Jeffrey Fairbrother, John Quayle. Alongside them were Jane How and Briony Glassco as their other halves; providing the fifth wheel to the farce in the comedy was Simon's old *tour-de-force* pal from *Hi-de-Hi!*, Su Pollard.

It was the first time Pollard and Simon had worked together since the end of *Hi-de-Hi!*, but their chemistry remained, as did the energy that she brought to the production, something director Farago had not previously encountered. He recalls, 'She was wonderful to work with. I was used to serious actors rather than variety turns. She would only take one breath at the start of coffee breaks!'[36]

The story within the show was that Quayle's character, married to How, was having an affair with Glassco. He would pretend that Glassco was actually Simon's character's girlfriend, unaware that Simon's character was actually having an affair with Quayle's on-stage wife. The arrival of Pollard's character throws the whole thing into chaos as farcical as farce can get.

Jane How felt that Simon had been a little distant from his fellow cast members, and certainly Briony Glassco recalls how herself, How, Quayle, and Pollard would gather to discuss where the laughs had been won or lost in the previous night's performance.

However, Simon was never one for over-analysing comedy. As the leading man, he was happy to take on the mantle of being the person to whom the cast would come when in need of any advice, performance or otherwise. Yet pulling apart comedy was not something that interested him, and never had done.

Back in 1973, Simon had written a review in *The Journal of the British Pantomime Association* of *A Funny Way To Be A Hero* by John Fisher. In his review, he was uncompromising in his critique of Fisher's work, saying: 'The minute you start to analyse such a spontaneous thing as comedy, the subject becomes tedious. What you cannot do is to say "Why", for instance, "does Eric Morecambe make me laugh?" To me, the thing that makes comedy is you never ask why you laugh.'[37]

Glassco recalls, 'Jane, John and Simon had a very clear idea that this was a sophisticated farce and everything had to be rooted in reality and truth. If it wasn't believable, it wasn't staying in. The play between John and Su and Simon was respectful and affectionate and you could feel that history and chemistry on the stage.'[38]

The critics were divided on *Don't Dress for Dinner*. *The Stage* said that Farago 'has a ball' directing the show, noting that 'Cadell and Quayle perform an hilarious double act of depression and ineptitude.'[39] However, the *Financial Times* said that 'as the actors change their identities for the tenth time you lose patience'.[40] The *Sunday Mail* said that, 'it amuses briefly, but not immoderately.'[41]

Perhaps the kindest of reviews was that of *The Sunday Times*, who reported that, 'The epicentre of the whole demented earthquake is Simon Cadell, hunter and hunted, shifty and charming, and looking in moments of dismay like a deposed Roman emperor. Cadell makes the whole thing look easy, but it isn't.'[42]

As ever, critical acclaim was not reflective of public opinion. There may have been an element of simply enjoying seeing Jeffrey and Peggy from *Hi-de-Hi!* reunited on stage, but even after Simon left, the play went on for a very lengthy run and an overseas tour lasting many years.

Glassco recalls that Simon, by now into his forties, was sweating profusely. 'He said that was why he never did any exercise, because it was exhausting enough doing the show eight times a week,' she remembered.[43] Curiously though, health was something that was becoming more prominent in Simon's mind.

Both Glassco and How recalled how intrigued he was by all things medical. 'He battled a sinus thing for a long time during our run,' remembers Glassco. 'It was always the most interesting thing ever. The government could be blowing up, but if he could hold your attention with the details of his latest cough, he was on fire.'[44]

It is a story echoed by How, who says, 'He was fascinated by illness. He would come to life if he knew you'd been ill and gone to the doctor. "Which doctor? Did you go to Harley Street? Which doctor did you see?" He was riveted by illness.'[45]

During filming of *Singles*, Simon had started to realise the damage being done by his years of smoking. For somebody whose living was so reliant on his smooth, silky vocal skills, he was wary of the damage a lifetime of smoking was starting to do. He told the *Western Mail* in 1991 of his albeit temporary decision to stop smoking his big cigars: 'It was the fact that my voice was suffering that made me stop. At the end of the week I would hardly have any voice at all, and as *Singles* is recorded on a Sunday night, that wasn't very good news.'[46] He also complained that his legs would ache after walking up two flights of stairs, and his toenails were starting to turn yellow.

One interview with the press found Simon woken by the reporter just fifty minutes before he was due to take to the stage. 'This only happens when I'm really exhausted,' he explained. 'I've been pushing myself a lot lately. But you know what they say. Never turn good work down.'[47]

The fascination with illness was not a new thing—he had always somehow been interlinked with health issues. He had missed entire terms at school with mystery ailments. Back when he was still with Stephanie Turner, he had become very ill one night and she made an urgent call to Gillian Cadell. 'Oh don't worry, he'll be alright tomorrow,' came the response from Simon's mother. 'It's just one of his turns.'

Stephanie recalls, 'I said "no, he looks really, really ill." He was shaking and shivering, but she insisted, "no, don't worry, he'll be alright". And he was. I think he maybe had three or four of these, which may have been because of his nervousness, I don't know.'[48]

With the acting treadmill continuing, there was no time then to be concerned with health issues. Simon's next and arguably finest stage role was just around the corner.

Come He Slow or Come He Fast

The relentless workload continued after Simon left *Don't Dress for Dinner*. His next venture was something that intrigued him from the start and would be seen my many as the pinnacle of his theatrical work. It would also give him an opportunity to display to a theatre audience the talents that he excelled at in his radio work.

Simon had always been a huge fan of the author Graham Greene, lending his voice to an audiobook of *The Quiet American* and children's story, *The Little Train*. When he heard of the opportunity to appear in a version of Greene's *Travels with My Aunt*, which had been given a new approach by director Giles Havergal, he jumped at the chance.

'I think it's the most original piece of theatre I've ever been involved in,' he later proclaimed. 'Novel adaptations in the theatre can be a little boring sometimes. The originality of the way the adaptation is done really makes this a very, very special evening indeed.'[1]

Havergal had adapted the comedy about a bored retired bank manager and his eccentric aunt in 1989 and had appeared in it himself when opening at the Citizens Theatre in Glasgow. He had been careful that every word spoken by the characters came from Greene's original book.

The story centres around Henry Pulling. Freshly retired from his job in the financial world, Pulling is leading a life of quiet solitude, pruning roses in his picture-perfect garden, but lacking any real quality in his days or direction in his life. The routine of his entire career pulled from under him, life changes when he meets up with the unstoppable force of nature that is Aunt Augusta at his mother's funeral.

Havergal's interpretation of the book is a most unusual one and is still regularly staged today. His adaptation involves four leading male actors, each sharing the role of Henry Pulling. However, they also carry out other acting duties for the variety of supporting characters, and the leading man not only plays Henry, but also the lively Aunt Augusta. This particular role Havergal initially gave to himself.

The director remembers that they went after Simon for the role, saying: 'It was very much "we would love you to do it. If you're interested in the part, it's yours."'[2] Anybody who has read the original novel, first released in 1969, will have found that the part of Pulling reads very much as a Simon Cadell vehicle, one that he could almost have been born to play; the added intrigue of performing the part of Aunt Augusta in the same show was too much of an opportunity to turn down.

Alongside Simon in the original cast were John Wells, Richard Kane, and newcomer Christopher Gee. Wells had met Simon briefly when doing voiceovers, but this was the first time that the pair would be working together. When writing in the *Evening Standard* a few months later, Wells recalled being immediately enamoured with his new friend:

> I realised that whatever else happened, we were going to enjoy ourselves. He immediately revealed a vast repertoire of wonderfully obscene jokes, including a collector's piece version of the teddy bears' picnic that had our director, Giles Havergal—hardened, one would have thought, by twenty years at Europe's greatest gay-dominated theatre, the Glasgow Cits [Citizen's]—howling.
>
> There was also a horrifying character he would assume—and who would continue to appear just before curtain-up on tour—of a deeply disgusting adenoidal old man of catholic sexual tastes and a distressingly direct approach to satisfying them.
>
> I have never had the good luck to work with anyone possessed of so much sheer theatrical skill.[3]

Fun it no doubt was, but Simon was throwing himself fully into the piece in his usual immersive way. Wells was amazed at how Simon went beyond simply performing his role, looking deeper into the mechanics of the theatre, the arrangements of the flying scenery in each of the venues of the pre-West End tour, and even the box office returns.

As for his characters, playing Henry was second nature to Simon, but playing Augusta required a great deal of imagination, given that there were no wardrobe changes to telegraph to the audience that he had changed role, and indeed, gender.

'He was very acerbic,' remembers Havergal of Simon's interpretation of Aunt Augusta. 'He would quite often turn something with bitterness and sharpness where somebody else might play it for fun.'[4] At different times, Simon confessed to drawing inspiration from an elderly aunt in Bournemouth and an old lady he had once seen in the General Trading Company, with bunions and an arthritic arm.[5]

Havergal felt at times that the elderly aunt needed to be overplayed, while Simon felt that he wished her to be less so for fear of turning her closer to a pantomime dame. Once again, his 'play it straight' schooling from his days at The Old Vic served him well. In the end, it was the flick of the eyebrow, a twist of the arm or foot and Simon would go from fifty-five-year-old retired bank manager to seventy-five-year-old jet-setting aunt in an instant. He felt that this was where his many years of radio performances came in particularly handy, reflecting on his belief that the aunt should be underplayed in order to let the audience create her:

> What the audience love about it is that it allows them to flesh out the characters in their own imagination. People always say that radio has the best scenery in the world because the scenery is in your own imagination. Well this is the theatre equivalent because people can create their own Aunt Augusta or Mr Visconte, this eighty-year-old war criminal hiding in Paraguay.
>
> It takes the average audience about half a minute then they're absolutely with you. It's a bit of a shock first of all when pretty much the first thing that happens is that I, playing this very staid, retired English bank manager, suddenly switch into Aunt Augusta and you can see people going 'What the hell are we in for?'[6]

After three weeks of rehearsal, *Travels with My Aunt* opened on a tour before settling into a stay at the Wyndham's Theatre. Wells, a comedy master craftsman himself, was in awe of Simon's prowess, suggesting that even from his vantage point on stage, 'evening after evening, matinee after matinee, I am convinced that Simon Cadell really is a sexually active seventy-five-year-old lady with a dubious past.'[7] His admiration for Simon's comic skills continued:

> Simon is a master of timing. The line in the play, after an American CIA man has explained how many hours a year we spend urinating, is 'Good heavens!' As the American, I imparted the information on the first night of our tour, and expected 'Good heavens!' The audience was laughing, but there was no line. I turned to look at him. His character, Henry Pulling, was clearly having trouble absorbing the information. His eyebrows shot up. He licked his lips. He was obviously wondering whether he had heard correctly. The audience was laughing more loudly. He looked at me, and seemed to lose himself again in thought. Then, controlling his amazement, he said, very flatly: 'Good heavens!' There was a huge laugh and he got the first sustained round of applause of the evening.
>
> In a way, Simon's timing is a kind of key to his life. That control over the audience extending to almost the whole activity of what the French call 'knowing how to live'.[8]

Havergal agreed with Wells, declaring that Simon's dual role was, 'a lovely big part played by an actor, not a comic. He's famous for being in a comedy series, but he was an actor who did comedy.'[9]

As ever, Simon's former agent, Patricia Lord, came to see her friend's work and Simon was keen to hear her thoughts. Patricia confesses that she felt that Augusta was indeed the pinnacle of Simon's achievements:

I thought it was such an extraordinary creation. There was marvellous physical work. He was never camp, he just sort of became her with the tilt of the head, which was one of Simon's great things, and the arrangement of the arm. If there wasn't a handbag, it was carried as though there was. And the body language changed and you absolutely understood and believed that it was the aunt, but it wasn't Danny La Rue or a camp character, which I thought was quite fascinating.[10]

Critical acclaim was swift and positive as were the box office sales; it became clear that Simon had secured a triumphant return to the West End. While quirky in its approach, with Simon and John Wells at the helm, *Travels with My Aunt* was garnering lavish praise from the majority of critics and takings were good.

When touring the production prior to its West End transfer, Martin Williams wrote in the *Bournemouth Evening Echo*: 'Simon Cadell, in particular, showed how much he has blossomed since throwing aside his *Hi-de-Hi!* image. His "off to a tee" interpretation of the English eccentric could be compared to anything that alternative comic genius Stephen Fry could conjure up.'[11]

The praise was no less forthcoming after the shows arrival at The Wyndham's. *The Times* compared the interpretation of the role of Henry Pulling to multiplying, 'Monty Python's archetypal suburbanite, Arthur Pewty, to a factor of three,' something which Simon himself found quite amusing. Benedict Nightingale's review suggested Simon's interpretation of Aunt Augusta was, 'a fluting blend of Lady Bracknell and Lydia Languish.'[12]

Even his co-stars were aware of the quality of Simon's performance, with John Wells remarking that, 'He always caught the character precisely, with the economy of a classic comedian.'[13]

With no immediate television work on the horizon, Simon was focused primarily on the play, alongside the radio work—continuing with some of the finest classics in the form of Evelyn Waugh—and his usual treadmill of voiceovers.

His old friend Joanna Lumley had been working on a new book for the Imperial War Museum called *Forces Sweetheart*. In it, she had compiled and edited a collection of some of the most moving and poignant pieces of wartime correspondence, love letters, and Dear John letters. They came from various conflicts from the First World War up to the Gulf War.

As a launch event for the book, Joanna decided to put together a stage show at the Queen Elizabeth Hall where they would read extracts and have some period songs. She needed a male vocal talent to go alongside her own fine diction, and who better suited than Simon? She called Simon and as he always did for his friends, he immediately agreed. He had always been a charitable friend and never refused work for a good cause, performing many times in fundraisers for charities, ailing theatres, and such like.

On Wednesday, 13 January 1993, the pair arrived at the Queen Elizabeth Hall on the South Bank for the event and it was a great success. Joanna remembers: 'Simon was brilliant in it, but he was sweating a lot and at the end of it, we were doing a curtain call and he said, "I'm going to have to go now."'[14]

Simon called for a taxi and headed home. By now, he was suffering thumping chest pains and shortness of breath, more pain than his usual nerves would ever inflict. As he said after the event, 'However bad your nerves are, it ain't nothing like having a heart attack.'[15] He considered heading straight for the hospital but decided that a night's rest at home would cure his ailments.

When he walked through the door, Simon just dropped into a chair and Beckie was startled to see him looking so poorly. When she grilled him as to what the matter was, he suggested that it was more than likely just some level of indigestion and a good night's sleep would sort him.

The Cadell's family dog, a jolly beagle called Sam, normally unconcerned by all manner of comings and goings, was behaving curiously. He was howling and fussing around Simon, something he had never done before. Whatever attempts Beckie made to calm him failed and he continued to stay around his master, seemingly sensing something was wrong. Beckie firmly believed that the dog's behaviour was a sign that he should call his GP, Dr Martin Scurr. Eventually, Simon did so. After firing off a number of questions, Dr Scurr insisted that this was definitely more serious than indigestion and Simon should be heading to A&E immediately.

As it turned out, he had unknowingly already suffered one heart attack some months before, while playing with the boys in the garden. On that occasion, he had also dismissed it as nothing more than indigestion. With the rich food, endless chain of cigars, fine wine, and the excessive workload, it was an easy mistake to make.

On this occasion, it was clearly not the case. The ambulance arrived and bundled Simon into the back. He never lost consciousness and once into the emergency vehicle, he received a number of injections to ease his symptoms. Simon reflected that courtesy of the drugs, 'you actually get very lackadaisical about the whole thing, all your cares dribble away really.'[16]

The trolley was wheeled into the Harley Street clinic and bundled into the elevator. 'The porter pressed button three—the cardiology unit,' recounted

Simon. 'Nothing happened at all. I heard him saying "oh fuck" behind me and I thought "well I suppose there must be better places to die."'[17]

Once the marooned lift burst into life, Simon was taken away for tests and stabilising; it was established that a triple bypass was needed. His years of smoking combined with the stressful overworking had brought him to an abrupt stop. Simon's arteries were blocked and he would need his bypass surgery urgently. He was honest about his part in his own downfall, admitting later that: 'It was smoking, it's as simple as that. I'm one of those people whose system can't cope with the smoke.'[18]

Smoking had been something Simon started as a youth and as a nervous support mechanism he had never been able or particularly inclined to stop. Gyles Brandreth remembered that he was able to blow perfect smoke rings when aged fourteen and during his time at the Bristol Old Vic Theatre School, his habit had reached as many as eighty Gitanes per day. Some smokers refuse to acknowledge the threat to their health, or at least prefer to bury it from their minds. Simon, however, fully acknowledged his contribution to his own downfall, recognising that, 'Heart problems don't suddenly develop overnight.'[19] Of his excessive smoking, he conceded that even when he moved on from his eighty per day habit, it was only to move onto cigars, which at times were smoked at a rate of twenty per day, and then finally bigger cigars with cigarettes.

The addictive personality that Simon had referred to previously was never more evident. Cigars seemed as much a part of his character as they were of Lou Grade or George Burns. Beckie recalls:

He was properly addicted. You'd wake in the morning and you'd hear this rattling and he literally hadn't even put the light on trying to find the ash tray. He'd find the ash tray that had the stub of the cigar, didn't even open his eyes. Being a non-smoker myself you were very aware.[20]

Ironically, Simon was able to draw some reassurance from his established obsession with all things medical: 'The funny thing is I was always glued to *Your Life in Their Hands* and loved watching other people undergoing open heart surgery. So when my time came I knew exactly what to expect and wasn't scared at all.'[21]

Long-time GP and family friend, Dr Scurr remembers well Simon's fascination with medical matters:

He was quite a polymath. He was a very intellectually accurate person. This was well before the internet and he would read things and look things up. Also he would receive information well. He'd ask for an explanation and when you gave an explanation he'd understand it, put it in his mind and store it. He was very easy to educate in that regard, and not given to flights of fancy into the world of complementary medicine. Not to decry any of that, but he was interested in science and progress and technology— evidence-based medicine before that phrase was ever thought of. He took an interest and that gave him confidence.[22]

It was perhaps with that knowledge that he considered that he 'never thought that I would do anything other than sail through the whole thing.'[23] Of the procedure itself, Dr Scurr continued:

> It was pretty major surgery. Bypass grafting was in its relatively early days. I became a GP in 1977 and one of my patients had a bypass graft in my first year and he was the twenty-third ever done in the world. So when Simon had his operation it was still a relatively new phenomenon—there was no such thing as angioplasty or stents which is now done for people who in his era would have had a bypass graft.[24]

Simon admitted that this second attack left him considering that he had been very fortunate, with his arrival at hospital coming in the nick of time. An extra bone for the Cadell dog for sure.

The surgery was a complete success. His *Travels with My Aunt* co-star John Wells recalled that Simon was, 'talking happily to his family the next morning, was ringing friends from his hospital bed within days, and was back at the theatre, watching the show from a box and then charging down, calling us "a lot of tired old queens."'[25] As Simon recuperated he felt he had been given a second chance. *Travels with My Aunt* would continue without him while its star spent a number of months under doctor's orders to rest, during which he determined to cut down his theatre workload once fully recovered.

As Simon began to acclimatise to his first extended break from the theatre, his health appeared to show the shoots of recovery. He began to exercise in moderation, finding swimming and walking his pet dogs to provide the most benefit. He also began to sleep better without the work commitments that his system had become so used to over the years.

'Although I'll be forty-four on 19 July, I feel better than I've felt for years,' Simon told Graham Bridgstock of the *Daily Express*. 'That's probably all the swimming. The trouble is chlorine and I don't get on too well. It irritates my sinuses.'[26]

Surgeon and cardiologist were both happy with Simon's progress and he began to take on gentle work, with a few voiceovers keeping the money coming in without the strain of nightly performances. His former Old Vic colleague Tim Pigott-Smith chatted to him about his recovery and Simon conceded that theatre was a particular drain on his energy. His old friend recalled:

One of the things he said to me when he was ill was that what he discovered was really bad for his health was to carry on acting on stage. He didn't mind doing television or film, but going back on stage was something that he thought was dangerous for him and he'd been advised against.[27]

Simon heeded the advice of his doctors. 'He was the perfect patient,' recalls Dr Scurr. 'He resolved—and not only that, stuck to his resolutions about getting fit, taking exercise, cutting back on his excesses.'[28]

John Arthur, who had starred alongside Simon in his two National Theatre plays under the tutelage of Sir Alan Ayckbourn, ran into him shortly after his operation. He recalls:

We met at a function at the National. Simon was just recovering from his surgery. He was terribly excited to be alive. He looked terrible, but he said he'd learned his lesson and he'd stopped drinking and he was going to change his lifestyle. He was so excited, he had such a new lease of life.[29]

Changing his lifestyle included the axing of the cigars, probably the one excess that Simon found most difficult to sacrifice. He would bemoan, 'I can't tell you how much that pains me. My only true luxury. After twenty years, it's hell. I'm allowed an occasional cigar, but I do miss it ... but it's a mug's game.'[30]

To further aid his recuperation, Simon, Beckie, and the boys took a trip to Barbados. They hired a nanny to spend some time with the boys and Simon was able to relax away from all the stresses of the dramatic profession and spend quality time with his family. While in the Caribbean, the Cadells decided to move permanently from their home in Notting Hill to Kettleburgh, where Simon was still within easy commute to London, but the family were closer to the Croft dynasty and the more relaxing surroundings of the Suffolk countryside.

Upon their return to the UK, Simon felt ready to return to work. He had enjoyed *Travels with My Aunt* and the run had continued to perform well in his absence, but he wanted to see out his commitment to his role at The Wyndham's, and return he did after what was a four-month spell on the sidelines.

Things picked up pretty much where they had left off. William Gaunt had joined the cast in Simon's absence, but otherwise all was well. Reviews and takings were still good and on 19 April 1993, Simon received the ultimate accolade. The Aunt Augusta/Henry Pulling combination had earned him victory in the Best Comedy Performance category at the Olivier Awards. Despite his lengthy list of credits on television and stage, this was the first time he had been recognised by his peers for his work and he was delighted.

Unsurprisingly, in his acceptance speech, he cheerfully thanked his doctors without whom he acknowledged he would no longer have been around to receive this accolade.

Shortly after returning to his theatre work, Simon was visited by Nick Renton. He had recovered sufficiently from his bypass and had proclaimed himself to be feeling better than ever. Renton, however, felt uneasy following his visit to his old friend:

> I remember going to see him in a matinee and I hadn't seen him for a bit. He'd had his heart op and he seemed fine but I kind of sensed there was just something going on, just a sort of sixth sense. We were just chatting away and then came a knock at the door. Two people, a man and a woman, and the man was Paul Eddington. Paul was really in the last stages of his cancer at the time. He simply didn't look like the same man and looking back on it, it was such a curious sort of moment. Whether he was feeling that something was not right I don't know. It was a very strange experience.[31]

For a long time, Simon had suffered with his sinuses. In an effort to continue his recovery, he was forced to look for swimming pools that did not use chlorine as these were said to irritate his sinuses. Briony Glassco remembered that he was regularly suffering during the run of *Don't Dress for Dinner* and he admitted that he once had to have them drained under a general anaesthetic. He suggested that it was simply an affliction that he had inherited from his father.

With that in mind, in the summer of 1993 and with a routine check-up due on his progress from the heart bypass, Simon booked in to see Dr Scurr. He seemingly had no prior concerns other than to mention that this particular bout of sinus trouble or cold, whichever it may have been, was proving persistent.

Dr Scurr had been friends with the Croft family before Simon had begun his relationship with Beckie. He had begun practising at a surgery in Notting Hill in the 1970s and the Croft family were already patients of the senior practitioner. Further cementing their friendship, Dr Scurr then bought the house the Crofts were selling in Talbot Road near to Kensington and Chelsea. When Simon registered as a patient, the pair got to know each other well and became good friends:

> He was one of those people who when you met him, you felt better afterwards. If you were in a foul mood or feeling miserable because it was Monday morning, it was raining, you were overly busy—you saw Simon, you'd cheer up. He was a sort of anti-depressant really, there are very few people who are like that.[32]

Dr Scurr knew that although Simon had a fair amount of ailments and an unusual fascination with medical subjects, he rarely visited without necessity. Simon recalled him saying, 'You're a good patient because I know when you come to see me you're not wasting my time.' Simon admitted, however, that his file was 'fairly thick!'[33]

So when Simon walked into his GP's office with ongoing sinus issues, a run of routine tests were done, all in conjunction with a general review of his ongoing recovery process. The heart operation had been a complete success and the visit was not expected to be anything other than to pass a verdict on this nagging cold.

Despite the expectation of a comparatively routine health-check along the road to recovery, the results of the test were brutal. Out of the blue, Dr Scurr had to deliver devastating news to his friend: Simon was dying.

13

Our Revels Now Are Ended

As Michèle Brandreth went to answer the telephone on 11 September 1993, she could not have imagined the horrifying news that the caller was bringing her. 'I'm in the Harley Street Clinic,' Simon began. 'It's not good news. I'm riddled with cancer. It could be just a matter of days.'[1]

The verdict on Simon's persistent cold could not have been worse. Tests showed that he was in fact suffering from non-Hodgkins lymphoma. Although most commonly diagnosed in people twenty years in advance of Simon's age at the time, he not only had the disease, but it was at an advanced stage and likely too advanced to avoid a swift, terminal conclusion.

For all the positive action Simon had taken since his heart operation, he had been dealt a knockout blow. From the time of his heart bypass through to this unrelated terminal diagnosis, he had had just months during which to spend some quality time with his family and reform his lifestyle. It was the cruellest of fates.

Selina Cadell could not help but wonder whether Simon's traumatic birth left him with an immune system that was deficient in some way: 'He was lucky to be alive after his birth. I think his immune system was slightly weaker than others. He always used to get slightly complicated colds. Whenever we had something, he had it worse than we did.'[2]

It is certain that Simon missed much of school through illness. Significant absences are noted throughout his time at both The Hall School and Bedales, causing him to miss both exams and an entire run of a play produced by good friend Gyles Brandreth while the pair were at boarding school. The turns that Stephanie Turner had recalled had happened several times during their relationship but they had never been diagnosed as anything more.

John Wells had spoken of Simon knowing how to live, and throughout his education, Simon was always in a rush to get to his acting life. It is perhaps evidence of a curious trait that was recalled by both Selina and Gyles that is somehow symbolic of some inner belief that Simon had of an early demise.

'He always said that he'd die young,' recalled Selina. 'I'd go "Why do you say that?", but he believed it. I don't know why he said it, but he was one of those people who was old before his time. I'm not sure old age held much of a prospect for him.'[3]

From his days at Bedales, Simon had always been in a rush to get to his desired profession, and in 1989, he said, 'I'm thirty-eight and heading towards forty and not liking it one bit. I feel there's so much to do and time is getting shorter.'[4]

The phone call from Simon to Gyles was clear. This illness was going to take him and it could be imminent. Simon was concerned because he was convinced the media had found out about his diagnosis and were preparing to break the news. He therefore decided that he would take ownership of the situation and make the announcement himself.

On 17 September 1993, just a few days after receiving his devastating news, Simon's diagnosis was out in the public domain. '"I am Dying," says *Hi-de-Hi!* star Simon,' and similar headlines covered the tabloids.[5]

The press release contained limited details of the nature of Simon's impending demise, other than to confirm that his condition was, 'inoperable and terminal.'[6] The statement confirmed that the hospital was only able to do whatever they could to make Simon's final days more comfortable and that he was returning home to spend his remaining weeks with his young family. In typical Simon fashion, he apologised for letting people down.

News of the unexpected development was met with the expected outcry of sympathy, both for the diagnosis itself and for the cruelty of it coming just months after surviving a heart attack and subsequent triple bypass.

Patricia Lord learned by mistake in a telephone call from Donald Sinden, who remarked to the unsuspecting agent how terrible the news was: 'When I heard that he was dying I absolutely fell apart. I've never reacted in the same way about any client, I was absolutely destroyed by it.'[7]

The common misconception, even within interviews for this biography some twenty years on, is that Simon's smoking habits proved to be his undoing. However, as Dr Scurr confirmed, although smoking was a direct contributing factor to Simon's heart attack, his terminal diagnosis was unlikely a result of his life-long tobacco addiction:

> We discussed all those things. I don't think anyone knows why one gets non-Hodgkins. There's all sorts of theories and ideas, but I don't think it's smoking related. What you always say to people in general health terms is that smoking is bad news for health and for immune systems, but I don't believe his smoking caused it.[8]

Simon's involvement with *Travels with My Aunt* came to an immediate end of course, and his agent Caroline Renton set about the sad task of cancelling the line-up of roles that he had been due to perform. Most immediate of those had been opposite Frances de la Tour, a long-time client of John Cadell's agency, in *Downwardly Mobile*. This was an ITV show that had been due to return Simon to where the British public knew him best—primetime comedy. He had been due to play a musical repair man with De La Tour as his psychotherapist wife. Yorkshire TV reluctantly recast Simon's role and pressed ahead with the show, but it was cancelled after only one series.

The intention was indeed for Simon to spend his final weeks at home with Beckie and the boys. Treatment from the hospital was expected to be of the pain-relieving variety rather than a combatant for the disease but Simon, despite his philosophical acceptance of his fate, determined to fight. Dr Scurr recalls:

> There's a spectrum so some people where it's relatively benign can respond to chemotherapy and in others, whatever you do treatment-wise there's a rapid downhill course. Some people give up and others say 'I'm going to beat this.' The gods were with him for a period of time.[9]

Selina remembered of Simon's approach during those first weeks after the announcement: 'He took his diagnosis in his stride, more than anyone I've ever known. He was very brave about it ... he wanted more time with his family.'[10]

Against expectations, chemotherapy began to have some effect. The initial prognosis that Simon may have just days, weeks at most, drifted out and he saw past Christmas 1993. As he began to get some of his strength back, he decided to return to work.

Stage work was off limits. Simon knew all too well that this was out of the question, with gruelling hours and endless stress. What he did opt for, however, was more voiceovers. However well his body was responding to treatment, he knew full well that it was most likely buying him time and that he should use it well. In typically giving style, he decided that he needed to provide for his family after he was gone, and so he began taking a great deal of voiceover work. It was fairly undemanding in terms of stress and energy and carried with it a significant income.

'He did so many voiceovers,' remembers Beckie of Simon's years of recording sessions. 'He'd get up at the crack of dawn and go and do four or five voiceovers at 6.30 in the morning. He'd get a taxi there, do the voiceovers, get a taxi back and go to the theatre or wherever.'[11]

Mexicans, peanuts, baked potatoes—you name it, Simon provided the voice for it. He appeared in adverts for cars, chocolates, and even an energy company in which he shared a screen with Mr Scott actor James Doohan in a *Star Trek* skit.

Voiceovers were something Simon had always done, believing that the income they commanded allowed him to be fussier when it came to taking theatrical or television roles. Indeed, a number of other actors credit Simon for persuading them to take on similar tasks.

During the brief run of *Musical Comedy Murders of 1940*, Simon and Tom Baker, another voice perfectly geared towards the commercials market, actually hired a rehearsal room separate from the one provided at the Greenwich Theatre in order to be closer to the voiceover studios, such was their audio workload.

Simon's tones had always been perfect for radio, but as he took on more audio work, he branched out from radio plays, recording a number of spoken word books, including further wonderful selections of Evelyn Waugh and P. G. Wodehouse. He had also emulated his father by venturing into voicing children's programmes, the aforementioned *Bump* bringing him into a line of work mirroring his father's pre-agency career.

Something Simon had never really turned his hand to during his career was writing. Perhaps it was his written skills left over from school, or maybe a timing thing—he bled theatre and so time writing would have been time not acting. Yet with stage performances now over and his health showing sparks of improvement, he decided to compose a book on one of his favourite subjects: wine.

Alcohol was a constant companion. Fine wines were perhaps not standard fare for poverty-stricken students at the Bristol Old Vic, but in the world of theatrical performers he was surrounded by, it was therefore easy for Simon to establish a healthy knowledge, and it was a topic that he never stopped learning about.

He recalled buying his first bottle of wine from the Hampstead Wine Company, a specialist independent wine merchant. Lined with wooden floors and adorned with wooden wine bins from floor to ceiling, the company was located near to the Everyman Cinema that Simon and his siblings would frequent with their Uncle Peter.

When he first ventured in and made a purchase, something for which his looking older than he was came in very handy, he chose a Château Rauzan-Ségla. He admitted that he bought the bottle based on looks over knowledge, but he consumed it with his parents the following weekend and was suitably impressed with his first venture into the wine market.

Unfortunately, income for a lowly acting student was not sufficient to indulge in learning about wine. Simon recalled:

It was a long time before I drank wine of such quality again. As a student of drama school I couldn't afford it and neither could I most of my time as a young actor. When I occasionally got a 'tele', then as now much better paid than the theatre, I would seek out a good wine merchant and buy a bottle of this and a bottle of that, take it home, taste it, drink it and try to learn from it. By the end of the seventies I had acquired a considerable knowledge of what I liked and disliked.[12]

His favourites were Chardonnay and Burgundy, and of course, he was always partial to champagne.

Simon's financial situation improved once the regular television work of *Enemy at the Door* and *Hi-de-Hi!* began to proffer a steady income. Subsequently able to expand his wine knowledge, he had built a storage area onto the outside of his Notting Hill flat, although he remained frustrated at the lack of a wine merchant with whom he could build a rapport and satisfy his quest for knowledge.

Experiencing the spectacle of his future father-in-law David Croft's wine cellar at the family home in Honington, Simon had still bemoaned the lack of a merchant until fate leant a hand.

The weekend visits normally involved Simon and Beckie arriving with a good supply of wines for the weekend, but on one occasion when the couple travelled separately Simon realised that he had neglected to buy any wines. Travelling on past Honington and into Thetford, he stumbled fortuitously into a store called T & W Wines—Simon was at home. He and owner Trevor Hughes became firm friends and Simon remained a customer and friend of Trevor's for the rest of his days.

Simon loved his fine food almost as much as he loved his fine wine, although he insisted that there was no snobbery on his part on either subject, saying, 'I'm not a snob about it. I'm perfectly happy with fish and chips, particularly when going home after the theatre or a TV recording.'[13]

That said, he got the most satisfaction from the finer choices, much to the amazement and sometimes frustration of some of his guests. Gyles Brandreth remembers one particular occasion when he had been paid in kind for a job working for Air France:

I had about £350 left. So I said to Simon I had this money left and there was this hotel in Piccadilly, the Meridien, owned by Air France. This was in the seventies, so £350 was a lot of money for dinner. There was the less expensive restaurant and we went to the hugely expensive restaurant. There was a vast wine list, but Simon said to the sommelier, 'Wasn't this a British Rail hotel once? You're bound to have something locked away in the cellar.'

So the wine waiter produced from the cellar, blowing dust off it, this fabulous bottle of wine. The long and short of it is that although we had £350 to spend, after we'd spent it there was still another £150 to pay. The girls were not amused![14]

It was one of many occasions where Simon simply wanted to enjoy life to the maximum that his budget would permit. 'That's the sort of world that Simon wanted,' Gyles recalls. 'He had this romantic view of life and he believed in living the high life with a certain style, and he achieved that.'[15]

With his passion and knowledge of wine, and with time on his hands without the theatrical work, Simon approached Trevor Hughes to discuss the merits of writing a book on wine, for which he would enjoy his friend's input. The pair had often taken trips to the Burgundy region and it was here that Simon asked for his friend's opinions.

Right Vintage: A Wine Lover's Companion is a collection of historical stories and anecdotes themed around the consumption of alcohol. Each is introduced or concluded by Simon with his own thoughts on the story, leading to his own choice of wine, where one was appropriate, that would complement such an occasion as that contained within the stories recounted. Intermingled with these are some entertaining teasers from Simon regarding his experiences of alcoholic anecdotes gained throughout his career.

Trevor Hughes remembers fondly some of the research for the book:

> We went to Burgundy on several occasions. I took him to some of the greater wine institutes in the area. He absolutely loved it. We found this restaurant and they had about twenty different variations of his favourite burgundies on their wine list. Although we didn't drink it, because we would have been dead, I think we had nine bottles with our lunch that day...and that was after some tastings and before some afternoon tastings as well.
>
> He was saying, 'We haven't tasted this wine producer yet, why don't we have a bottle of that? I must taste it.'[16]

Trevor's recounting of Simon's enthusiasm and thirst for wine knowledge is by no means an isolated one. Constantine Gregory, who would co-star with Simon in his final television role in *Circle of Deceit*, remembers a similar occasion, albeit in rather more unlikely circumstances—a motel off the M1 near Barnsley:

> One evening we got a taxi to take us to Brooklands in a village called Dodworth. Brooklands itself was very unprepossessing, a motel with swirly carpets. The wine list was more of a thick book, with wines from all over the world. Simon was flabbergasted as he read the list, and the prices! The owner bought good wines at auction, and the prices were historical, i.e. what he had bought them for plus a profit—a fifth or less of what one would expect to pay.
>
> The very young waiter took our order and Simon made a very educated selection. The boy said, 'Ah—if you like that, may I suggest this?' and he

would point to a wine Simon didn't know, also cheaper. That was the red and he made another brilliant suggestion for the white. We had an evening of laughter and astonishment at the extraordinary value of the wines, which arrived properly decanted and served.[17]

Despite Simon's affection for wines and the frequency of their consumption, getting drunk on such pleasures was not something he ever did. 'I never saw Simon drunk, never,' recalls Trevor Hughes. 'He got very happy at times, but never did I see him staggering or falling about. I think it would have spoilt his appreciation of the next bottle.'[18]

It is a theory shared by Selina Cadell, who believed that her brother, 'drank the best wine and he stopped when he could no longer notice that it was the best wine. He was always a measured, expert drinker.'[19]

Simon's capacity for alcohol was significant. Two or three bottles over dinner was not uncommon, and with Beckie rarely consuming more than half a bottle herself, his seeming never to be significantly drunk was all the more remarkable. 'He drank for the taste, not to get drunk,' remembers Beckie. 'He used to giggle a lot, which maybe was his kind of being drunk. But the kind of incoherence—he just never did.'[20]

As his book neared completion, Simon was continuing to respond to treatment. While clearly still not a well man, he remained committed to making the most of his days and investing time in ventures away from the theatre.

He made his first public appearance since his gloomy diagnosis in the spring of 1994, presenting the Best Comedy Performance award at the Oliviers to Griff Rhys Jones. When John Sessions announced his arrival on stage, Simon was greeted with a heart-warming standing ovation from his appreciative peers at the London Palladium.

Nick Renton remembers watching the awards at the time: 'I can remember him coming onto the stage and the audience erupted. That is something else—that is about a public that loves what that actor is.'[21]

'It's been an exciting week for me,' Simon announced at the ceremony before handing out the award. 'They have been searching for a new James Bond. If Keith Chegwin fails, there's always a chance for me.'

Simon began to let the outside world know of his against-the-odds recovery, his legion of fans encouraged by his progress. 'I am still under treatment and I am just taking it one day at a time,' he declared, uneasy at tempting fate. 'As you can see, I am still here today and I am feeling very well.'[22]

Although resisting any temptation to return to the stage, the work Simon had been doing in the voiceover studio, although financially rewarding, was not challenging for a born actor. With his treatment leading to a more positive outlook, and his having resurfaced in front of an audience, he decided that it was time to venture back into acting work.

The next time audiences would see Simon Cadell was in probably his most disturbing role, one in which he would be as far away from the sitcom comfort of Jeffrey Fairbrother as one could ever imagine. In 1994, Rudolf van den Berg, a Dutch film director, was attempting to cast his upcoming project, *The Cold Light of Day*, a remake of a 1958 film, *It Happened in Broad Daylight*.

Unfamiliar with British television and as yet unproven in making English language films, van den Berg was particularly keen to find somebody with the right levels of eccentricity and intrigue to play the part of a child serial killer. He approached casting director Karen Lindsay-Stewart and she suggested Simon for the killer and Richard E. Grant as the policeman on his trail.

Van den Berg was looking for his killer to have more depth than the standard bad guy in a thriller. He wanted to explore the mind of the man whose victims were solely young girls. Simon was responding well enough to his treatment to be intrigued by the chance to appear in the film. He and van den Berg arranged to talk face to face, a meeting the Dutchman remembers well more than twenty years on:

> I was so under the spell of this man. He was so pleasant to be with, but he didn't have mainstream looks. That attracted me very much because that's the first you see of this character—his eyes, his face. That was something slightly unusual about him, but at the same time there was something warm about him.[23]

Simon was understandably a little anxious about the role. Even then, after twenty-five years in the business, this was a step into the unknown. Aside from his brief cameo in *The Meteor*, Simon had steered away from feature films. Here, the loveable Englishman the British public had taken to their hearts across five series of *Hi-de-Hi!* and three series of *Life Without George* would be seen as a sinister murderer preying on young girls, setting child-sized dolls in a circle in the woods, and having angry exchanges with these inanimate objects.

Despite the wild leap into the unknown, Simon was very keen to take the role, seemingly relishing the opportunity to still test himself with something unlike anything he had done previously.

It was not lost on either Simon or van den Berg that the pair were making a film about a child murderer at a time when both had toddler-aged children. In an interview for genre magazine *Fangoria*, van den Berg confessed to stopping reading any time a story appeared about the murder of a child. However, he would start to read again in the hopes of trying to understand the mind of the killer in order to avert the danger. Indeed, the Dutchman thinks that Simon's concerns were less about the reception of the public and more about the intensity of the role:

His anxieties were more about his inner self. He was such a good actor, you could feel it coming from inside. There are some very frightening scenes where he's playing with this little girl and I think that's what worried him most—that he had to transform into something he hated. I don't think he was worried about his audience, he was more challenged by the fact that he was asked to do something so evil.[24]

Simon's character in the movie was technically a supporting role, with the central figure being Richard E. Grant's policeman, who takes the dangerous approach of using a young girl as live bait to try and capture the depraved killer. In the end, it is van den Berg's belief that it was Simon's role that actually made the movie his most successful venture:

Whenever I think of that film I think of Simon. He was not the lead, but a very important character. Where you see the scenes where she [Perdita Weeks] was sitting on the lap of Simon, she was really scared. She didn't like those scenes at all, he really radiated that danger. Richard E. Grant did a great job, very credible and authentic in his part, but the special nature of the film was thanks to Simon.[25]

Filming took place in and around Prague, and with a fairly limited schedule, Simon was able to film without it affecting his health or his ongoing treatment. His charm played his way into van den Berg's heart, the director remembering that at the completion of shooting, Simon arrived at his caravan with a bottle of fine wine to share before his return home.

'I can still see him and hear him,' recalls van den Berg affectionately. 'If I hear him mentioned or see photos of him, I think, "This was a very dear person." A lot of the time you have some actors who after you have worked with them, belong in the past. Simon is still here.'[26]

The film itself unfortunately suffered a fairly limited theatrical release. A Dutch director making an English language movie was quite harshly judged in Holland. Elsewhere, the production company involved was being taken over by Universal and so the film, when it eventually arrived in January 1996, went largely unnoticed from a commercial perspective.

As for critical acclaim, Fangoria described Simon's performance as 'convincing and disturbing.'[27] It was not a role that went unnoticed at home. After a segment of filming was complete, Simon brought home one of the puppets with whom his character had rather one-sided disagreements. Beckie remembers: 'He did just a little section of the person and I said, "You're never bringing that puppet into the house again and I do not want to see that man."'[28]

There is certainly no doubt when watching the film today that the killer in Simon's hands is at once convincing and thoroughly sinister and is as far away from anything Simon ever appeared in during his career, making the role a unique, if somewhat disturbing addition to Simon's CV.

In terms of his health, Simon was just holding his own. He would be well enough to also make a television return in *Circle of Deceit*, a vehicle for Dennis Waterman. Simon would again turn away from mild-mannered Englishman, providing a chilling portrayal of an angry and corrupt merchant banker.

Circle of Deceit was a run-of-the-mill collection of made-for-television films, with Simon's role of Brendan Rylands appearing in one particular edition, *Kalon*. While again perhaps not getting the greatest of receptions when it was eventually released, it does nevertheless show Simon in a different light once more. His rage and aggression in his characterisation are again aspects of a personality that he had not been asked to portray on television before, and it is a standout performance in an otherwise mediocre offering.

It was January 1996 when *The Cold Light of Day* received its limited release. As is often the case with patients receiving chemotherapy, it is not the cancer that itself that brings about the demise, but the immune system's inability to fight off other threats. Around the same time as the film was first seen, Simon's progress had stopped and his condition was deteriorating. Dr Scurr made regular trips up to Suffolk for his ailing friend:

> I would get in the car early on a Sunday morning, blast up there and spend an hour or two with him—have a coffee, tweak his treatment or do whatever was necessary and then drive back to London before lunchtime. In that era—let's say treatments have moved on since then. What gets the better of people in the end is they get infections and they get pneumonia and other immune deficiencies from the chemotherapy.[29]

During one of these visits, Simon gave his friend a beautiful glass inkwell as a thank you for his efforts and support, something that remains on Dr Scurr's desk to this day and is a reflection of Simon's thoughtfulness even during such dispiriting times.

In the early stages of 1996, Simon's health deteriorated. It became obvious that the fight against his illness was starting to turn. Beckie was regularly bringing the boys down from Suffolk to London, but when it became clear that Simon was into his final weeks, they decided to remain in the capital.

When Simon was finally forced into hospital, he went into a Harley Street Clinic room where he would fight his final days with the same spirit, kindness, and naughty humour that he had led his life with. His friends despaired at his fate and flooded the family with letters of good wishes and reminders of better times.

It would be wrong to think, however, that Simon's popularity among his fellow professionals was somehow a sign of distance from his public. He had always believed that class should not dictate how one was perceived nor treated. True to his beliefs, he treated everybody with whom he came into contact with the same level of courtesy and warmth as he did those in his own profession.

A reflection of this came one day in the hospital. Selina was in Simon's room with Penny Croft when one of the nursing staff poked her head around the door. 'Selina, we've got a big card for Simon downstairs,' she announced, and curious as to know why she would need to go down to get it, Selina obliged.

What awaited Selina in the foyer was a remarkable testament to the charm and popularity of her brother. A huge 'get well' card contained countless pictures of taxis. Simon had lived in taxis, going from club to club, theatre to theatre in them.

'I opened it up with Simon,' recalled Selina, 'and inside, 600 black taxi drivers had signed this get well card. All of them said things like "You know guv', you're the best," and "Never talk down to us, treat us like one of you." There aren't many people who would get 600 signatures, all of whom just talked about how they loved him.'[30]

As the days went by and Simon's destiny drew closer, fewer and fewer friends were able to file through the doors as he became weaker. On 29 February, Gyles Brandreth said his goodbyes to his best friend for the last time. They had never led the kind of friendship that had involved deep discussions over feelings, instead having an almost intuitive appreciation of their position in each other's lives. As such, although Gyles acknowledges that those final days were very grim, the pair nonetheless simply continued to tell Ralph Richardson and John Gielgud stories. It was how they had always been, and as Gyles says now, 'that, essentially, is the essence of him.'[31]

Nick Renton recalled: 'I can remember Gyles saying somewhere that there isn't a day goes by when he doesn't think about this man, which kind of summed it up really.'[32]

Even in his final hours, Simon still had time to show an extraordinary gesture of his kindness towards others. Just a few days prior to his passing, he made a request for somebody to return to Suffolk and collect a set of bottles of a particular red wine. Simon's knowledge was such that he knew this particular vintage was not going to be at its best for another year, but he was determined not to depart this world without it going to good use.

The request was duly adhered to and the wine arrived at the clinic having been kept on its side for the duration of the journey. Simon disliked the fact that so many stores sold good wines that were stored upright instead of being laid flat. This was not conducive to their remaining at their best.

What Simon had planned was not to down these bottles himself, but to throw a party. This was not to be just any party though. Such was his affection for the medical staff and for them having helped prolong his life so much beyond his original diagnosis that they were the people the party was for. Selina recalled:

> We had to go and get the chef from downstairs and we left Simon plotting and planning. The chef came up with the perfect recipe for this burgundy. This was a chef who was used to making meals for Arab princes and he was terrific, so Simon had this party in his room. The upshot was this most incredible meal for all the doctors, heart doctors and cancer doctors. We were not invited, this was just for the doctors.[33]

Selina wondered whether Simon had secretly hoped this would be his own private send off. The pain of saying farewell to his beloved wife and boys was enormous and Selina considered whether the combination of rich food and the red wine might just be enough to send him on his way, sparing Beckie and his family any more painful goodbyes. Although his system was shutting down, his heart was of course now made of sturdier stuff and so the party was not his final send-off.

In his hospitalised days, Simon still retained his humour in spite of the emotional and physical pain. Gyles Brandreth mentioned in the foreword Simon's reaction to a nurse's warning of, 'just a little prick'—'there's no need to be insulting'.[34] It was a line in the finest Croft and Perry mould and one which typified his dignified surrender to his condition.

Trevor Hughes dropped in to bring his friend half a bottle of wine and as Simon lost his ability to feed himself, Selina lovingly fed her brother some champagne through a straw. With the final curtain due, Beckie took the decision that the boys had experienced enough pain and she would prefer not to have them see their father slip away. When she returned home the phone call came from Selina's husband Michael Thomas that Simon had gone. He lost his fight with non-Hodgkins at 7 p.m. on 6 March 1996, surrounded by his grief-stricken mother and siblings, just a few hours before his tenth wedding anniversary. He was forty-five years old.

David Croft took care of the announcements the following day. As expected as the news had been for some time, friends and fans alike were no less devastated. At such a young age, one of the leading theatrical lights of the British stage had been cruelly snuffed out. 'A brilliant career cut tragically short,' was the accurate phrasing used by Croft as he said goodbye to his friend, son-in-law, and one of the brightest stars to have graced the Croft and Perry stable of success.[35]

Tributes flooded in from all angles. John Wells, who had become such a strong friend during *Travels with My Aunt*, perhaps summed things up most succinctly when he described his fallen pal as, 'a great comedian, famously good company and an irreplaceably nice bloke.'[36] The pair had actually bought the television rights to *Travels* in the hope of adapting it together.

Another project Simon had hoped to be involved in was a return to the life of Larry Wade. *Life Without George* had ended not in cancellation, but simply because time had moved on. The eponymous George had been out of the picture and Larry and Jenny had been all set for parenthood. Penny Croft had written the new series and had even retitled it as *Happy as Larry*. One can only pine for the show that might have been.

After the airing of *Circle of Deceit* a few days after Simon's death, there was still one more chance for the British public to hear his vocal talents, and it is perhaps a piece more consistent with Simon's career. Completed a few weeks before his illness took a turn for the worse, *Noël Coward from His Diaries* had been completed for Radio 4. The show had been a combination of extracts from Coward's own interviews, a new interview with his lover Graham Payne, and some passages read by Simon, all narrated and edited together by producer Tony Staveacre. Whether simply keen to get the programme completed while he was in the groove or whether he was simply acutely aware of having limited time, Simon finished his recording in one day at a voiceover studio in Wardour Street. Staveacre remembers:

> People think narration is easy to do, but they couldn't be more wrong. It's just a kind of instinctual thing. Simon had a lovely little flavour of Coward—the clipped voice that people poke fun at. He had just enough of it. It was very subtle and very lovely. He was quite frail, but we didn't know when we did it that his life was going to end quite so soon. There's some quite touching stuff about the end of his [Coward's] life so there was quite a resonance from that.[37]

There is indeed a certain poignancy about hearing some of Coward's lines on the topic of death. Even though when he wrote them in 1961, Coward expected to live considerably longer, and indeed did so, his words when spoken by Simon carried an uneasy poignancy:

> Ah me! This growing old. This losing of friends and breaking of links with the past ... It is an inevitability one must prepare the heart and mind for. I wonder how long it will be before I make my last exit.[38]

The Stage review was aptly respectful of Simon's final bow, noting of the well-received piece that: 'Even in the last weeks of his life, Cadell's standard of professionalism never slackened.'[39]

The end of any life at such a young age is always tragic. That Simon's knockout blow should have been dealt just when he was discovering a new lease of life was especially cruel. For the Cadell family's great friend Donald Sinden, the pain was mirrored in an even more intolerable way. Jeremy

Sinden, Donald's oldest son who had been born within months of Simon and with whom Simon had struck up a wonderful friendship, also lost a fight with cancer, at the same age within just a few months of Simon's own passing.

A private funeral for only family and the closest of friends was held at Honington in Suffolk. The inscription on Simon's headstone is a quote from Shakespeare's *The Tempest*—'Our Revels Now Are Ended'. Far too few years had passed since Simon had first watched John Gielgud deliver Prospero's lines on stage, but he had indeed enjoyed plenty of revels in his tragically short life. In his own memoir, *Do You Know Who I Am?*, Tim Pigott-Smith admitted that when playing Prospero himself in 2012, he, 'became convinced that it was a farewell from the actor.'[40] Looking at the full passage, it is not difficult to see why, and certainly using the opening sentence seems a fitting farewell to Simon Cadell, who had been so entranced by Gielgud's Prospero nearly forty years previously:

> Our revels now are ended. These our actors,
> As I foretold you, were all spirits and
> Are melted into air, into thin air:
> And, like this baseless fabric of this vision,
> The cloud-capp'd towers, the gorgeous palaces,
> The solemn temples, the great globe itself,
> Yea, all which it inherit, shall dissolve
> And, like this insubstantial pageant faded,
> Leave not a rack behind. We are such stuff
> As dreams are made on; and our little life
> Is rounded with a sleep.[41]

During his later few years, Simon never courted sympathy for his condition. He faced the challenges of both of his medical ailments with courage, humour, and determination and it is perhaps this, along with his desire to grab some more precious time with his wife and two boys that allowed him to outperform his terminal diagnosis by more than two years. At the same time, Roy Castle had been battling his own terminal cancer, who had attributed his lung cancer diagnosis to passive smoking caused by years of playing music at smoke-filled clubs. Simon had the utmost admiration for Castle's approach to his fate, despite facing the same destiny himself with such courage and dignity.

'I don't ask "Why me?" because that really would be a waste of time,' Simon once said of his fate. 'But overall, I know I've had a wonderful life. It's been great fun.'[42]

If Love Were All

When word of Simon's passing was first given to Beckie, she gathered the boys to pass on the news that no parent should ever have to give to children of their age. In a charming moment that Simon would have found the humour in, Alec gave an unusual response, given that he was just six years old.

'What a waste,' he told his mother. It seemed a deep remark from such a young boy, and Beckie went to clarify that he meant his father's passing at such an age, or with so much future success now denied. Yet that was not the reason for his comment: 'No. I mean what a waste of all that Coke in the fridge.'[1] It is a small piece of humour only utterable by one of such tender years, but somehow makes such an intolerably cruel passing a little more human.

Simon Cadell was buried in the small churchyard at Honington, just a few minutes away from the Croft family home. His is an inauspicious headstone—no fancy decoration or showy materials, just an ordinary stone among the rows of others, with the Prospero quotation, which was perhaps applicable given Simon's belief that he was no more significant than any other.

Although finally released from his pain, Simon's talents continued to be heard. Among his catalogue of voiceovers had been a recording of the 'Mind the gap' message for Gatwick and London Underground stations. Simon's voice gently warned the patrons for some time after his death.

On 5 August 1996, a memorial service was held for Simon at the St James's cathedral in Piccadilly. The cathedral was understandably packed to the rafters with mourners there to celebrate the life of their friend. Readings were given by Selina, Tim Pigott-Smith, Joanna Lumley, John Wells, Peter Howell, and Donald Sinden, while Gyles gave an address. There were musical contributions charged with emotion, Patricia Hodge singing 'If Love Were All' and Su Pollard contributing 'Look for the Silver Lining'.

Simon's colleagues from his biggest successes on stage and screen reassembled for the memorial. Among them was Jeffrey Holland, who remembered a curious incident:

> The first speaker was Gyles Brandreth and he had a microphone. As soon as he started to speak into the microphone, it cut out completely. When Selina got up to speak she said, 'That was Simon.' He hated amplified sound—he was a trained actor, people use their voices. She reckoned he sabotaged it![2]

Understandably, many of those attendees that gave their time in the research for this book struggled to recall specifics of the memorial, such was the power of the occasion. Joanna Lumley was unable to recall what passage she read: 'When Gyles did the piece talking about him at the end, I was fit for rags. I couldn't really see, I was crying so much. Simon was so young and the death was so cruel. So heart-stabbingly dreadful.'[3]

Tim Pigott-Smith felt that the service was perfect—a little lightness, but a particular sadness for the loss of such talent when it hadn't been allowed to reach its full potential:

> It was rightly emotional, but there were some light moments as well. I don't like memorials that are all just fun and flippant. If you don't actually feel the loss of the person you're there for, it's pretty bloody pointless. Gyles Brandreth did a quite brilliant speech in which he rescued us from gloom and misery. There's a ghastly sadness in the air of somebody that young, of somebody one felt was just on the edge of potential greatness as an actor.[4]

As mentioned in the acknowledgements section of this book, while conducting my research, Tim Pigott-Smith passed away unexpectedly at the age of sixty-nine. We had spoken at length of their time at The Bristol Old Vic Theatre School and of their various subsequent meetings. He was a delight to speak to and viewed the entire Cadell family with great affection.

When we were wrapping up our interview, Tim gave one of the warmest tributes that I heard throughout my research:

> He was a wonderful, generous man, both privately and professionally. I still think about him quite a lot and I feel quite strongly of my debt to him and his family for their generosity towards me and what they gave me towards the business.[5]

Our interview came shortly after the announcement that he had been awarded an OBE. Simon would have found a delicious irony in the idea that such an announcement would come after the filming of *King Charles*, in which Tim starred as a future Prince Charles being freshly promoted to King and which would irk some of the less tolerant royal-loving critics.

I cannot help but think that these two events, which were so sadly among his final ones, were perhaps reflective of where Simon might have found himself had circumstances been different. A poke at society, at the same time as taking on a hefty role as the King of England would certainly have been of appeal to Simon. Back in the early 1980s, he had already been seen in a few sketches as a chain-smoking Prince Philip, destitute on a park bench with his beloved Elizabeth, in the guise of a bearded Kenny Everett.

There is also a common belief that Simon himself would have found his way into favour with the honours committee, with a number of interviewees suggesting that he would by now have been either Simon Cadell OBE, or indeed Sir Simon Cadell. His great friend Gyles Brandreth believed that he was ready to take on the role that Sir Donald Sinden held until his own death—the dramatic royalty who had played every role, been afforded every accolade, and assumed a place at the head of the profession.

'One of the many tragic things about his dying was that he was literally just growing into his face,' Tim Pigott-Smith felt. 'He'd arrived at that perfect moment where all his experience and all his powers, the way he looked and the way he was, were just ready to springboard off into a fantastic career.'[6]

Simon's work on *Hi-de-Hi!* is of course readily available. As long as we are born with chuckle-muscles, as Ken Dodd would have put it, there will be demand for the full range of Croft and Perry box sets, and *Hi-de-Hi!* will always be at the forefront of the range. Looking back on the programmes now, there are still many laugh out loud episodes and there is no denying that Simon's performance as Jeffrey Fairbrother is indeed one of the finest in television comedy. To achieve the amount of laughs that he did without ever having a joke to tell is quite remarkable.

Enemy at the Door and *Blott on the Landscape* are also easily available and represent something different within Simon's arsenal of talents. Of Herr Reinicke, Simon said that even some of his friends commented on being amazed just how nasty he was capable of making the role, and that still comes through today, though somehow not nearly as disturbing as his Vladimir Kozant in *The Cold Light of Day*.

Sadly, Simon's other two successful jaunts into sitcom land, *Singles* and *Life Without George*, remain commercially unavailable. *Life Without George* may have stirred some controversy upon its release, but it is a timid forerunner to the numerous comedy-dramas that have subsequently populated the television screens. If promotion of promiscuity was the criticism then, *Sex and the City* now makes it look like an Edwardian piece on chastity. Quite why the BBC have held on to a show that pulled in as many as 13 million viewers is anybody's guess.

The greater amount of Simon's work available is his audio pieces. Greene, Waugh, Wodehouse, *The Lord of the Rings*—there is a great deal out there if you look hard enough, and perhaps it is appropriate that Simon's recognisable voice is more easily available than some of his television appearances.

Simon's theatre work was expansive and pretty much unbroken from Theatre School through to the abrupt end of *Travels with My Aunt*. Of these pieces, very little evidence remains. There is the occasional glimpse of the 1989 incarnation of his *Noël and Gertie* role online, having performed it with Patricia Hodge in the Queen Mother's Birthday Royal Gala. That aside, one can only trust those who saw them first hand as to how strong his performances were. It is perhaps one of the reasons I felt this book needed to be written. As I spoke to more and more of his colleagues, it became apparent just what an extraordinary talent Simon was and just how many great roles theatre missed out on when he passed so early.

Selina Cadell's acting career goes from strength to strength. She regularly writes for *The Guardian*, can still be seen treading the boards in the West End, and has been a regular member of the cast in the popular television show *Doc Martin*. Simon was understandably a huge influence on her career, and whenever she is faced with an acting challenge, she ponders what Simon might have done, and she nearly always finds the answer she needs.

Brother Patrick, who opted for the production side of the movies for such hits as *Raiders of the Lost Ark* and *A Passage to India*, remained behind the camera, but he has changed camera type now, mostly focusing on still photography.

Simon's boys have grown into fine young men. They chose not to follow their ancestors into the acting profession, albeit Alec did put a toe in the water. He progressed to a late stage of auditions for Ron in the Harry Potter movies, having appeared briefly on television in *Zip and Hollow*, written by his aunt Penny Croft, directed by former *Hi-de-Hi!* producer Roy Gould, and including among its cast Rosalind March, the original Amanda in *Life Without George*. It was a path he moved away from, as did older brother Patrick. They may not have followed their father into the business, but while there are not an abundance of similarities immediately obvious, they have a charm and amiability about them that Simon would have been justly proud of.

The generations of Cadells on stage and screen will not end with Selina, however. The son of Selina and Michael Thomas, Edwin, carries a striking resemblance to Simon and having carved out a career in the dramatic arts, a fifth generation flourishes.

At the turn of the millennium, Gyles Brandreth took to his diaries to pen a note to his fallen friend. After much consideration as to whether to reproduce the letter, previously published in Gyles's diaries, I have decided to do so. The friendship between Gyles and Simon was integral to Simon's life. That this deeply personal letter radiates affection for a lifelong pal, with whom discussing their friendship was never on the table, speaks volumes as to the strength of the relationship and I am indebted to Gyles for allowing its reproduction here.

Saturday, 1 January 2000
Framlingham, Suffolk
Dear Simon,

How are you? Stupid question, of course. You're dead. All the same, I thought I'd write to you today because it's the first day of a new year—some say it's the first day of a new millennium—and I'm here, sitting on your old sofa in your old home, thinking of you.

We have had a memorable night, thanks to your in-laws. We went over to Honington Hall where they wined us (royally) and dined us (splendidly) and then entertained us with a special showing of *Inspector Gadget*—possibly the worst film in the history of cinema. (I don't think you could have sat through it: you'd have twitched until you exploded.) The children enjoyed the movie while the adults drank steadily. As midnight approached, the film ended and we switched to TV. That's when the real horror began. The poor Queen had been dragged from Sandringham to take part in the 'festivities' at the Millennium Dome. As midnight tolled, she was obliged to stand in line holding hands with Tony Blair, singing 'Auld Lang Syne'. It was truly the sight of the century—Her Majesty, with barely concealed disgust, allowing her Prime Minister to take hold of the tips of her fingers and yank her arm up and down in time to the music. It said everything we needed to know about Blair's Britain at the dawn of the twenty-first century.

And if we'd had any lingering doubts, they were washed away when we switched to live coverage of the millennium fireworks. As Big Ben finished striking the hour, we had been promised a spectacular 'River of Fire'— two-hundred-foot flames rising above the Thames and sweeping, surging, leaping, coursing at 775 mph, in just ten seconds, from Tower Bridge to Vauxhall. Alas, it was not to be: the spin out-performed the delivery: we held our breath and nothing happened: the River of Fire turned out to be a dribble. It was so feeble it was funny. In fact, it was all so ghastly, I rather enjoyed it. I suspect it would have made you very angry.

But you'd have enjoyed the party. David and Anne [Croft] are lovely people and generous hosts—none more so. (We need more generosity in this mean-spirited world.) Your extended family was all there. We talked about you. (Well, some of us did.)

And while you will be pleased to know, even though it's nearly four years since you died, you have not been entirely forgotten by the wider public either. Predictably, it's not for your stage work that they remember you: your Mercutio, your Hamlet, Oswald in *Ghosts*, that archetypal silly-ass in *Tons of Money* at the National, Elyot in *Private Lives* (those would be my top five), not even for your award-winning performance in *Travels with My Aunt*. No, your immortality, such as it is, seems to rest on your portrayal of the holiday camp manager in the TV sitcom *Hi-de-Hi!*. (You are allowed to smile. If I am remembered at all, it will be as the man who wore silly jumpers on breakfast TV.)

We still get plenty of *Hi-de-Hi!* repeats on the box. And because, for so long, you were one of the masters of the commercial voice-over, you still crop up in some unexpected places. The other morning I stepped out of the London Underground at Bank Station and, suddenly, over the loudspeaker system, I heard you booming at me: 'Mind the gap!' It's not much of a line, but you do it brilliantly. (Do you remember how, at school, Rachel loved to quote Stanislavsky: 'There are no small parts, only small actors'?) I stood on the station platform and let three trains come and go just to listen to you. I could picture you in the recording studio: a small cigar in your right hand, left hand cupped behind your ear, your lopsided mouth close to the microphone, taking such pleasure in pitching it so perfectly. It was good to hear that voice again: crisp, energetic, fruity, lived-in.

Where are you, old friend? It's 12 noon. You should be in here serving me a glass of champagne with crème de pêche. That's what we do on New Year's Day. (Actually, any day will do.) Do you realise it's thirty-five years since we met—in 1964, when the Beatles and the Rolling Stones were all the rage, but you and I (bless us) were living in another era. Our heroes were Gerald du Maurier and Jack Buchanan. I played you my Noël Coward records: you played me your Flanagan and Allen. We spoke of Sir Ralph and Sir John, Sir Michael and Dame Peggy as though we knew them—and as it happens, one day we would. (We took that for granted)

I see now what a quaint couple we must have seemed: an absurd pair of prematurely middle-aged teenagers who thought they knew it all. In fact, while I had long sensed (at least since I was 7) that I understood everything— absolutely and completely—when I met you I had to concede that, in terms of sophistication and a thorough understanding of the ways of the world and the pleasures of the flesh, you were the undoubted master.

At 13, you could blow perfect smoke rings (at that stage you preferred Gitanes to Gauloises); at 14, you could tell the difference between a Chablis and a Montrachet at a hundred paces; at 15, girls would do things for you that the rest of adolescent Britain could only dream of. (Do you remember that brief dalliance I had with the nurse in the sanatorium? I suppose I was 17 and she was 23. It seemed to me to be the most thrilling thing that had happened in the long history of desire—until I gave you the details and you explained to me, quite kindly, that by your standards, my tentative kissing and cuddling was very thin beer indeed.)

Why did our friendship work?

We had common interests and shared values. We were equally narcissistic, self-absorbed, ambitious, but never in competition with one another. We were never critical of one another either. In time, our wives might tell us to spend less, drink less, improve our posture, hold our stomachs in, but we simply accepted each other, exactly as we were, without qualification, without question. Neither of us was ever judgemental. If you had reservations about my politics (which you did) you never said so. If I had reservations about your women (and the assortment was varied) I never spoke a word.

Our friendship may have been profound, but our conversation wasn't. We avoided introspection. (That's one of the secrets of happiness: my new friend, Professor Anthony Clare, has just told me so.) We didn't discuss our feelings, ever, not even when you were dying, possibly because we were middle-class Englishmen of a certain vintage but perhaps, too, because, instinctively, each knew how the other felt and there really wasn't any need. We never had a cross word—not once in thirty-five years.

Our relationship was totally secure and wonderfully uncomplicated. There was no jealousy, no envy, no confusing desire. That's the joy of friendship: sex never gets in the way. A love affair is fun, thrilling (the highs so high), but it's unsettling, dangerous, exhausting too; and, if you've been around the block, you know it always ends in tears. Marriage (I think I understood this better than you) is magnificent—fundamental, essential, and, when it works, (thank you, Lord), a blessing like non other—but it isn't easy. Living a lifetime with your lover/husband/wife calls for energy, staying power, infinite care, eternal compromise. Ours was an altogether easier lot. A friendship that begins in childhood is simply a favourite cardigan: you don't need to keep it in good repair, you simply need to slip it on.

We were good companions, you and I. We made each other laugh (without fail), telling the same stories in the same funny voices, year after year. We had awarded ourselves a special licence (irrevocable) to quaff (the best champagne), to scoff (the finest caviar), to gossip until dawn.

We both went along with the Noël Coward line that 'on the whole work is more fun than fun'. That doesn't mean to say that we didn't take our pleasures where we found them. (Do you remember the menu gourmand at the Hôtel du Cap at Antibes? Our wives said, 'Eleven courses and a different wine with every course? You can't!' We did.) But essentially, we were defined by our work rather than by our family lives or our relationships. Our careers came first. Yours was more satisfactory, of course, because you never had any doubt about what you wanted to do. I've meandered: that's been a mistake. Being an actor was your life: you were most alive in a studio or on a stage. You relished and understood your craft. (You were also very ready to share your experience. When I was an MP and a Government Whip, you and I discussed John Major's distracting way with words, his curious sing-sing speaking voice and his annoying way of saying 'want' as 'wunt'. You suggested I suggest to the PM that you give him some help with his pronunciation. Did I tell you that I did? Mr Major was not amused.)

There was an unspoken conspiracy between us, wasn't there? It was our world and whatever we wanted of it could be, would be, must be ours. Do you remember one summer turning up in the south of France at the villa your parents had rented and finding the sky hopelessly overcast? You opened a bottle of champagne and stood there, glass in hand, staring at the heavens, commanding the clouds to part. Of course, they were happy—they were honoured—to oblige.

We thought we were invincible and then, one day, we had our comeuppance. On the morning of Saturday 11 September 1993—I can tell you the date: I keep a diary, as you know: I am writing this in my diary now—I was standing in the kitchen at home, squeezing the orange juice when the telephone range. 'You are going to have to be brave,' you said. 'I'm in the Harley Street Clinic. It's not good news ... Of course I'll want you to do the address at the service. We must talk about that. And the music. I think a combination of Charles Trenet and the Battle Hymn of the Republic, don't you?'

In the event, you struggled on for two and a half more years, with such grace and style and indomitable joie de vivre. John Wells (who followed you all too quickly to the grave) put it perfectly: 'Simon showed us how to live and then taught us how to die.'

Four years on, what's the news at this end? Not much: Tony Blair is Prime Minister; John Birt is a lord, Henry Cooper is a knight and Shirley Bassey and Julie Andrews are dames (I kid you not: all as of yesterday); and, apart from *Frasier* and repeats of *Inspector Morse*, there's still nothing worth watching on the box.

On the domestic front, the big news is that your wife has a new man. Don't worry. He's okay. In fact, he's lovely. She often says you must have sent him. He's younger than you, taller, better-looking, better-read, calmer, easier-to-live-with. (He isn't an actor, so he must be. Actors are impossible. We know that.) I like him a lot now, but at first I found it difficult to be in the room with him. It was nothing personal. He's intelligent, thoughtful and kind. I just couldn't bear to see him sitting in your chair, drinking from your glass.

He is wonderful with your sons. He does those dad-like things with them (watching football, playing games) that you (and I) were never very good at. The boys seem happy: the tension that was in the air during the years when you were dying has gradually disappeared. They are 12 and 14 now, looking good, growing tall, winning prizes. You've got plenty to be proud of. (So have I. My children are the light of my life.)

Your mother is pretty perky too. In truth, she's the one I feel for. I can imagine nothing worse in the whole world than losing your child. At her house in France, she created a glorious sundial in your memory. You'd love it, and you'd be proud, too, if you could see the way she soldiers on. No doubt, in the still watches of the night she feels quite bleak, but she's British and she's brave and she doesn't let it show.

And how am I? I'm fine. I lost my seat at the general election—a relief really. Michèle hated the life. I could have gone back. I was offered a crack at the first by-election that came along—a safe seat, too. But I couldn't do it to her. She has given me her life. I owe her something. (In truth, I owe her everything.) And ten years in opposition? Fifteen, maybe? And then what? Secretary of State for Hairpins—or possibly the Arts. No, I shan't be Prime Minister: I missed the boat—too busy faffing around on the quayside. But I'm not downcast: a new millennium dawns and I have plans … a novel, a play, a film—I am going to get one thing right, *completely right*, before I'm done. I shall make my pitch for immortality.

Meanwhile, here I am, starting 2000 at the forefront of the second division. I don't complain. I'm a hack, but a happy one: doing radio, TV, journalism. Working all day, every day. It's fun. I'm well paid. I travel the world meeting interesting people. I pursue my projects. I make my plans. I've lost weight. I drink less. I even exercise now and again. And the curse of cholesterol means I've given up the pate de foie gras. It's all okay. It's really very good. I want for nothing and I surround myself with famous, funny and delightful people. Oh yes, there's still laughter at my end of the table—but, old friend, let's face it: without you, it isn't quite the same.[7]

'Not a month goes by in my life without someone mentioning him,' says Selina. 'He doesn't go away … and I feel very lucky.'[8]

List of Performances

What follows is a comprehensive listing of the performances of Simon Cadell. While every effort has been made to ensure accuracy, any omission is purely accidental. No attempt has been made to cover Simon's extensive catalogue of commercial voiceovers. There are a number of earlier performances that Simon was known to have appeared in, but despite best efforts, no character name is known.

Stage Appearances

Ivan the Fool, 1962, Ivan the Fool (Dunhurst)
A Passage to India, 1963, Major Callendar (Bedales)
Measure for Measure, 1964, Pompey (Bedales)
A Study in Sherlock, 1964, Sherlock Holmes (Bedales)
Thirty Minutes in The Street, 1965, An Actor (Bedales)
Zigger Zagger, 1967, Chairman (National Youth Theatre)
The Enemies, 1968, Zakhar Ivanovich Bardin (Bristol Old Vic Theatre School)
Twelfth Night, 1968, unknown role (Bristol Old Vic Theatre School)
The Duenna, 1968, Father Paul (Bristol Old Vic Theatre School)
A Midsummer Night's Dream, 1968, Egeus, Father of Hermia (National Youth Theatre)
Richard II, 1968, Edmund, Duke of York (National Youth Theatre)
The Great Stage of the World, 1968, The King/The Peasant (alternating) (Bristol Old Vic Theatre School)
The Poet's Heart, 1969, Lord Kettering (Bristol Old Vic Theatre School)
The Alchemist, 1969, Subtle (Bristol Old Vic Theatre School)
Major Barbara, 1969, Stephen
Macbeth, 1969, unknown role.
The Servant of Two Masters, 1969, Magistrate
It's A Two Foot Six Inches Above the Ground World, 1969, P.C. Beamish
The Boy Friend, 1969, Gendarme
Oh, What A Lovely War, 1970, unknown role
As You Like It, 1970, Sir Oliver Martext, Jaques do Boys, Forester

The School for Scandal, 1970, Snake, Moses
Arms and The Man, 1970, Nicola
The Importance of Being Earnest, 1970, Lane
A Close Shave, 1971, Celesin,
Antigone, 1971, Chorus
The Balcony, 1971, Chief of Police
Geneva, 1971, The Betrothed
Lloyd George Knew My Father, 1972, Simon Green
The East Blows Cold (son et lumiere), 1972, company of voices
Son-et-lumiere, 1973, voices of Sir Christopher Wren and John Henry
The Beaux Stratagem, 1973, unknown role
Edith Grove, 1973, Justin Jackson
Dangerous Corner, 1974, Gordon Whitehouse
Romeo And Juliet, 1974, Mercutio
Ghosts, 1974, Oswald Alving
How the Other Half Loves, 1974, William Featherstone
The Thing-Ummy-Bob (That's Going to Win the War), 1974, Andy
The Case in Question, 1975, Julian Underwood
Lies, 1975, Justin Jackson
How the Other Half Loves, 1976, William Featherstone
Widowers Houses, 1976, Dr Harry Trench
Landscape & Silence, 1976 (Uncredited stand-in)
The Amazons, 1977, Andre, Count de Grival
Sybil, 1977, company (Tribute to Dame Sybil Thorndike)
Caught in The Act, 1981, Martin Barclay
Private Lives, 1981, Elyot Chase
A Night in Old Peking, 1981, The Wicked African Magician
Caught in The Act, 1982, Martin Barclay (touring production of 1981 show)
Celia Johnson Memorial Gala, 1982, Mr Holst
You Should See Us Now, 1983, Ernest
May Day Gala, 1983, Host (Oxford Playhouse benefit performance)
Noël and Gertie, 1983, Noël Coward
Hi-de-Hi!, 1983, Jeffrey Fairbrother
Hamlet, 1984, Hamlet, Prince of Denmark
Raffles, 1984, A. J. Raffles
Jumpers, 1985, Archie
Blithe Spirit, 1985, Charles
Tons of Money, 1986, Aubrey Henry Maitland Allington
A Small Family Business, 1987, Benedict Hough
Musical Comedy Murders of 1940, 1988, Eddie McCuen
Double Act, 1988, George
The Parasol, 1989, Alexei Fyodorych Laptev
Noël and Gertie, 1989, Noël Coward
Queen Mother Royal Gala, 1990, guest performance from *Noël and Gertie*
High Flyers, 1990, Ashley Stockton-Wood
Don't Dress for Dinner, 1991, Robert
Travels with My Aunt, 1993, Henry Pulling and Aunt Augusta

Television Roles

Hadleigh, 1969, John Scully (Yorkshire Television)
Hine, 1971, unnamed official (ATV)

Love Story, 1972, John (ATV)
The Love School, 1975, Oxford undergraduate (BBC)
Plaintiffs and Defendants, 1975, Sallust (BBC)
Two Sundays, 1975, Schoolmaster (BBC)
The Glittering Prizes, 1976, Ken Hobbs (BBC)
The Dame of Sark, 1976, Dr Braun (Anglia Television)
The Promise, 1977, Leonodik (Anglia Television)
Wings, 1978, Major Colin McAdam (BBC)
She Fell Among Thieves, 1978, Candle (BBC)
1990, 1978, Robert Jessup (BBC)
Enemy at the Door, 1978-9, Hauptmann Reinicke (London Weekend Television)
Edward And Mrs Simpson, 1978, Major John Aird (Thames Television)
Hi-de-Hi!, 1980–3, Jeffrey Fairbrother (BBC)
The Executioner (Play for Today), 1980, Fowler, (BBC)
Square Mile of Murder, 1980, David Cook (BBC)
Rifleman, 1980, Harry Kincaid (BBC)
Minder, 1980, Simon (Thames Television)
Name for The Day (Play for Today), 1980, Dr Nethersole
When the Boat Comes In, 1981, Philip Martin (BBC)
Miss Europe, 1981, Compere (BBC)
Take the Stage, 1981, recurring guest participant (Granada Television)
Tales of The Unexpected, 1981, Co-pilot (Anglia Television)
Bergerac, 1981, Hedley Cross (BBC)
The Kenny Everett Television Show, 1982, Prince Philip (BBC)
Where Is Betty Buchus? (Saturday Night Thriller), 1982, Mr Murkitt (London Weekend Television)
Children in Need, 1983, studio guest (BBC)
David Frost's End of The Year Show, 1983, studio guest (Channel Four)
Tales of the Unexpected, 1984, Sam Luke (Anglia Television)
Blott on the Landscape, 1985, Dundridge (BBC)
Life Without George, 1987-9, Larry Wade (BBC)
Comic Relief, 1988, guest (BBC)
The Dog It Was That Died, 1989, Hogbin (Channel Four)
A Wanted Man, 1989, Leslie Payne QC (BBC)
Minder, 1989, William Pierce (Thames Television)
Anything More Would Be Greedy, 1989, voiceover (Anglia Television)
Pride and Extreme Prejudice, 1989, Wilson (ITV)
Bump, 1990, Narrator (BBC)
About Face, 1991, Graham (Thames Television)
Singles, 1991, Dennis Duval (Yorkshire Television)
Perry And Croft: The Sitcoms, 1995, contributor (BBC)
Circle of Deceit (Kalon), 1996, Brendan Rylans (Yorkshire Television)

Radio Appearances

Evan Harrington, 1976, Evan Harrington
The Grand Babylon Hotel, 1976, Prince Aribert of Posen
The Loved and The Unloved, 1977, Gilles Salone
The Pickwick Papers, 1977, Charles Dickens
Invitation to The Waltz, 1978, Rollo
The Girl Who Didn't Want to Be, 1978, Timothy Turner
Janus, 1978, Robin Loxley

The Weather in the Streets, 1979, Rollo
A Dance to The Music of Time, 1979, Charles Stringham
Prudence, 1979, Jack (Capital Radio)
Engaged, 1980, Cheviot Hill
The Sitting Tenant, 1980, Gordon Whitehouse
First Love, 1980, Vladimir, Voldemar
A Love Match, 1980, Perdican
Little Dorrit, 1980, Charles Dickens
Story Time: The Moon in The Cloud, 1980, narrator
Gardens, 1980, poetry reader
The Lord of the Rings, 1981, Celeborn
Story Time: The Boys, 1981, narrator
Story Time: The Black Monk, 1981, narrator
Bleak House, 1982, Charles Dickens
The New Nightingale, 1982, poetry reader
The Christmas Story, 1982, narrator
The Hidden Years, 1984, narrator
Our Mutual Friend, 1984, Charles Dickens
Story Time: Salad Days, 1985, narrator
Pygmalion, 1986, Professor Higgins
Murder for Christmas, 1986, Nigel Strangeways
Martin Chuzzlewit, 1987, Charles Dickens
Right Ho Jeeves, 1988, Bertie
The Family Reunion, 1988, Harry Lord Monchensey
Rogue Male, 1989, Sir Ben
Put Out More Flags, 1990, Basil Seal
P. G. Wodehouse's Golf Omnibus, 1990, narrator
Waugh On Five Fronts, 1992, narrator
Forces Sweetheart, 1993, narrator
Waugh On Five More Fronts, 1994, narrator
The Wodehouse Letters, 1994, narrator
You, 1995, narrator
The Diary of Samuel Pepys, 1995, Lord Anglesey
Noël Coward—From His Diaries, 1996, Noël Coward

Film Appearances

Europe After the Rain, 1978, narrator
Watership Down, 1978, voice of Blackberry
Meteor, 1979, BBC reporter
Cold Light of Day, 1996, Vladimir Kozant

Audiobooks

Scoop by Evelyn Waugh
Gulliver's Travels by Jonathan Swift
The Quiet American by Graham Greene
The Little Train & The Little Fire Engine by Graham Greene

Endnotes

Where at all possible I have attempted to provide the original source for information. Some of Simon's own thoughts were not always attributable to one specific source so I have provided information of that used during the research of this book, aware that this may have been a secondary quote. There have been occasions where only a cutting remains in the Cadell family's archives from some newspaper sources, so specific dates are unavailable.

Chapter One

1   *Hi-de-Hi!*, opening scene of the pilot episode, transmitted 1 January 1980.
2   *Ibid.*
3   *Ibid.*
4   *Western Evening News*, 10 November 1882.
5   Comment quoted in *The London Stage 1900–1909: A Calendar of Productions, Performers and Personnel.*
6   *London Evening Standard*, 23 February 1907.
7   Hewlett, *Cadell* (1988), p. 11.
8   *Ibid.*, p. 12.
9   *Ibid.*, p. 15.
10 *Edinburgh Evening News*, 10 March 1903.
11 *London Evening Standard*, 19 June 1906.
12 *London Daily News*, 19 June 1906.
13 *The Era*, 23 June 1906.
14 *The Scotsman*, 6 April 1909.
15 *Islington Gazette*, 14 April 1909.
16 *The Era*, 10 April 1909.
17 *The Scotsman*, 17 June 1909.
18 *Ibid.*
19 *The Era*, 16 June 1909.
20 *The Evening News*, 6 July 1911.
21 *The London Daily News*, 6 July 1911.
22 National Archives, WO339/20543, letter dated 24 March 1915.

23   National Archives, WO339/20453, proceedings of medical board, 11 March 1915.
24   National Archives, WO330/20453, letter dated 24 March 1915.

Chapter Two

 1   *The Sporting Times*, 29 May 1926.
 2   Selina Cadell, interview with the author, 20 July 2017.
 3   *The Lorettonian*, 31 March 1933.
 4   *The Lorettonian*, 28 March 1934.
 5   Patrick Cadell, interview with the author, 13 October 2017.
 6   Selina Cadell, interview with the author, 20 July 2017.
 7   *Ibid.*
 8   *Radio Times*, 26 September 1948.
 9   Patricia Lord, interview with the author, 27 February 2017.
10   Sarah Berger, interview with the author, 16 May 2017.
11   Patricia Lord, interview with the author, 27 February 2017.
12   Selina Cadell, interview with the author, 20 July 2017.
13   *Ibid.*
14   Cadell, *The Right Vintage: A Winer Lover's Companion* (1995), p. 7. Simon's collection of stories and recollections on wine was subsequently reprinted under the title of *Good Vintage*.
15   Selina Cadell, interview with the author, 9 November 2016.
16   Selina Cadell, interview with the author, 20 July 2017.
17   *Ibid.*
18   Cadell, *op. cit.*, p. 7.
19   Simon Cadell, BBC Radio Two interview, 1993.
20   Patrick Cadell, interview with the author, 13 October 2017.
21   *Ibid.*
22   Patricia Lord, interview with the author, 27 February 2017.
23   The Hall School report, Summer 1960.
24   Letter to The Hall School, 18 September 1960.
25   *Ibid.*
26   Dyslexia Action website, www.dyslexiaaction.org.uk.
27   Intelligence test report, 22 September 1960.
28   *Ibid.*
29   *Ibid.*

Chapter Three

 1   Bedales website, www.bedales.org.uk.
 2   Badley, Bedales, *A Pioneer School* (1923).
 3   John Caird, interview with the author, 15 November 2016.
 4   Badley, *op. cit.*
 5   Simon Cadell, *Woman's Weekly*, 1983.
 6   Dunhurst School report, spring 1962.
 7   Selina Cadell, interview with the author, 20 July 2017.
 8   Dunhurst School report, summer 1962.
 9   Bedales school report, summer 1965.
10   Selina Cadell, interview with the author, 9 November 2016.
11   *A Study in Sherlock* flyer, 1964, courtesy of Gyles Brandreth.
12   Patrick Cadell, interview with the author, 13 October 2017.
13   Gyles Brandreth, interview with the author, 21 April 2017.

14 *Ibid.*
15 Brandreth, *Something Sensational to Read in the Train* (2009), p. 70.
16 Gyles Brandreth, interview with the author, 21 April 2017.
17 *Ibid.*
18 Patricia Lord, interview with the author, 27 February 2017.
19 Gyles Brandreth, interview with the author, 21 April 2017.
20 *Ibid.*
21 *Ibid.*
22 *Ibid.*
23 Bedales school report, summer 1965.
24 Bedales school report, summer 1966.
25 Bedales school report, winter 1966.
26 Gyles Brandreth, interview with the author, 25 October 2017.
27 Gyles Brandreth, interview with the author, 21 April 2017.
28 Terson, *Zigger Zagger/Mooney and His Caravans* (1970), p. 25.
29 Esta Charkham, interview with the author, 1 August 2017.
30 Robert Eaton, email to the author, 6 May 2016.
31 Anthony May, email to the author, 16 May 2016.
32 Esta Charkham, interview with the author, 1 August 2017.
33 *Ibid.*
34 Bedales school report, summer 1967.
35 *Ibid.*

Chapter Four

1 Bristol Old Vic, *Not In The Script* (1992), p. 39.
2 Brown, *Bristol Old Vic Theatre School: The First 50 Years* (1996), p. 9.
3 Michael Hadley, interview with the author, 23 November 2016.
4 *Ibid.*
5 *Ibid.*
6 Biggins, *Just Biggins* (2008), p. 38.
7 John Caird, interview with the author, 15 November 2016.
8 *Ibid.*
9 *Ibid.*
10 Tim Pigott-Smith, interview with the author, 6 January 2017.
11 John Caird, interview with the author, 15 November 2016.
12 Nick Turnbull, interview with the author, 7 June 2016.
13 Carol Hayman, interview with the author, 23 June 2016.
14 John Oxley, email to the author, 21 June 2016.
15 Tim Pigott-Smith, interview with the author, 6 January 2017.
16 Simon Cadell, interview with *Bromley & Croydon Advertiser*, 1990.
17 John Caird, interview with the author, 15 November 2016.
18 Beckie Croft, interview with the author, 9 February 2017.
19 Selina Cadell, interview with the author, 9 November 2016.
20 John Caird, interview with the author, 15 November 2016.
21 Tim Pigott-Smith, interview with the author, 6 January 2017.
22 *Ibid.*
23 Joanna Lumley, interview with the author, 19 August 2016.
24 John Caird, interview with the author, 15 November 2016.
25 *Ibid.*
26 *Ibid.*
27 Tim Pigott-Smith, interview with the author, 6 January 2017.

28 Selina Cadell, column in *The Guardian*, 3 January 2017.
29 Selina Cadell, interview with the author, 9 November 2016.
30 Jane Morgan, interview with the author, 1 June 2016.
31 Stephanie Turner, interview with the author, 26 January 2017.
32 Tim Pigott-Smith, interview with the author, 6 January 2017.
33 Simon Cadell, interview with Richard Littlejohn, 1993.
34 Beckie Croft, interview with the author, 8 February 2017.
35 Michael Hadley, interview with the author, 23 November 2016.
36 Tim Pigott-Smith, interview with the author, 6 January 2017.

Chapter Five

1 Patricia Lord, interview with the author, 27 February 2017.
2 Beckie Croft, interview with the author, 10 November 2016.
3 Tim Pigott-Smith, interview with the author, 6 January 2017.
4 Simon Cadell, interview with *TV Times*, 13 July 1991.
5 *Ibid.*
6 Michael Hadley, interview with the author, 23 November 2016.
7 Cadell, *op. cit.*
8 *Ibid.*
9 *Ibid.*
10 Simon Cadell, *Daily Express,* 19 November 1983.
11 Beckie Croft, interview with the author, 9 February 2017.
12 Patricia Lord, interview with the author, 27 February 2017.
13 Joanna Lumley, interview with the author, 19 August 2016.
14 David McKail, email to the author, 4 April 2017.
15 Gyles Brandreth, interview with the author, 21 April 2017.
16 Nick Renton, interview with the author, 27 February 2017.
17 Beckie Croft, interview with the author, 9 February 2017.
18 Tim Pigott-Smith, interview with the author, 6 January 2017.
19 David Schofield, email to the author, 10 September 2017.
20 Charlie Waite, email to the author, 13 March 2017.
21 Tim Pigott-Smith, interview with the author, 6 January 2017.
22 John Caird, interview with the author, 15 November 2016.
23 Simon Cadell, *You Magazine*, 1985.
24 Janet Henfrey, email to the author, 18 February 2017.
25 Cadell, *Right Vintage – A Wine Lover's Companion* (1995), p. 221.
26 Brandreth, *Something Sensational to Read in the Train* (2009), p. 267.
27 Patricia Lord, interview with the author, 27 February 2017.
28 Cadell, *Right Vintage – A Wine Lover's Companion* (1995), p. 149.
29 Nick Renton, interview with the author, 27 February 2017.
30 Chris Ellis, email to the author, 16 March 2017.
31 *The Stage*, 13 July 1972.
32 Ray Cooney, email to the author, 17 March 2017.
33 Selina Cadell, interview with the author, 20 July 2017.
34 Nick Renton, interview with the author, 27 February, 2017.
35 Miller, Ralph Richardson (1995), p. 246.
36 Simon Cadell, interview with Steve Jones, 1988.
37 Ray Cooney, email to the author, 17 March 2017.
38 Brandreth, *Something Sensational to Read in the Train* (2009), pp.262–263.
39 Gyles Brandreth, interview with the author, 21 April 2017.
40 Nick Renton, interview with the author, 27 February 2017.

41 *Ibid.*
42 *The Stage*, 15 November 1973.
43 Sheila Brownrigg, letter to Simon Cadell, 11 November 1973.
44 *Ibid.*
45 Nick Renton, interview with the author, 27 February 2017.
46 *The Times*, 22 October 1975.

Chapter Six

1 Conversation recalled by Gyles Brandreth, interview with the author, 21 April 2017.
2 Beckie Croft, interview with the author, 9 February 2017.
3 Simon Cadell, interview with Richard Littlejohn, 1993.
4 *The Times*, 11 March 1975.
5 Jane Morgan, interview with the author, 1 June 2016.
6 Tim Pigott-Smith, interview with the author, 6 January 2017.
7 Jane Morgan, interview with the author, 1 June 2016.
8 *Ibid.*
9 *Ibid.*
10 *Ibid.*
11 *Ibid.*
12 *Ibid.*
13 Sir Alan Ayckbourn, email to the author, 6 January 2017.
14 *The Times*, 6 April 1976.
15 Neil Stacy, interview with the author, 14 January 2017.
16 *Ibid.*
17 *Ibid.*
18 *Ibid.*
19 Stephanie Turner, interview with the author, 26 January 2017.
20 Neil Stacy, interview with the author, 14 January 2017.
21 Nick Renton, interview with the author, 27 February 2017.
22 *The Stage*, December 1983.
23 Stephanie Turner, interview with the author, 26 January 2017.
24 *Radio Times*, 18–24 March 1989.
25 Stephanie Turner, interview with the author, 26 January 2017.
26 *Daily Express*, February 1985.
27 Richard Heffer, interview with the author, 26 May 2016.
28 *Ibid.*
29 *Ibid.*
30 *Ibid.*
31 *Ibid.*
32 Simon Cadell, *Woman's Weekly*, 1983.
33 *Ibid.*
34 Simon Cadell, *News of the World*, 1 March 1981.
35 Simon Cadell, *The Sun*, 5 January 1980.

Chapter Seven

1 *News of the World*, 1 March 1981.
2 Stephanie Turner, interview with the author, 26 January 2017.
3 Richard Heffer, interview with the author, 26 May 2016.
4 Cope & Fury, *Hi-de-Hi! Companion* (2009), p. 23.
5 Perry, *A Stupid Boy* (2002), p. 301.

6   Stephanie Turner, interview with the author, 26 January 2017.
7   Croft, *You Have Been Watching...* (2004), p. 212.
8   Cope & Fury, *Hi-de-Hi! Companion* (2009), pp. 30–31.
9   Simon Cadell, BBC Radio Two, 1993.
10 Simon Cadell, interview with Rob Cope, 1992.
11 Stephanie Turner, interview with the author, 26 January 2017.
12 Jeffrey Holland, interview with the author, 30 June 2016.
13 Simon Cadell, *Woman's Weekly*, 1983.
14 Jeffrey Holland, interview with the author, 30 June 2016.
15 *Sunday Mirror*, 1984.
16 Jeffrey Holland, interview with the author, 30 June 2016.
17 *The Stage*, 14 March 1996.
18 David Webb, interview with the author, 25 October 2016.
19 Simon Cadell, *Daily Mirror*, 30 November 1982.
20 Simon Cadell, *Western Mail*, 27 July 1991.
21 Simon Cadell, *Daily Mail*, 20 April 1981.
22 Simon Cadell, interview with Rob Cope, 1992.
23 Stephanie Turner, interview with the author, 26 January 2017.
24 Jeffrey Holland, interview with the author, 30 June 2017.
25 Beckie Croft, interview with the author, 8 February 2017.
26 *Ibid.*
27 Penny Croft, interview with the author, 10 November 2016.
28 Beckie Croft, interview with the author, 10 November 2016.
29 *Ibid.*
30 *Ibid.*
31 Various press, January 1984.
32 Penny Croft, interview with the author, 10 November 2016.

Chapter Eight

1   Unknown magazine cutting.
2   *Woman's Weekly*, 1983.
3   Beckie Croft, interview with the author, 10 November 2016.
4   *Ibid.*
5   *Kentish Mercury*, 13 January 1983.
6   *News of the World*, 1983.
7   Joanna Lumley, interview with the author, 19 August 2016.
8   *Ibid.*
9   Gillian Bevan, email to the author, 17 April 2017.
10 *Ibid.*
11 Kenn Oldfield, interview with the author, 15 June 2016.
12 Gillian Bevan, email to the author, 17 April 2017.
13 *Time Out*, 1983.
14 *Ibid.*
15 Morley, *Asking for Trouble: The Memoirs of Sheridan Morley* (2003), p. 282.
16 Evening Standard, May 1983.
17 Joanna Lumley, interview with the author, 19 August 2016.
18 Simon Cadell, interview with Rob Cope, 1992.
19 John Caird, interview with the author, 15 November 2016.
20 Jeffrey Holland, interview with the author, 30 June 2016.
21 *News of the World*, 1983.
22 *Daily Express*, February 1985.

23   *The Stage*, December 1983.

24   *Daily Mail*, 1985

25   Jeffrey Holland, interview with the author, 30 June 2016.

26   Interview with Hilary Samson for *Double Act* programme, 1988.

27   *Ibid.*

28   Peter Farago, interview with the author, 10 November 2016.

29   *Ibid*

30   *The Times*, 21 December 1983.

31   *London Evening Standard*, April 1984.

32   *Ibid.*

33   Nick Renton, interview with the author, 27 February 2017.

34   Simon Cadell, *Watford Observer*, 1984.

35   Simon Cadell, *You Magazine*, 1985.

36   *Daily Express*, 9 February 1985.

37   Unknown newspaper cutting, 1991.

38   *Financial Times*, April 1984.

39   *Guardian*, April 1984.

40   *Daily Telegraph*, April 1984.

Chapter Nine

1   Orwell, *Raffles and Miss Blandish*, October 1944.

2   *Watford Observer*, September 1984.

3   Sarah Berger, interview with the author, 16 May 2017.

4   *The Stage*, September 1984.

5   *Watford Observer*, September 1984.

6   Sarah Berger, interview with the author, 16 May 2017.

7   *Daily Mirror*, 1985.

8   *Daily Mail*, 1985.

9   *Radio Times*, 9 February 1985.

10   *Sunday Mirror*, 4 August 1991.

11   Penny Croft, interview with the author, 10 November 2016.

12   Beckie Croft, interview with the author, 10 November 2016.

13   *Radio Times*, 9 February 1985.

14   *You Magazine*, 1985.

15   Eddington, *So Far, So Good* (1995), p. 184.

16   *Ibid*, p. 187.

17   *Ibid*, p. 186.

18   Nick Renton, interview with the author, 27 February 2017.

19   Selina Cadell, interview with the author, 20 July 2017.

20   *Ibid.*

21   *The Times*, 1 February 1986.

22   *The Stage*, 13 February 1986.

23   Simon Cadell, *Woman's Weekly*, 1983.

24   *Ibid.*

25   Simon Cadell, *TV Times*, 13 July 1991.

26   Beckie Croft, interview with the author, 8 February 2017.

27   Simon Cadell, undated *Titbits* interview.

28   Simon Cadell, *You Magazine*, 1985.

29   Beckie Croft, interview with the author, 8 February 2017.

30   *Ibid.*

31   *Ibid.*

32 *Ibid.*
33 *Ibid.*
34 *Ibid.*
35 *Ibid.*
36 Patrick Cadell (son), interview with the author, 25 October 2017.
37 Beckie Croft, interview with the author, 8 February 2017.
38 *Ibid.*
39 *Ibid.*
40 Simon Cadell, *Today*, 23 March 1989.

Chapter Ten

1   *Daily Mail*, 26 November 1986.
2   Selina Cadell, interview with the author, 9 November 2016.
3   *London Standard*, 15 January 1987.
4   *What's On*, 6 November 1986.
5   *Ibid.*
6   *Ibid.*
7   *Country Life*, November 1986.
8   *The Telegraph*, 10 November 1986.
9   *The Month*, January 1987.
10 John Arthur, interview with the author, 11 April 2017.
11 Penny Croft, interview with the author, 10 November 2016.
12 *Radio Times*, 18 March 1989.
13 Penny Croft, interview with the author, 10 November 2016.
14 *Radio Times*, 18 March 1989.
15 *Ibid.*
16 *Today*, March 1988.
17 *Western Mail*, 13 March 1987.
18 Penny Croft, interview with the author, 10 November 2016.
19 Michael Thomas, interview with the author, 12 December 2016.
20 Unknown magazine article, 1989.
21 *The Stage*, 19 March 1987.
22 Penny Croft, interview with the author, 10 November 2016.
23 *Ibid.*
24 *The Stage*, 19 March 1987.
25 *Ibid.*
26 *Ibid.*
27 Penny Croft, interview with the author, 10 November 2016.
28 *Ibid.*
29 *Ibid.*
30 *Ibid.*
31 Interview with Nicki Household, 1988.
32 Unknown magazine article, 1989.
33 *Financial Times*, 8 June 1987.
34 *The Independent*, 8 June 1987.
35 *The Sunday Times*, 21 June 1987.
36 *The Times*, 6 June 1987
37 *London Evening Standard*, 8 June 1987
38 Sir Alan Ayckbourn, email to the author, 6 January 2017
39 Simon Cadell, interview with Steve Jones, 1988
40 Unknown magazine article, 1989

41 Simon Cadell, *Today*, 23 March 1989
42 Unknown magazine article, 1989

Chapter Eleven

1 Simon Cadell, interview with Steve Jones, 1988.
2 Simon Butteriss, interview with the author, 15 December 2016.
3 Peter Farago, interview with the author, 10 November 2016.
4 *The Stage*, 4 April 1988.
5 *The Sunday Times*, 3 April 1988.
6 Simon Butteriss, interview with the author, 15 December 2016.
7 Interview with Hilary Samson for *Double Act* programme, 1988.
8 *Ibid.*
9 *The Sunday Times*, 25 September 1988.
10 *The Stage*, 6 October 1988.
11 Nick Renton, interview with the author, 27 February 2017.
12 *The Times*, 16 September 1989.
13 *The Stage*, 21 September 1989.
14 Tim Luscombe, email to the author, 6 May 2016.
15 *The Times*, 12 December 1989.
16 *The Guardian*, December 1989.
17 *Daily Mail*, December 1989.
18 Morley, *Asking for Trouble: The Memoirs of Sheridan Morley* (2003), p. 285.
19 *The Stage*, 4 January 1990.
20 Unknown press cutting, 1990.
21 Morley, *Asking for Trouble: The Memoirs of Sheridan Morley* (2003), p. 284.
22 Simon Cadell, interview with *Bromley & Croydon Advertiser*, 1990.
23 *Ibid.*
24 *Ibid.*
25 Simon Cadell, *Western Mail*, 3 July 1991.
26 *Radio Times*, 7 June 1991.
27 *Daily Mirror*, 1991.
28 *TV Times*, 13 July 1991.
29 *Ibid.*
30 Simon Cadell, interview with *Bromley & Croydon Advertiser*, 1990.
31 Peter Farago, interview with the author, 10 November 2016.
32 Selina Cadell, interview with the author, 9 November 2016.
33 Peter Farago, interview with the author, 10 November 2016.
34 Simon Cadell, interview with Rob Cope, 1992.
35 Jane How, interview with the author, 13 January 2017.
36 Peter Farago, interview with the author, 8 February 2017.
37 Fisher, *The Journal of the British Pantomime Association* (1973).
38 Briony Glassco, email to the author, 26 March 2016.
39 *The Stage*, 9 May 1991.
40 *Financial Times*, March 1991.
41 *Sunday Mail*, March 1991.
42 *The Sunday Times*, 31 March 1991.
43 Briony Glassco, email to the author, 26 March 2016.
44 *Ibid.*
45 Jane How, interview with the author, 13 January 2017.
46 Simon Cadell, *Western Mail*, 27 July 1991.
47 *Sunday Mirror*, 4 August 1991.

48 Stephanie Turner, interview with the author, 26 January 2017.

Chapter Twelve

1   Simon Cadell, interview with Richard Littlejohn, 1993.
2   Giles Havergal, interview with the author, 8 May 2016.
3   *Evening Standard*, 20 September 1993.
4   Giles Havergal, interview with the author, 8 May 2016.
5   The elderly aunt reference was made by John Wells in his Evening Standard piece of 20 September 1993, while Simon told others he based her on an elderly aunt in Bournemouth.
6   Simon Cadell, interview with Richard Littlejohn, 1993.
7   *The Sunday Times*, 15 November 1992.
8   *Evening Standard*, 20 September 1993.
9   Giles Havergal, interview with the author, 8 May 2016.
10 Patricia Lord, interview with the author, 27 February 2017.
11 *Bournemouth Evening Echo*, 22 September 1992.
12 *The Times*, 19 November 1992.
13 *Daily Mail*, 8 March 1996.
14 Joanna Lumley, interview with the author, 19 August 2016.
15 Simon Cadell, interview with Richard Littlejohn, 1993.
16 *Ibid.*
17 Simon Cadell, *The Telegraph*, 6 December 1995.
18 Simon Cadell, interview with Richard Littlejohn, 1993.
19 *Daily Mail*, 1994.
20 Beckie Croft, interview with the author, 8 February 2017.
21 *Daily Mail*, 1994.
22 Dr Martin Scurr, interview with the author, 31 July 2017.
23 Simon Cadell, interview with Richard Littlejohn, 1993.
24 Dr Martin Scurr, interview with the author, 31 July 2017.
25 *Evening Standard*, 20 September 1993.
26 *Daily Express*, 1993.
27 Tim Pigott-Smith, interview with the author, 6 January 2017.
28 Dr Martin Scurr, interview with the author, 31 July 2017.
29 John Arthur, interview with the author, 11 April 2017.
30 Simon Cadell, interview with Richard Littlejohn, 1993.
31 Nick Renton, interview with the author, 27 February 2017.
32 Dr Martin Scurr, interview with the author, 31 July 2017.
33 *Daily Mail*, 1994.

Chapter Thirteen

1   Brandreth, *Something Sensational to Read in the Train* (2009), p. 555.
2   Selina Cadell, interview with the author, 20 July 2017.
3   Selina Cadell, interview with the author, 9 November 2016.
4   *Today*, 23 March 1989.
5   *Daily Mirror*, 17 September 1993.
6   Family press release, September 1993.
7   Patricia Lord, interview with the author, 27 February 2017.
8   Dr Martin Scurr, interview with the author, 31 July 2017.
9   *Ibid.*
10 Selina Cadell, interview with the author, 20 July 2017.

11 Beckie Croft, interview with the author, 8 February 2017.
12 Cadell, *Right Vintage: A Winer Lover's Companion* (1995), p. 8.
13 *Woman's Weekly*, 1983.
14 Gyles Brandreth, interview with the author, 21 April 2017.
15 *Ibid.*
16 Trevor Hughes, interview with the author, 11 April 2017.
17 Constantine Gregory, email to the author, 25 July 2017.
18 Trevor Hughes, interview with the author, 11 April 2017.
19 Selina Cadell, interview with the author, 21 April 2017.
20 Beckie Croft, interview with the author, 8 February 2017.
21 Nick Renton, interview with the author, 27 February 2017.
22 *Today*, 27 July 1994.
23 Rudolf van den Berg, interview with the author, 26 October 2016.
24 *Ibid.*
25 *Ibid.*
26 *Ibid.*
27 *Fangoria*, November 1996.
28 Beckie Croft, interview with the author, 8 February 2017.
29 Dr Martin Scurr, interview with the author, 31 July 2017.
30 Selina Cadell, interview with the author, 9 November 2016.
31 Gyles Brandreth, interview with the author, 21 April 2017.
32 Nick Renton, interview with the author, 27 February 2017.
33 Selina Cadell, interview with the author, 20 July 2017.
34 Various family interviews, 2017.
35 Family statement, March 1996.
36 *The Times*, 8 March 1996.
37 Tony Staveacre, interview with the author, 29 September 2017.
38 Coward, diary entry 1961.
39 *The Stage*, 2 May 1996.
40 Pigott-Smith, *Do You Know Who I Am?* (2017), p. 286.
41 Shakespeare, *The Tempest*, Act IV, Scene I.
42 Simon Cadell, *Daily Telegraph*, 6 December 1995.

Epilogue

1 Beckie Croft, interview with the author, 8 February 2017.
2 Jeffrey Holland, interview with the author, 30 June 2016.
3 Joanna Lumley, interview with the author, 19 August 2016.
4 Tim Pigott-Smith, interview with the author, 6 January 2017.
5 *Ibid.*
6 *Ibid.*
7 Brandreth, *Something Sensational to Read in the Train* (2009), pp. 678–683.
8 Selina Cadell, interview with the author, 9 November 2016.

Bibliography

Biggins, C., *Just Biggins* (Great Britain: John Blake Publishing, 2008)

Brandreth, G., *Something Sensational to Read in the Train* (Great Britain: John Murray, 2009)

Brown, S., *Bristol Old Vic Theatre School* (Great Britain: BOVTS Productions Ltd, 1996)

Cadell, S., *The Right Vintage: A Wine Lover's Companion* (London: Robson Books Ltd, 1995)

Croft, D., *You Have Been Watching...The Autobiography of David Croft* (Great Britain: BBC Books, 2004)

Eddington, P., *So Far, So Good: The Autobiography* (Great Britain: Hodder and Stoughton, 1995)

Hewlett, T., *Cadell* (London: The Portland Gallery, 1988)

Morley, S., *Asking for Trouble: The Memoirs of Sheridan Morley* (Great Britain: Hodder and Stoughton, 2002)

Not in the Script (Bristol: Redcliffe Press Ltd, 1992)

Perry, J., *A Stupid Boy* (Great Britain: Century, 2002)

Pigott-Smith, T., *Do You Know Who I Am: A Memoir* (Great Britain: Bloomsbury Publishing plc, 2017)

Terson, P., *Zigger Zagger/Mooney and His Caravans* (Great Britain: Penguin Books, 1970)